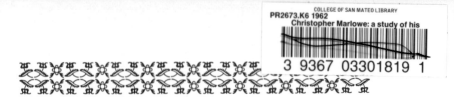

CHRISTOPHER MARLOWE

A Study of his Thought, Learning, and Character

CHRISTOPHER MARLOWE

A Study of his Thought,
Learning, and Character
By PAUL H. KOCHER

NEW YORK
RUSSELL & RUSSELL · INC
1962

To
ANN

PREFACE

It is a salutary thing for a writer to count his obligations
and to realize, when his work is done, how little of it
is wholly his. To the Trustees of the Folger Shakespeare
Library I am grateful for the grant of a fellowship in
the year 1940-41 which gave me leisure to do uninter-
rupted research. During that year at the Library, its
Director, Dr. Joseph Q. Adams, was a genial and ener-
gizing presence, receptive of question and most generous
in his interest. I also remember with pleasure the assistance given me by other friends on the Library staff.

Over a period of years Professor Hardin Craig of the
University of North Carolina has given continuous
friendly help and has made suggestions upon the manuscript. Needless to add, the faults which, I am conscious,
remain in the book are of my own making.

Likewise I am indebted to Dr. Louis B. Wright of
the Henry E. Huntington Library for many kindnesses
and much practical advice. The staff of the Huntington Library has always been most cordial in its aid.

I wish to acknowledge the courtesy of the editors of

Journal of English and Germanic Philology, Modern Philology, Philological Quarterly, and *Studies in Philology* in allowing the incorporation of materials which I originally published in those journals. My thanks are due also to Methuen & Co. Ltd. for permission to reprint the Baines note from Professor Tucker Brooke's *Life of Marlowe.*

Possibly it may be well for me to emphasize here what will become evident to anyone who reads on into the book. My intention has not been to present an exhaustive study of all phases of Marlowe's learning. That would require a volume several times the size of the present one. Rather, I have selected subjects which seem significant in themselves and at the same time representative of widely different facets of the dramatist's mind and character. To each of these I have given a full and detailed treatment. I am confident that by this method the essential truths about him can be made to emerge.

November, 1945

P. H. K.

CONTENTS

IV

CHARACTER

V

SYNTHESES

I

INTRODUCTION

1. CROSSROADS OF INTERPRETATION

THE FIRST OBLIGATION OF A STUDY OF THE MIND of Marlowe is to interpret all the available biographical evidence of his thought. This basic material, the Rosetta stone for all that follows, is here treated at the head of the section on religion, since it falls almost exclusively within that field. The extant plays and poems are next to be interpreted, only secondarily as separate works of art, and primarily as mirrors of the thought, learning, and character of their creator.

Thus the crucial problem of all interpretation of Marlowe, the problem of the degree of his subjectivity as a dramatist, presents itself immediately. It is not a question on which complete agreement can reasonably be expected. Those who dislike the romantic propensity to self-revelation or who cherish an ideal of drama as an objective art are quite naturally reluctant to concede subjectivity. Indeed, findings of subjectivity have often been very unwisely made in some dramatists, notably Shakespeare. Each dramatist, however, is a separate case. Shakespeare may conceal, whereas Marlowe may reveal, his nearest thoughts and feelings.

At the outset it is quite clear that no theory of subjectivity which depends solely on the intuitions of the critic is

3

likely to reach the truth. The whole broad body of the evidence must be construed. Now what is this evidence for the
meaning of any given play? It is the dramatist's choice and
treatment of sources—what he omits, what he uses, and how
he uses it. It is the background of the thought and custom of
the period. It is the practice of other dramatists. It is the
dramatist's own practice in the remainder of his work. It is
his own personally held ideas, as supplied by biographical
data. It is his manipulation of emphasis within the play by
the placement, length, frequency, and eloquence of the various speeches and by the good or bad standing of the
speakers to whom they are allocated. When these indications all point in the same direction, judgment is easy. But
when they conflict, then, in the last analysis, the choice between them can be made by each critic only in accordance
with his total estimate of the nature of the dramatist's genius
and his place in his epoch. And such an estimate is, inevitably and desirably, a matter partly of intellect and partly
of intuition.

Taking all these factors into consideration in their broadest possible scope, Marlowe stands out, it seems to me, as one
of the most highly subjective playwrights of his age. In some
degree every dramatist is bound to disclose in his work the
major processes of his mind and emotion. Even Shakespeare's plays are not, of course, just anybody's plays,
fatherless and unrelated to one another; they are *Shakespeare's* plays, all bearing the general stamp of one personality, however difficult that personality may be to delimit.
Marlowe's plays are Marlowe's not only in this general
sense but also as projections of some of his more particular
ideas and passions. Criticism of Christianity, for example,
appears in all the biographical documents as the most absorbing interest of his life. And likewise in his plays it is the
most anxiously, skillfully, and passionately reiterated theme

of dramatization. It is clear to us where his sympathies lie, and we can watch him maneuvering to express them in ways not too dangerously obvious. The equivocation of Christians can be stressed in the Orcanes episode of 2 *Tamburlaine*, but it must be shown as avenged by Christ; Faustus can freely blaspheme, but he must be damned for it in the end; Barabas can be given the best of the argument in his criticism of Christian morals, but he must be painted as a dire villain. And so forth. Again, Marlowe is subjective in his use of irony. The same ironic undertone which sounds in the anti-Christian quotations reported by Baines and Kyd is audible almost everywhere in the plays. Thus the good gifts of the white witch of biography give us a unique vantage for the understanding of the dramatic work.

They suggest, moreover, certain criteria for determining the existence of subjectivity in topics other than religion. The religious utterances in the plays have the following characteristics: they are diffused generally through almost the whole Marlowe canon; they are given most passionate expression; and they clash vividly, in many respects, with the accepted ideas of the times, whether on or off stage. These criteria apply exactly to the desires for power and knowledge felt by all of Marlowe's great protagonists. That these aspirations and sorrows are the poet's own is indicated by their superb eloquence, the highest of which Marlowe was capable, and, more conclusively, by the manner in which the same type of character—I had almost said the same character—is evoked over and over again. Marlowe was never able really to visualize any other. Many critics have noted that Tamburlaine, Faustus, Barabas, Gaveston, Mortimer, and Guise are but the embodiments of a craving for illimitable power in varied forms, and few have hesitated to attribute this passion to the dramatist himself. Ambitions so gigantic were not known on the stage before the coming of Marlowe, and were, of course, anathema to the Elizabethan moral code.

One caution, however. It would be absurd to say that when Faustus cried, "Why, the Signory of Emden shall be mine!" he was voicing Marlowe's own specific desire. Less absurd, but still untenable, is the inference that Marlowe craved power through magic because Faustus did. But Faustus' wish for power and knowledge in general does probably represent Marlowe's wish, since it is the same wish expressed in the other plays. The principle, therefore, must always be kept in mind that the more general an idea or emotion in one of the plays, the more likely it is to be close to Marlowe, and the more particular, the farther away. In the particulars the materials of the story make their exactions felt. Thus any given play is a series of compromises between Marlowe's subjectivity and the sources of the story he is using. On the other hand, it is worth noting that the original choice of the story may be, and indeed probably is, a personal one. As far as we know, the selection of a plot was not dictated to Marlowe by the theatrical company for which he wrote. He established new fashions, did not have to follow old ones. And his choice of basically the same type of material for most of his plays likewise indicates his freedom. Again, he had liberty, after the plot had been selected, to mold it according to his own convictions. Therefore the mere fact that an idea or theme of the play is to be found in the sources is by no means conclusive against its having a subjective element also. The test must always be its generality of use, its outstanding eloquence of statement, and its congruity with other ideas presumptively or certainly Marlowe's.

The ripest fruit of all in the interpretation of any literary figure is attainment of some comprehensive and unified view of his nature in its relations with his work. For this ultimate generalization, something resembling a hypothesis in the physical sciences is necessary—some theory which will save all the known phenomena and will, at the same time, be most fruitful for later study. The contrast with a hypothesis in science is, of course, that such a theory cannot be proved by experiment. It can only be offered in the hope that through its consistency and probability it will bear the sign of truth and win the assent of other students. The perils of rising to a final generalization for Marlowe, who has left only a small body of work, and dramatic work at that, are obvious to all, and not least to the present writer. But to be content with less, where the prize is great, is to rest indeed "attemptless, faint, and destitute."

Study of Marlowe's religion is the core of this book, because religion was the core of Marlowe's thought and feeling. The chapter on witchcraft presents attitudes and materials in the related subject of the supernatural. Some aspects of the poet's social thinking are next dealt with in the chapter on politics and ethics. Here also is first outlined tentatively a comprehensive theory of his psychology as the wellspring of his thought. His astronomy is then taken as representative of his knowledge of natural science, and his art of war as a favorite subject closer to the sphere of action. The topic of the succeeding two chapters is Marlowe's personality as a changing entity. Especially in the chapter on the development of his character, further amplification of the psychological theory is attempted. The whole is bound together in the final chapter of syntheses.

THE SCHOOL OF NIGHT

Before we proceed, however, comment is in place on Marlowe's relations with a possible School of Atheism or School of Night centering in Sir Walter Raleigh, whose influence is thought to be visible in the religious, philosophical, and scientific ideas expressed by the dramatist. Some recent scholarship [1] has sought to draw together into one intimately related group such men as Raleigh, Marlowe, Harriot, Chapman, Royden, Warner, the second Lord Hunsdon, and the earls of Derby and Northumberland, and to oppose this Raleigh circle to the Essex-Southampton circle. The theory has sometimes even advanced so far as to work out for the Raleigh group a community of religious and scientific doctrine. These are excesses which result from several types of false assumption.

For example, when Kyd names as Marlowe's associates in atheism "such as he conversed withall, that is (as I am geven to understand) with Harriot, Warner, Royden, and some stationers in Paules churchyard," we are not warranted in assuming that all the men named are necessarily members of a compact group and then going further to assume that because Harriot was an intimate of Raleigh, therefore all the others were his familiars also. In mathematics things equal to the same thing are equal to each other, but in the complexities of human character the friends of a friend are by no means always the friends of each other. Marlowe may have been friendly with both Harriot and Royden and yet these two may have been to each other no more than the coldest of acquaintances. Harriot may have played Aristotle to Raleigh's Alexander, and the stationers of Paul's churchyard never have exchanged a word with Raleigh himself. Almost as dangerous is the additional assumption that because one man stands to another in the relation of patron or intellectual whetstone or even friend, therefore their ideas are the same on all

1. See especially M. C. Bradbrook, *The School of Night* (Cambridge, 1936), and the edition of *Love's Labour's Lost* by Sir Arthur Quiller-Couch and John Dover Wilson (Cambridge, 1923).

important subjects. Taking this argument at its strongest, if we consult our experience we know that even good friends often differ radically. Chapman may have dedicated poems to Royden, Raleigh may have listened to Marlowe's atheist lecture, and Marlowe have admired Harriot's scientific brilliance without there being a unanimity of damnation among them all. Surely it is necessary to look at the evidence to see whether there is such a closeness of connection of each supposed member of the group not merely with one or two of the other members but with most or all of them, and such a mutual display of unique ideas in science and philosophy or dangerous ideas in religion as to justify the conclusion that a School of Atheism in any significant sense existed.

There were, of course, strong popular suspicions that Raleigh and his immediate entourage were tainted with atheism. Parsons' well known reference,

Of Sir Walter Rawleys school of Atheisme by the waye, & of the Conjurer that is M[aster] thereof, and of the diligence used to get yong gentlemen of this schoole, where in both Moyses, & our Sauio', the olde, and the new Testamente are iested at, and the schollers taughte, amonge other thinges, to spell God backwarde,

names Raleigh and hints at Harriot. The Government thought it worth while in March, 1594, to appoint a commission to take depositions on the subject at Cerne Abbas near Raleigh's estate of Sherborne in Dorset. Several witnesses testified that Harriot, Carew Raleigh, and Thomas Allen, all members of Raleigh's household, had attacked the Scriptures and the doctrines of the resurrection and the Deity.[2] It is noteworthy, however, that none of the

2. Specifically, the charges against Harriot were that he "hath brought the godhedd in question" and "hath ben convented before the Lordes

numerous witnesses once mentioned Chapman, Royden,
Warner, and the others now put forward as constituents
of the "school." Against Raleigh himself the testimony was
chiefly of a vague and general sort, to the effect that he
was "suspected of Atheisme." The single exception was the
report of a conversation held by Minister Ralph Ironside
with Raleigh about the definition of man's soul and of God.
Raleigh had simply stated that he had never been able to
understand what either was, and had declared himself un-
enlightened by the circular argument offered by the
minister. At the end of the discussion he had asked that grace
be said. This was an orthodox conclusion to a completely
orthodox opinion. No Christian professed to know what
either God or the soul was in any last analysis, and Raleigh
had merely been pressing the question to its ultimate. Later,
in his *History of the World,* he maintained a perfect consistency when he wrote:

I confess it, that to enquire further, as of the essence of God,
of his power, of his art . . . is not an effect of reason . . . but
they grow mad with reason, that enquire after it. . . . For seeing both reason and necessity teach us . . . that the world was
made by a power infinite; and yet how it was made cannot
teach us; and seeing the same reason and necessity make us
know that the same infinite power is every where in the world;
and yet how every where it cannot inform us;—our belief
hereof is not weakened, but greatly strengthened by our
ignorance; because it is the same reason that tells us, that such

---

of the Counsell for denyinge the resurreccion of the bodye"; against
Carew Raleigh that he said "there was a god in nature" and that he
made light of death "as beinge common to all sinner and rightuous";
against Thomas Allen, that he denied the immortality of the soul, spoke
blasphemously of God, and used leaves of the Bible to dry tobacco on.
Oliver, Allen's servant, was reported to have "sayde Moyses had lii
whores" and spoken "manye other thinges in derogacion of God & the
scriptures and of the immortallitye of the soule."

a nature cannot be said to be God, that can be in all conceived by man.[3]

Similarly, Raleigh's *The Sceptic* is not inconsistent with Christianity, because however much it may argue for the unreliability of man's senses and his reason, it never impugns the validity of his faith. *The Soul* voices only conceptions current since Aristotle and long since incorporated into Christian theology. The truth is that Raleigh never wrote anything which was not clearly reconcilable with the better elements of Christian belief. Impressions to the contrary today are due largely to a persistent underestimation of the refinement and spirituality of the religious thought of his time. Attempts, therefore, to see something strange and meaningful in the similarity between Raleigh's description of God as "an understanding which only itself can comprehend, as essence spiritual and eternal" and Orcanes' invocation to the Deity in 2 *Tamburlaine* (II, ii, 36ff.) are mistaken. Both Raleigh and Marlowe are writing in the highest Christian tradition in these passages. Consequently their resemblance is no proof whatever of mutual influence. Exactly the same comment may be made upon their parallel treatments of the soul.[4]

Upon searching farther for signs of important mental contact between the two writers we are confronted only by negatives. Marlowe seems never to have been a sceptic. On the contrary, everything suggests that he was dogmatic and positive. He may have believed, as did his Tamburlaine,

3. Raleigh, *The History of the World* (Edinburgh, 1820), Preface, I, lv. This passage is quoted in an admirable essay by E. A. Strathmann ("*The History of the World* and Ralegh's Skepticism," *Huntington Library Quarterly* III [1940], 265-87), who anticipates me in some of the views I have expressed about Raleigh in this chapter. See also G. T. Buckley, *Atheism in the English Renaissance* (University of Chicago Press, 1932), chap. xi.

4. See the evidence presented *infra* in the discussion of religion in *Tamburlaine*.

that knowledge was infinite and beauty not to be prisoned in words, but he never questioned the worth of the knowledge already attained and the possibility of attaining ever more, or the truth of the impressions beauty made upon his senses. Affirmation is the pith of his character. And a comparison with Raleigh in the matter of specific attitudes towards Christian dogma yields further sharp contrasts. Raleigh in all his writings accepts the authority of both testaments of the Bible, computes the chronology of Genesis in the conventional way on the basis of its texts, and reveres Moses. What Marlowe's opinions on these items were we know from the Baines note. Thus wherever the two great Elizabethans vary from the accepted thought of their day they are in direct opposition to each other, and it is only where they are conventional that their ideas seem to be alike. If this is the discord between the two minds, it is useless, of course, to try to extract a harmony from the mere fact that Marlowe read his anti-Christian polemic before Raleigh and others or was friendly with Harriot. One recalls that Raleigh sat up one night talking religion to a Jesuit in prison without being particularly intimate with Jesuits or having Jesuitical leanings, and advocated religious toleration for the Brownists without belonging to a school of Brownism.

The difficulty of framing a central creed for a hypothetical Raleigh school is likewise evident in the differences between Raleigh himself and such of his undoubted intimates as his half-brother Carew and Harriot. Anti-Scriptural opinions ascribed to the latter two men in the Cerne Abbas investigation are not reconcilable with any of Raleigh's known attitudes.[5] Anthony à Wood wrote of Harriot:

5. The only possible indications to the contrary, so far as I am aware, consist in Parsons' description of Raleigh's School of Atheism,

But notwithstanding his great skill in mathematics, he had strange thoughts of the creation of the world, and could never believe that trite position, Ex nihilo nihil fit. He made a Philosophical Theology, wherein he cast off the Old Testament, so that consequently the New would have no foundation. He was a Deist, and his doctrine he did impart ... to Sir. Walt. Raleigh when he was compiling the History of the World....

But if Harriot did so impart it he did a very bad job, for the *History* assumes the divine inspiration of the Old Testament and takes the orthodox view of the creation of the world.[6]

It is between Harriot and Marlowe that there exists something approaching a real congruity of thought about religion, well authenticated by Marlowe's personal reference

---

quoted above, and Aubrey's biographical note: "He was scandalised with Atheisme, but he was a bold man and would venture at discourse which was unpleasant to the church-men. I remember Lord Scudamour sayd, 'Twas basely sayd of Sir W. R. to talke of the anagramme of Dog. In his speech on the scaffold, I heard my cosen Whitney say ... that he spake not one word of Christ, but of the great and incomprehensible God with much zeale and adoration, so that he concluded that he was an a-christ, not an atheist." The manner of his death showed, says Aubrey, "that he had a certain expectation of a better life after it." To the extent that this is anti-Christian—and it is a limited extent—it appears to me far outweighed by the orthodoxy of Raleigh's other utterances. Aubrey's statement partially negatives itself, because Raleigh cannot have meant the anagram very seriously if he had such adoration for God. The conjuration by Faustus, "Within this circle is Jehovah's name / Forward and backward anagrammatiz'd" (I, iii, 8-9), does not refer to the same blasphemous anagram but to the transposition of the letters of the Hebrew name of Jehovah. See the chapter on Witchcraft, *infra*.

6. Preface, pp. xli ff. It is true that Raleigh agrees with Harriot in rejecting the doctrine that *Ex nihilo nihil fit* (p. xliv). But Wood is in error if he means to imply that there was anything un-Christian in Harriot's position on this point. It was the Aristotelians, believing that the world had always existed, who championed the doctrine that nothing can come of nothing. Christianity had always contended that God created the world out of nothing.

to the scientist in the Baines note and by an over-all similarity in their Biblical criticism. On the other hand, Harriot's
influence upon Marlowe's ideas in the field of astronomy
is not demonstrable, as many critics assume. Marlowe showed
so elementary a knowledge of this science that it seems
impossible he could have been in touch with Harriot's
research while writing his plays.[7] Also it is worth remembering that our evidence for Marlowe's acquaintance with
the astronomer comes only at the very end of his life, and
that this is precisely the period in which Marlowe's work
(if we accept the 1589 date for *Faustus*) contains least of
astronomical learning.

Let us now consider the case for the inclusion of Royden,
Chapman, and Warner in a Raleigh circle. Royden's few
acknowledged poems have nothing to do with religion or
science and, although of fine literary quality, display no
unusual learning. External evidence of connection is likewise completely lacking. He dedicated no work to Raleigh
and is never mentioned as having been in his presence. We
have only Kyd's naming of Royden as a friend of Marlowe, which, I have stressed, means little for a relationship
with Raleigh, and Chapman's dedication of *The Shadow
of Night* (1594) and *Ovid's Banquet of Sence* (1595) to
Royden in very friendly terms.

But Chapman's connection with Raleigh is itself in
doubt. The belief in it rests partly on the dedication of
the two poems to Royden, together with the School of
Night theory built around them. This argument is obviously circular. Leaving the poems aside for a moment, what
is the *independent* evidence that Chapman was an initiate
of a Raleigh "school"? The strongest is his blank verse
poem, *De Guiana* (1596), praising Raleigh's explorations

7. See the chapter on astronomy and meteorology, *infra*.

in the Orinoco country and urging the Queen to support and reward them. This poem was published as a preface to *A Relation of the second Voyage to Guiana* by Lawrence Keymis, a devoted follower of Raleigh. Moreover, in 1598 Chapman wrote a poem to Harriot whom he called "My Admired and Soule-Loved Friend," and published as well his continuation of Marlowe's *Hero and Leander*. But it is seldom remembered that in the same year, 1598, Chapman dedicated to the Earl of Essex, Raleigh's deadliest enemy, the first two sections of his important translation of Homer, *Seaven Bookes of the Iliades of Homere* and *Achilles Shield*. This catholicity of dedication suggests that Chapman was a free lance inviting patronage wherever he could, rather than a fixed satellite of Raleigh. In fact, of all his scores of dedications to various noblemen, not one was ever made to Raleigh, nor is he known to have received at any time the slightest patronage or any other attention from him.

In Chapman's writings there is, of course, everything to show that he felt the same passion for knowledge that animated Harriot and Marlowe and Raleigh. But, contrariwise, there is nothing to show that he had any interest in religious heterodoxy. Chapman's Christianity was always ardent. This author of *A Hymne To Our Sauior on the Crosse*, this "person of most reverend aspect, religious and temperate," as Wood calls him, bears no impress of the creedal iniquities of Marlowe and Harriot, or the scepticism of Raleigh.

Now to return to *The Shadow of Night*. If this was the grand manifesto for the School of Night that it is sometimes believed to be, then Chapman was acting rather peculiarly, to say the least, when he wrote in the dedication to Royden,

...I remember my good Mat. how ioyfully oftentimes you reported unto me, that most ingenious Darbie, deepe searching Northumberland, and skill-imbracing heire of Hunsdon had most profitably entertained learning in themselues....

without even mentioning Raleigh, supposed to be the moving spirit of the group, or Harriot, its best scientific brain. And, in fact, it may be gravely doubted whether Chapman really intended the poem as a declaration against the Southampton-Essex group or anybody else in particular. The hypothesis that this was his intention is based primarily not on the poem itself, which looks unpointed and harmless enough, but on Shakespeare's supposed ridicule of it in *Love's Labour's Lost,* and on the assumption that Chapman was of the Raleigh inner circle, which in turn is based on the very dubious indications we have already considered. Now whether Shakespeare was indeed ridiculing a Raleigh coterie is itself open to most serious question. The sole textual evidence for it, embodied in the lines,

> O paradox! Black is the badge of hell,
> The hue of dungeons, and the school of night,
>
> (IV, iii, 250-51)

has been vigorously and, as it seems to me, successfully attacked in a recent study.[8] Once this textual foundation is removed, the various subtleties of personal allusion which some commentators see in the play lose whatever persuasiveness they may have had. Nor should it be overlooked that the School of Night theory is antagonistic to the other widely current theory that Chapman is the rival poet of Shakespeare's sonnets, because Chapman is unlikely to have been competing with Shakespeare for Southamp-

8. E. A. Strathmann, "The Textual Evidence for 'The School of Night,'" *MLN*, LVI (1941), 176-86

ton's favor and at the same time attacking Southampton in *The Shadow of Night*.

From all this dubiety we may well emerge with one conviction—that a close relationship of either Chapman or Royden to Raleigh or to a school surrounding him is very far from being proved. They were close to each other, and Chapman was close to Harriot, but we are not dealing with syllogisms which can extend the intimacy any further. And what of the Warner named by Kyd as one of Marlowe's friends? We are not even sure whether he is William Warner, the poet of *Albion's England*, or Walter Warner, the mathematician who was friend and editor to Harriot. In the latter case, nothing is known of his personal beliefs, certainly nothing to indicate that he was disposed to advanced religious speculation, although his interest in science may be taken for granted. In the former, the poems show only a uniform ordinariness of thought, with none of the "strangely-intellectual fire" which is supposed to distinguish the School of Night. If the characterization of God in *Albion's England* as "Unpassive, unmaterial, uncompounded, Infinite" is like that given by Raleigh, it is also like that given in hundreds of Elizabethan theological treatises.

In what sense, then, was there a Raleigh School of Atheism? Not in the sense that there was a tightly interrelated group. Not in the sense that they had a definite and uniform doctrine. The whole situation is much more amorphous. Instead of a rounded circle we must conceive of a number of separate broken lines intersecting each other at different points. Instead of one attitude common to all we must understand extremes of temperament and creed. The only discoverable principle of unity among the several individuals is an earnestness of desire for knowledge. But it is not proved that they all satisfied it cooperatively.

To designate as a Raleigh School, whether of Atheism or of Night, men so loosely related is profoundly misleading.

The net result for a study of Marlowe is to replace the question of group influence with the more pertinent question of the interaction between him and specific individuals like Harriot and Royden. It also makes less likely than ever the theory that Marlowe's great protagonists were portraits of Raleigh himself or of members of his circle. Marlowe does not seem to have been this kind of topical dramatist.

Finally, certain elementary decisions as to the authenticity and chronology of the dramas and poems have to be made. I shall consider only those works which are accepted as genuine by all modern editors. There is a risk in excluding such plays as *The Contention betwixt the Two Famous Houses of York and Lancaster* and *The True Tragedy of Richard Duke of York*, but it is smaller than the risk of including them. The chronological order of Marlowe's writings I take to be *Dido* (*ca.* 1586), *Tamburlaine* (1587), *Faustus* (1588 or 1589), *The Jew of Malta* (*ca.* 1590); then *Edward II* and *The Massacre at Paris*, or vice versa (both *ca.* 1591); and, last, *Hero and Leander* (1593-). A number of authorities prefer to date *Faustus* 1592.[9] I have given elsewhere my reasons for believing wholeheartedly in the 1588 or 1589 dating. Since *The Massacre at Paris* offers little that is new, its standing relative to *Edward II* is not of great consequence.

9. See the Introduction to Boas' edition of the play, and Tucker Brooke, "The Marlowe Canon," *PMLA* XXXVII (1922), 367-417. I have argued to the contrary in "The English Faust Book and the Date of Marlowe's *Faustus*," *MLN*, LV (1940), 95-101; "Some Nashe Marginalia Concerning Marlowe," *MLN*, LVII (1942), 45-49; "The Early Date for Marlowe's *Faustus*," *MLN*, LVIII (1943), 539-42.

II

RELIGIOUS THOUGHT

2. THE BIOGRAPHICAL EVIDENCE

THE RECORD OF MARLOWE'S RELIGIOUS HETERODOXY begins unobtrusively with his failure to take holy orders upon graduating from Cambridge in June, 1587. As the holder of an Archbishop Parker scholarship he was expected to study for the ministry, and in fact no doubt accumulated during his years at the university much of the theological learning which he later used in attacking Christianity. His decision not to enter the church, reached probably against considerable pressure from his college, is best attributed, at least in part, to a powerful distaste for the creed he would have been asked to teach.

Shortly before the date of his graduation, the rumor ran through the university that Marlowe, like many another young man from Cambridge and Oxford at this time, had turned Catholic and gone to study in the school for seminary priests at Rheims. The rumor, however, was false, for he was absent instead on some kind of government service. So much is clear from the letter, dated June 29, which the Privy Council sent to the Cambridge authorities: [1]

1. See C. F. Tucker Brooke, *The Life of Marlowe* (London: Methuen & Co., 1930), p. 32. Most of the other biographical evidence to be cited here is conveniently assembled in the Appendices of this book,

Whereas it was reported that Christopher Morley was determined to have gone beyond the seas to Reames and there to
remain, their Lordships thought good to certify that he had
no such intent, but that in all his actions he had behaved himself orderly and discreetly, whereby he had done her Majesty
good service and deserved to be rewarded for his faithful
dealing. Their Lordships' request was that the rumour thereof
should be allayed by all possible means, and that he should be
furthered in the degree he was to take this next Commence-
ment. . . .

He did not go abroad as a Catholic: this is the single fact
of immediate concern which the letter supplies. Whether
Marlowe's service to the government was merely as some
sort of confidential agent to the Low Countries or as a
spy upon Catholic plots in England or France, whether
this service ceased in 1587 or continued intermittently in
the after years, whether it was connected in some way with
his death at the hand of Ingram Frizer in 1593—these are
all matters on which at present there is little or no real
evidence and much diverse conjecture.[2] As nearly as
may be judged, the connection of these questions with
Marlowe's religion is problematical and remote. Holding
almost any kind of faith, he might have been almost any
kind of spy and have met almost any kind of death. For-
tunately, we need not rely on such conjectures. Direct
evidence as to the nature of his religious thought is most
abundant.

---

commencing on page 83. For the remainder see the same author's article,
"The Reputation of Christopher Marlowe," *Transactions of the Connecticut Academy of Arts and Sciences*, XXV (1922), 347-408.

2. The sanest interpretation of all the facts seems to me to be given
by Brooke, *Life*, pp. 32-37. *Cf.* also A. K. Gray, "Some Observations on
Christopher Marlowe, Government Agent," *PMLA*, XLIII (1928), 682-
700; Ethel Seaton, "Marlowe, Robert Poley, and the Tippings," *RES*,
V (1929), 273-87; Samuel Tannenbaum, *The Assassination of Christopher Marlowe* (1928).

The first inkling of "atheism" after the start of Marlowe's career as dramatist sounds in Greene's epistle to the prose romance, *Perimedes the Blacksmith* (1588): [3]

...I could not make my verses iet upon the stage in tragicall buskins... daring God out of heauen with that Atheist Tamburlan, or blaspheming with the mad preest of the sonne: but let me rather openly pocket up the Asse at Diogenes hand: then wantonlye set out such impious instances of intollerable poetrie, such mad and scoffing poets that haue propheticall spirits as bred of Merlins race....

Marlowe here appears as an impious scoffer whose blasphemy is reflected in his drama. Greene's more famous appeal in the *Groatsworth of Wit* (1592), emphasizing again Marlowe's personal irreligion, addresses him as one "who hath said... like the foole in his heart, There is no God...." The comment has special value as coming from one who probably knew Marlowe personally. The two men were both graduates of Cambridge, frequenters of theatrical circles in London, and possible collaborators in several plays.

Envy, of course, may have colored Greene's opinion, but considering that he was on his deathbed when he wrote the *Groatsworth* and was engaged in the repentant moralizing natural to the occasion, an actual falsification is quite unlikely. As it was, for Marlowe's sake Chettle cut out the more damaging parts of Greene's exhortation before it reached print. Chettle's refusal to apologize to Marlowe for the publication as he did to Shakespeare for the "only Shake-scene in a countrie" passage, together with his tart remark that he did not care to make Marlowe's acquaintance, is further testimony of the latter's bad repute at the end of 1592.

3. Brooke, "Reputation," p. 351. The following quotation from Greene's *Groatsworth of Wit* is given on page 352.

What the poet had been doing to earn this ill name can be glimpsed in the accusations made against him by Thomas Kyd in June, 1593, soon after Marlowe's death. Kyd had been arrested on suspicion of complicity in the writing of inflammatory literature against foreigners. When Arian quotations from John Proctor's obscure little book, *The Fal of the Late Arrian*,[4] were found in manuscript in his room, Kyd hastened to assure the authorities that they belonged to Marlowe, who, two years ago, had been "wrytinge in one chamber" with Kyd and had left the papers there by mistake. The story sounds likely enough, despite the obvious existence of a motive on Kyd's part for shifting the blame to a dead man. Marlowe probably was doing a bit of research for the treatise which, according to several later reports, he wrote against Christianity. Kyd also made several other accusations which are more difficult to impugn, including the statement that the Lord (probably Lord Strange) for whose company of players both dramatists had been writing, cast Marlowe off,[5] "ffor never cold my Lord endure his name, or sight, when he heard of his conditions, nor wold in deed the forme of devyne praier used duelie in his Lordships house, haue quadred with such reprobates." Since a declaration of fact like this could be verified, it was one which Kyd could not afford to fictionize. Moreover, he named the names of Marlowe's associates, "Harriot, Warner, Royden, and some stationers in Paules churchyard" from whom corroboration might be obtained. This willingness to particularize is not the sign of guilt. Most important of all, he gave a highly concrete

4. Published as long ago as 1549. Proctor took up each Arian argument in turn and gave a refutation. The manuscript found in Kyd's room contained the Arian matter only, omitting the refutations. See W. D. Briggs, "On a Document Concerning Christopher Marlowe," *SP*, XX (1923), 153-59.

5. Brooke, *Life*, p. 104.

description of Marlowe's attitudes and sayings, such as he could remember: [6]

...ffirst it was his custom when J knewe him first & as J heare saie he

contynewd it in table talk or otherwise to iest at the devine scriptures

gybe at praiers, & stryve in argument to frustrate & confute what hath byn

spoke or wrytt by prophets & such holie men.

1 He wold report St John to be our saviour Christes Alexis J cover it with reverence

and trembling that is that Christ did loue him with an extraordinary loue.

2 That for me to wryte a poem of St paules conversion as J was determined

he said wold be as if J shold go wryte a book of fast & loose, esteming

paul a Jugler.

3 That the prodigall Childes portion was but fower nobles he held his

purse so neere the bottom in all pictures, and that it either was a iest

or els fower nobles then was thought a great patrimony not thinking it a parable.

4 That things esteemed to be donn by devine power might haue aswell been don

by observation of men all which he wold so sodenlie take slight occasion to

slyp out as J & many others in regard of his other rashnes in attempting

soden pryvie iniuries to men did ouerslypp though often reprehend him for it....

As persuasive as any feature of Kyd's letter is the close resemblance between his allegations and those appearing

6. *Ibid.*, p. 107.

in the note sent by Richard Baines to the Privy Council at about the same time. Whether Baines had any motive in thus exposing Marlowe, other than his expressed one of bringing to book a dangerous member of the community, is not known. But the paramount fact is that both his memorandum and that of Kyd ascribe to Marlowe the same gibes against the homosexuality of Jesus and the divine origin of miracles, the same contempt for St. Paul, and the same type of critical humor, most trenchant, bawdy, and sardonic. Both, moreover, mention Harriot as an associate of Marlowe.[7] And both dwell on the persistence of the poet's attacks on the holies of Christianity. His efforts, as described, amount to a campaign against the religion; he does not merely speak at random but engages in purposeful debate. "... it was his custom ... in table talk or otherwise to iest ... & stryve in argument to frustrate & confute ...," says Kyd. And Baines: "These things, with many other shall by good & honest witnes be aproved to be his opinons and Comon Speeches and that this Marlow doth not only hould them himself, but almost into euery Company he Cometh he perswades men to Atheism...."[8] Baines's offer to produce other "good & honest witnes," it will be noted, was not one which could be rashly made to the Queen's Privy Council.

7. A further indication of the truth of Baines's allegations is that the statement he attributes to Marlowe "that he was acquainted with one Poole a prisoner in Newgate who hath greate Skill in mixture of mettals..." can be, in part, verified. A John Poole, a coiner, had been imprisoned in Newgate in 1589 at the time when Marlowe himself was there for his share in the killing of William Bradley. Cf. Mark Eccles, *Christopher Marlowe in London* (Harvard University Press, 1934), pp. 36-37; and "Marlowe in Newgate," *TLS*, Sept. 6, 1934, p. 604.

8. Eccles, *Marlowe in London*, p. 99. See for collections of the available information about Baines, *ibid.*, pp. 100-3; F. S. Boas, *Christopher Marlowe* (Oxford, Clarendon Press, 1940), pp. 245 ff.; F. S. Boas and E. Vine Hall, "Richard Baines, Informer," *Nineteenth Century*, CXII (1932), 742-51.

Some effort, indeed, has been made to discredit Baines's testimony on the ground that he was implicated in slightly shady business dealings and that he may have been the Richard Baines who, for some crime unknown, was hanged at Tyburn in 1594. But it may have been another Richard Baines who was hanged,[9] and if we should discredit all Elizabethans who were off color in business ethics, few would be left capable of giving evidence in any court. Baines may not have been a saint, and certainly he was a busybody, but even the testimony of a busybody carries weight if it is specific, detailed, consistent with itself and with other testimony, and backed by an offer to produce corroboration before the Privy Council, a body not likely to put up with any nonsense.

Efforts to sully the motives of those who bring the charges against Marlowe are, I think, unprofitable. There are too many such charges, some by reputable, others by disreputable, men, and too many points of agreement between them. Baines and Kyd cannot be shown to have colluded with each other in any way, yet their accounts possess a sameness which is the guarantee of truth. In turn, they both receive support from two Harleian manuscripts, undated but probably written in 1593, itemizing the dangerous sayings of Richard Cholmley. This was the same Cholmley who, according to Baines, "hath confessed that he was perswaded by Marloe's Reasons to become an Atheist." In one manuscript Cholmley is quoted as saying "that Marlowe is able to show more sound reasons for atheism than any divine in England is able to give to prove

9. Besides several ineligibles, two men named Richard Baines have been found who might have been Marlowe's accuser. One lived, apparently, with all virtue; the other possibly, but not certainly, committed business sins. One died on the gallows, the other in his bed. But we do not know which life to match with which death, nor which life-death to assign to the betrayer of Marlowe.

divinity, and that Marlowe told him that he hath read the atheist lecture to Sir Walter Raleigh and others." [10] The emphasis again is on Marlowe's gathering of arguments against divinity and his labors to disseminate his views, this time by laying them before Raleigh and others. As before, Cholmley cannot be connected personally with either Baines or Kyd.

A second manuscript, in the same handwriting as the first, ascribes to Cholmley many of the specific blasphemies ascribed by Baines to Marlowe, together with some new ones:

His seconde course is to make a ieste of the Scripture with these fearefull horrible & damnable speeches, that Ihesus Christe was a bastarde St. Mary a whore & the Aungell Gabriell a Bawde to the holy ghoste that Christe was iustly persecuted by the Iewes for his owne foolishness. That Moyses was a Iugler and Aaron a cosener the one for his miracles to Pharao to prove there was a god, & the other for takinge the eareringes of the children of Israell to make a golden calfe with many other blasphemous speeches of the devine essence of God which I feare to rehearse.

The language about Christ, the Virgin, the Angel Gabriel, and Moses is almost identical with that of the Baines note.[11] On the other hand, there are new details about Moses, and completely new observations about Aaron and "the devine essence of God." Unfortunately we do not know the identity of the man who wrote the two manuscripts. Danchin believes he was Baines, on the argument that the handwriting is the same as that in the Baines

10. Both Harleian manuscripts are published in full by F. C. Danchin, "Etudes Critiques sur Christopher Marlowe," *Revue Germanique,* IX (1913), 566-87. The first MS likewise is printed by Tucker Brooke (*Life,* pp. 64-66).

11. See *infra,* pp. 34-39.

note;[12] Tucker Brooke doubts the sameness. In either case, the likelihood is that we get through the two Harleian manuscripts a picture of Cholmley repeating the "reasons" of the dramatist who persuaded him "to become an Atheist." His new matter about Aaron and Moses, not given in the Baines memorandum, has the true ring of Marlowe.

Marlowe's death provoked a number of significant allusions. Within a few months Gabriel Harvey was describing him as one "that nor feared God, nor dreaded Diu'll" and "a Lucian," or mocker of the gods.[13] Personal venom against Marlowe as Nashe's friend may have dictated these attacks, but they are of a piece with his general reputation. Much more factual is Beard's puritanical denunciation of the dramatist four years later, in 1597, as an atheist who "not only in word blasphemed the trinitie, but also (as it is credibly reported) wrote bookes against it...."[14] The sources of Beard's information about the dramatist's life are not known, but since many of his facts are accurate, although others are distorted, what he says is entitled to some credence. William Vaughan's account in *The Golden Grove* (1600) seems to draw on independent springs of knowledge about the poet even closer to the truth. Interesting, therefore, is his repetition of the same report: "Not inferiour to these was one Christopher Marlow by profession a playmaker, who, as it is reported, about 7 yeeres a-goe wrote a booke against the Trinitie...."[15] Quite the most circumstantial mention, however, is that which Simon Aldrich made to the Kentish poet, Henry Oxinden, entered

---

12. Danchin, *op. cit.*, p. 576; Brooke, *Life*, p. 66. I have not had an opportunity to examine the holograph.

13. Brooke, *Life*, pp. 111-12; Hale Moore, "Gabriel Harvey's References to Marlowe," *SP*, XXIII (1926), 337-57.

14. Brooke, *Life*, p. 112.

15. *Ibid.*, p. 114.

in the latter's commonplace book in 1640.[16] Aldrich had
been a Cambridge scholar and fellow in the years 1593 to
1607, and as a man of critical and cultured mind was a
most creditable witness. He told Oxinden "that Marlo
who wrot Hero & Leander was an atheist & had writ a
booke against Scripture; how it was all one man's making,[17] & would have printed it but could not be suffered."
Aldrich also spoke of a "mr Fineux of Dover was an
Atheist ... he learnd all Marlo by heart & divers other
bookes: Marlo made him an Atheist." The fact that a
Thomas Fineux entered Corpus Christi, Marlowe's own
college at Cambridge, in 1587, gives this narrative a distinct air of truth. And the pattern, we notice, is always the
same: Marlowe is making converts by his skill in dialectic;
Marlowe is writing a polemic against Christianity.

In a moment I shall give reasons for believing that the
arguments of this lost polemic, many of them actually
couched in Marlowe's own wording, are preserved in the
Baines note. First, however, certain general conclusions

16. Mark Eccles, "Marlowe in Kentish Tradition," *N&Q*, CLXIX
(1935), 20-23, 39-41, 58-61.

17. The contention that the various books of the Bible had not been
written by their purported authors had long been one of the chief
avenues of attack on Christianity. St. Augustine of Hippo in his *Reply
to Faustus the Manichean* (*Works*, ed. Dods; Edinburgh, 1872, V, Bk.
XXXIII, 552) quotes Faustus as arguing: "Besides, as we have proved
again and again, the writings are not the production of Christ or of His
apostles, but a compilation of rumours and beliefs made, long after their
departure, by some obscure semi-Jews. ..." Calvin (*Institution of Christian Religion*, London, 1578, fol. 22) attempts to refute the same argument as applied to the books of the Old Testament. Philip de Mornay's
The Trewnesse of the Christian Religion (trans. Sidney and Golding;
London, 1587, p. 417), deals more specifically with Marlowe's point:
"And if any man ... will step foorth and say, that our Scriptures are an
Historie gathered out of the Registers of many ages, by some one
author; as we see Berosus hath done for the Chaldees, Duis for the
Phenicians, Manetho for the Egiptians, and such others; let him tell
us then (I hartily pray him,) in what age of the world that Author is
lykely to haue liued."

about the biographical evidence as a whole require sharp
stress. The charges against Marlowe come from too many
different people, complete strangers to one another, to be
the outgrowth of either individual malice or criminal col-
lusion. They are, furthermore, much too concrete and circumstantial to be merely loose scandalmongering. They are
contemporaneous with Marlowe. They cohere together
remarkably in matters of detail. Still better, they are unopposed by any direct evidence to the contrary. I am not
speaking now of the indirect evidence of the plays, which
will be examined in due time, with results sufficiently un-
favorable to any view of Marlowe's religious orthodoxy.
But on the strictly biographical level, neither Marlowe
himself, nor anybody else in his period, ever spoke word or
did act, so far as we know, to assert his acceptance of
Christian dogma after he left the university. We could
scarcely ask for more widely distributed, more mutually
substantiated, and more overwhelming evidence of any
fact over three centuries old. It makes untenable the theory,
sometimes raised, that the poet was actually a Catholic.
No Catholic could have scoffed at the virgin birth and accused Jesus of homosexuality, as Marlowe did.[18] Nor—to
counter another theory—can one well imagine him uttering such blasphemies in order to conceal his role as a spy,
since they would hardly be likely to win him the confidence of either the Catholics or the Puritan left wing, the
parties whom the government most wished to keep under
surveillance. Rather, the cumulative force of the whole

18. The statement attributed by Baines to Marlowe, "That if there be
any god or any good Religion, then it is in the papistes because the
service of god is performed with more Cerimonies, as Elevation of the
mass, organs, singing men, Shaven Crownes & cta" does not, of course,
alter this fact. All the other statements of the Baines note would seem
utterly vile to a Catholic, and even the "if" clause would not please
him. As will be shown later, Marlowe merely uses the comparison with
Catholic ritual in order to deride the Protestants.

multitude of charges gathering against Marlowe in the active years of his life is to show him as a propagandist and instigator of revolt against Christianity, anxious to proselytize others to his views. On this point the evidence seems to me quite decisive.

3. THE BAINES NOTE

MUCH THAT HAS BEEN SUMMARILY OUTLINED IN the foregoing analysis receives new reality from a patient study of that master key to the mind of Marlowe, the Baines note. On minute examination it appears that the statements attributed to Marlowe, even as they stand, reveal a progress and transition of ideas which strongly suggest that they form parts of an organized dissertation against Christianity. And if some transpositions are made in their order, unity of structure emerges even more convincingly. Baines seems to be taking notes either direct from a manuscript written by Marlowe or from some lecture which he delivered. Particularly interesting is the "that" clause into which each statement is cast (e. g. "That the first beginning of Religioun was only to keep men in awe"), resembling the typical section or chapter heading of the Renaissance treatise on theology. Thus the list as a whole has all the air of a series of formal propositions, each capable of support by a section of detailed argument, and all articulated into a single overarching design.

As to why transpositions are needed, one may suggest either that Baines, jotting down his notes hurriedly on slips of paper while listening to Marlowe's atheist lecture, did not rearrange them properly, or that he leafed through the manuscript rather haphazardly, noting those section headings that caught his eye. The strong probability that some of the statements represent *ad lib.* conversational additions by Marlowe must also be allowed for, in view of the highly personal nature of a few, like those referring to Poole and Cholmley. Suppositions of this kind must of course justify themselves, as the argument progresses, by their utility in affording a more credible and meaningful view of the Baines memorandum than could otherwise be attained.

Baines's allegations are here reproduced in the order in which he made them,[1] but the numerals in the left margin opposite each indicate a proposed rearrangement based on community of subject matter.

> A note Containing the opinion of on Christopher Marly Concerning his damnable <opini> Judgment of Religion, and scorn of Gods word.

1a   That the Indians and many Authors of antiquity haue assuredly writen of aboue 16 thousand yeares agone wheras <Moyses> Adam is <said> proued to haue lived within 6 thowsand yeares.

1b   He affirmeth that Moyses was but a Jugler & that one Heriots being Sir W Raleighs man Can do more than he.

1d   That Moyses made the Jewes to travell xl yeares in the wildernes, (which Jorney might haue bin done in lesse then one yeare) ere they Came to the promised land to thintent that those who were privy to most of his subtilties might perish and so an everlasting superstition Remain in the hartes of the people.

1e   That the first beginning of Religioun was only to keep men in awe.

1. Reprinted from Brooke, *Life*. Words in brackets were scored through in the original.

1c   That it was an easy matter for Moyses being brought up
      in all the artes of the Egiptians to abuse the Jewes being a
      rude & grosse people.

2b   That Christ was a bastard and his mother dishonest.

2c   That he was the sonne of a Carpenter, and that if the
      Jewes among whome he was borne did Crucify him theie
      best knew him and whence he Came.

2d   That Crist deserved better to dy then Barrabas and that
      the Jewes made a good Choise, though Barrabas were both
      a thief and a murtherer.

3a   That if there be any god or any good Religion, then it
      is in the papistes because the service of god is performed
      with more Cerimonies, as Elevation of the mass, organs,
      singing men, Shaven Crownes & cta. That all protestantes
      are Hypocritical asses.

3c   That if he were put to write a new Religion, he would
      vndertake both a more Exellent and Admirable methode
      and that all the new testament is filthily written.

2e   That the woman of Samaria & her sister were whores &
      that Crist knew them dishonestly.

2f   That St John the Evangelist was bedfellow to Christ and
      leaned alwaies in his bosome, that he vsed him as the
      sinners of Sodoma.

2g   That all they that loue not Tobacco & Boies were fooles.

3d   That all the apostles were fishermen and base fellowes
      neyther of wit nor worth, that Paull only had wit but he
      was a timerous fellow in bidding men to be subiect to
      magistrates against his Conscience.

3e   That he had as good Right to Coine as the Queen of
      England, and that he was aquainted with one Poole a
      prisoner in Newgate who hath greate skill in mixture of
      mettals and hauing learned some thinges of him he ment
      through help of a Cunninge stamp maker to Coin ffrench
      Crownes pistoletes and English shillinges.

3b   That if Christ would haue instituted the sacrament with
      more Ceremoniall Reverence it would haue bin had in

more admiration, that it would haue bin much better being administered in a Tobacco pipe.

2a   That the Angell Gabriell was baud to the holy ghost, because he brought the salutation to Mary.

4a | That on Ric Cholmley <hath Cholmley> hath Confessed that he was perswaded by Marloe's Reasons to become an Atheist.

These thinges, with many other shall by good & honest witnes be aproved to be his opinions and Comon Speeches and that this Marlow doth not only hould them himself, but almost into every Company he Cometh he perswades men to Atheism willing them not to be afeard of bugbeares and hobgoblins, and vtterly scorning both god and his ministers as I Richard Baines will Justify & approue both by mine oth and the testimony of many honest men, and almost al men with whome he hath Conversed any time will testify the same, and as I think all men in Cristianity ought to indevor that the mouth of / so dangerous a member may

4b be stopped, he saith likewise that he hath quoted a number of Contrarieties oute of the Scripture which he hath giuen to some great men who in Convenient time shalbe named. When these thinges shalbe Called in question the witnes shalbe produced.

Richard Baines

It will be observed that the accusations fall under four main topics: (1) attacks on the theological version of early history with respect to the Old Testament figures, Adam and Moses; (2) scoffs at Christ as to the virgin birth, his divinity, and his sexual looseness; (3) criticism of the "methode" of the Christian religion; (4) statements of Marlowe's efforts to secure converts to atheism. This fourth division is shaky, and perhaps no attempt should be made to set up such a topic, since it seems to consist of the left-overs of Baines's notations. The other three topics, however (with some reservations as to topic 3), not only are well compacted within themselves but can be seen to flow readily into one another. That this is so will be more convincingly demonstrated if an interpretation and paraphrase of the whole is given. We may express its spirit and tendency, without claiming an impossible accuracy in details, somewhat in this fashion:

The theological explanation of early history, Marlowe may be thought to declare, is false. It teaches (1a) that mankind began with Adam less than 6,000 years ago, whereas we know that there are accounts of a history much earlier. It is also false (1b) in holding Moses to be a true performer of miracles.[2] He merely performed juggling tricks which Harriot can better today. By them (1c) he was easily able to hoodwink the Jews, who were an unsophisticated people. In order to conceal these deceits and perpetuate superstition (1d) he secured the death of his confederates by multiplying the hardships of the journey in the wilderness. Therein he was a typical founder of religion. Religions are begun by unscrupulous men as a device to attain power (1e).

Christ is another pretender and false leader. If the theological account of his conception through the Holy Ghost is to be credited, the Angel Gabriel was a bawd (2a). But of course the account is trumped up. Christ was in fact a man like any other, and his claim of divine sonship was merely a humbug. He was either the bastard son of an adulterous union (2b) or else merely the legitimate son of a carpenter (2c). The Jews, who knew him all his life, were in the best position to realize his true origin and were justified in crucifying him (2c). He deserved death because

2. The underlying connection in Marlowe's mind between the first two assertions may be the thought of Harriot. See Nashe's possible allusion to Harriot in *Pierce Penniless* (1592): "I heare that there be Mathematicians abroad that will prove men before Adam."—F. S. Boas, *Marlowe and his Circle* (Oxford, 1929), p. 70. But *cf.* footnote 6, *infra*.

his deception of the people was worse than murder or thievery (2d) and because he was in addition sexually impure. Did he not fornicate with the woman of Samaria and her sister (2e) and have unnatural relations with St. John the Evangelist (2f)? However, he can scarcely be blamed for the latter, since all sensible men do the like (2g)—and smoke tobacco.

The fact of the matter is that, considering the frauds of prophets and messiahs, no organized religion is worthy of credence; and indeed we may go further and ask whether any God at all can be believed in.[3] But certain established religions are wiser than others in the method of their appeal. Catholicism is superior in this respect to Protestantism because it has insight enough to know that men's religious feelings are best aroused by the use of elaborate ceremonial (3a). Protestants censure Catholics for employing a ritual but are hypocrites since they themselves use a different, though inferior, one (3a).[4] Christ was foolish in not seeing this psychological principle and building his religion more firmly by surrounding the sacrament of holy communion with more impressive ceremonies (3b). Why not administer it in a tobacco pipe, for example (3b)? Moreover the presentation of Christianity has been bungled in other ways; the abominable style of the New Testament is an instance (3c). Christ made another error of strategy in choosing ignorant, worthless fishermen as his apostles to spread his doctrine (3d). Paul was the only man of brains

3. This bridge of ideas can only be conjectural. Between sections 2 and 3 there is a lacuna which, although not impassable, requires some structure of speculation. It should also be admitted that unity and consecutiveness are more difficult to see in the allegations which I have grouped as topic 3 than in the earlier allegations. Baines's notes seem to grow more jumbled as he proceeds.

4. Baines's inclusion of the statement of Protestant hypocrisy in the paragraph dealing with ceremonies tends to indicate that Marlowe attacked Protestants in that particular rather than in general.

among them, but he was a coward, as is shown by his violation of his conscience in bidding men obey the law of the state (3d). Many laws unjustly encroach upon the rights of the individual and should not be obeyed. The present English law against coining is just such a law, and I for one do not intend to obey it (3e).

Everything makes it plain that Christianity is a bugaboo from whose tyranny men must be freed. I have succeeded in converting Cholmley to my views (4a) and have written a pamphlet, which I have given to certain great men, pointing out the self-contradictions in the Bible (4b).

Too much should not be claimed for this attempt to re-build the dissertation, of course. It is completely tentative and is intended rather to suggest the running of a general current of continuity through the whole than to maintain the correctness of any one of the proposed transpositions or links of thought. In the nature of the case, we cannot suppose that Baines reported every detail completely or intelligently or fairly. It is enough if the whole exhibits an essential unity of design.

Whence, then, comes this unity? It derives, I believe, from the lost, unpublished tract which Marlowe wrote against Christianity. We have already noticed briefly Aldrich's statement that Marlowe "had writ a booke against Scripture; how it was all one man's making...," and Cholmley's "that Marlowe told him that he hath read the atheist lecture to Sir Walter Raleigh and others." The most probable meaning of "read the atheist lecture" is that Marlowe did literally read a manuscript, perhaps the identical one mentioned by Aldrich, to Raleigh's circle. The whole context of Cholmley's assertion indicates [5] that Marlowe

5. The full text reads: "That he saith and verily believeth that one Marlowe is able to show more sound reasons for atheism than any divine in England is able to give to prove divinity, and that Marloe

presented to Raleigh's group a formal argument; and the most likely occasion for a presentation of that kind would be the author's reading of a work newly written, not yet published.

Most interesting of all, however, is what Thomas Beard writes only four years after Marlowe's death. Marlowe, he says,

fell (not without iust desert) to that outrage and extremitie, that hee denied God and his sonne Christ and not only in word blasphemed the trinitie, but also (as it is credibly reported) wrote bookes against it, affirming our Sauiour to be but a deceiuer, and Moses to be but a coniurer and seducer of the people, and the holy Bible to be but vaine and idle stories, and all religion but a deuice of pollicie.

Beard makes a specific distinction between what the dramatist said and what he wrote. Then under the latter heading are listed four blasphemous opinions, of which three appear in almost exactly the same form in the Baines document and the fourth is implicit there. Not one iota of evidence exists to show that Beard either knew Baines or had access to the Baines document, which was filed with the papers of the Privy Council and was no doubt treated as a secret of state.

Why, then, have the two sets of allegations so singular a similarity? The most plausible explanation is that Baines

---

told him he hath read the atheist lecture to Sir Walter Raleigh and others." It would not be surprising if this "atheist lecture" included the list of contradictory Biblical texts which Baines refers to in his last paragraph: "...he saith likewise that he hath quoted a number of Contrarieties oute of the Scripture which he hath giuen to some great men who in Convenient time shalbe named." The verb "giuen" implies a manuscript (left with some of the audience after being read), and the "great men" are not likely to be any but Raleigh and his associates since these are the only prominent men, interested in advanced religious speculation, thought to have been close enough to Marlowe to warrant his taking the risk of communicating dangerous papers to them.

either had access to the manuscript of the book (or books) Beard mentions or else heard Marlowe himself reading from it in the course of his lectures against Christianity.

If this hypothesis is correct, we can get from an examination of the more seriously intentioned items in the Baines list a notion, distorted perhaps but nevertheless illuminating, of the real nature of the book which Marlowe wrote. It was a work attacking Christian dogma on rationalistic and historical grounds. It was primarily concerned not to disprove the existence of God, although that may possibly have been Marlowe's ultimate objective, but to discredit the authority of Scripture. Here the choice of Moses and Christ as the chief subjects of attack is highly significant. Renaissance religion considered Moses, giver of the Law, and Christ, redeemer of men condemned by the rigor of the Law, the two main underpropping columns of Christianity. If these could be destroyed the whole edifice must crumble. Marlowe strikes not by denying that such men as Moses and Christ ever lived but by stripping them of divine authority and explaining them as ambitious men seeking power under the pretext of religion.

We cannot say whether Marlowe wrote only one such treatise, as might be inferred from Aldrich, or several, as Beard avers. The former seems on the whole the more likely. But even if he produced several, the dominant homogeneity of subject-matter in the Baines charges tends to show that they stem from only one. Whether as manuscript or manuscripts, Marlowe's unpublished writing seems to have circulated with some freedom: it was heard of by Beard, heard of or seen by Aldrich, perhaps shown to Cholmley and Fineux, and listened to by Raleigh and others from Marlowe's own lips.

SPECIFIC MEANINGS

It is time now to become very inquisitive about the specific meanings of the dramatist's statements recorded by Baines, especially in their connection with the religious controversies of his own and earlier periods. In spite of the impossibility of exhausting so huge a subject, I hope to make it clear that the Marlowe of the Baines note, far from being a mere jester at religion, was a serious thinker who had for his views both ancient precedent and contemporary parallel; furthermore, that his utterances represent a carefully designed attack on Christian dogma, often with very dexterous use of the language of Scripture itself. Greatly daring, brilliantly sardonic, and fortified with Scriptural learning, he was an heir of all the ages of protest against Christianity and a voice for the inarticulate and nameless of his own day. From the paraphrase of the Baines note given above it seems evident that Marlowe's argument against Scripture was quite the opposite of random. It was drawn up chronologically and directed against the central elements of faith.

The first charge is, "That the Indians and many Authors of antiquity haue assuredly written of aboue 16 thousand yeares agone whereas Adam is proued to haue lived within 6 thowsand yeares." It is usual to say that Marlowe got this idea from Harriot, who has left notes on the chronology of Genesis.[6] Perhaps he did. We should be a little wary of this conclusion, however, because calculation of Old Testament chronology was a favorite occupation of the sixteenth century. Placing creation of the world vari-

6. Harriot's notes have never been published, and no descriptions of them have been available to indicate whether or not his calculations were unorthodox, and if so, to what extent. One notices that Marlowe based his objection on the authority of the ancients, not on science or mathematics.

ously between 5505 B.C. and 3759 B.C., all orthodox computations were based solely on Biblical texts.[7] Nevertheless, many of them found it hard to ignore and even harder to reconcile the very different accounts given by Greek, Egyptian, Babylonian and other ancient historians. Philip de Mornay's way of disposing of the Chaldee records is characteristic:

...they make their vaunt that they haue the natiuities of Childred noted & set downe in writing...for aboue the space of three and fortie thousand yeres afore the reigne of the great Alexander. And that is true. But...when they speake after their Schoolemaner, they meane alwaies (as witnesseth Diodorus) the moneth yeere, that is to say, euery moneth to be a yeere.[8]

This is a very convenient method. Raleigh, therein markedly differing from Marlowe, likewise applied it in his *History of the World* to Egyptian traditions said to be 13,000 years old.[9] Clearly, the possibility that the world might be older than Scripture permitted was something to be reckoned with. In one form, the idea was even imputed to the Family of Love by John Rogers, who said, "They holde, that there was a worlde before Adams time,

7. See M. Hanmer, *A Chronographie* (London, 1585), p. 554; Iohn More, *A Table From the Beginning of the world to this day* (Cambridge, 1593); and many others.

8. *Trewnesse of the Christian Religion* chap. VIII, p. 115. This work, over six hundred pages long, contained one of the finest compilations of anti-Christian arguments ever assembled during the Renaissance, each accompanied by Mornay's reply. See similarly, Calvin, *The Institution of Christian Religion* (trans. T. Norton, London, 1578), Lib. I, chap. VIII, fol. 20ʳ; Nicholas Gibbens, *Questions and Disputations Concerning the Holy Scripture* (London, 1601), chap. II, p. 56.

9. Oxford University Press, 1829, Bk. I, chap. VIII, sec. xi, p. 298. Lodowick Lloyd's *Consent of Time* (London, 1590, p. 142), also refers to the 13,000 years of Egyptian antiquity and explains them in the same way.

as there is now." [10] In fact, the issue had a long history and was probably as old as the church itself. It was debated for the Christians as early as *ca.* A.D. 170 by Theophilus of Antioch.[11] And the amount of pagan authority which had to be denied or explained away was very great. For example, Egyptian history was said by Herodotus to go back more than 17,000 years, by Diodorus Siculus 23,000 years, by Pomponius Mela above 13,000, by Plato 8,000, by Diogenes Laertius 48,000.[12] Babylonian claims of an antiquity of over 400,000 years were reported by Alexander Polyhistor and Abydenus, but ridiculed by Cicero.[13] A Persian civilization 6,000 years before the fall of Troy is mentioned by Diogenes Laertius.[14] Finally, Aristotle and many other philosophers held that the world had always existed. Marlowe, therefore, had good reason to say that "many Authors of antiquity" opposed the Christian chronology. He chose a limit of 16,000 years apparently because sixteen contrasted to six made a good rhetorical jingle, and because the figure was conservative. But why he specified Indian writers is not so easy to discover. Most of the accessible references to Indian antiquities were vague.

10. John Rogers, *Displaying of...the Familie of Loue* (London, 1578), sig. K2r.

11. *Theophilus to Autolycus* (Ante-Nicene Christian Library, Vol. III), Bk. III, chap. XVI, p. 120. Here Apollonius the Egyptian is quoted as declaring the world to be 153,075 years old. Our question was usually merged into the question whether the books of Moses were the oldest writings of mankind. On this point the Church fathers were vehement. Each nation contended that its own records were oldest and therefore most reliable.

12. Herodotus (Loeb Library) Bk. II, sec. 43, p. 329; Diodorus Siculus (Loeb) Bk. I, sec. 44, p. 157, also pp. 73, 77, 83; Pomponius Mela, *The Situation of the World* (trans. A. Golding; London, 1590), p. 19; Plato, *Timaeus* (Loeb), p. 37; Diogenes Laertius (Loeb), Bk. I, Prologue.

13. Extracts from Alexander Polyhistor and Abydenus are given by I. P. Cory, *Ancient Fragments* (London: Wm. Pickering, 1832), pp. 21, 26, 32, 33. Cicero, *De Divinatione* (Loeb) Bk. I, xix, 37.

14. Bk. I, Prologue.

Strabo and Diodorus Siculus, for instance, wrote descriptions implying great age for the Indian nation but risked no particular date whatever. The most definite figures I have seen appear in Arrian's *Indica* [15] and in the *Polyhistor* of Julius Solinus,[16] where events in India considerably more than 6,000 years before the conquest by Alexander the Great were narrated.

In the succeeding portion of the Baines note, Marlowe shifts his attack from the Mosaic cosmogony to Moses himself, saying "that Moyses was but a Jugler & that one Heriots being Sir W Raleighs man Can do more than he." This type of argument was giving some concern to Renaissance divines, as can be seen in Calvin's *The Institution of Christian Religion:* [17]

But because the matter was plainlier knowen, than that the prophane coulde deny that miracles were done by Moses: the father of lyeng hath ministered them an other cauillation, saying that they were done by Magicall artes and sorcerie.... Truely no such deceiuer useth his iugglinge castes, but that he studieth to amase the mindes of the people to get himselfe a fame. But what doth Moses? ... he crieth out, that himselfe and his brother Aaron are nothing, but doth onely execute those things that God hath appointed ... how oft did sometime the people prowdely and impudently make insurrections ... how could he haue begyled their furor with illusions?

15. Loeb, Bk. VIII, chap. IX, p. 333. But Marlowe may be thinking of the Indians of America. See Nashe's *Christs Teares Over Ierusalem* (ed. McKerrow, II, 116), describing modern atheists: "Impudently they persist in it, that the late discouered Indians are able to shew antiquities thousands before Adam."

16. Trans. A. Golding; London, 1587, sig. Dd2ᵛ. L. Thorndike (*A History of Magic and Experimental Science*, New York, 1923, II, 898), says that Petrus de Abano's *Conciliator* lists "various estimates of the number of years since creation ... up to the enormous figure of 1,474, 346,290 years given by the Indians and Persians."

17. Lib. I, chap. VIII, fol. 21ʳ.

The questions troubling Calvin had been raised long ago in various quarters hostile to Jew and Christian. Of those classical writers who were aware of the existence of Moses, a few, like Strabo, gave him a favorable character, as a man of superior intelligence and leadership, but the majority considered him an evil worker in magic.[18] Flavius Josephus, the first-century Jewish historian so often cited by the Elizabethans, thus rebukes certain of the Greeks: "Apolonius Molon, and Lysimachus, and certaine others, partly for ignorance, partly for madnesse, haue most iniuriously belied our lawmaker Moses, and the lawes he made, detracting him as a deceitfull Magician, and then as the author of all malice and impietie amongst us."[19] A century later, Celsus struck at Christianity through Judaism with the same charge: "Those herdsmen and shepherds who followed Moses as their leader, had their minds deluded by vulgar deceits" and "they worship angels and are addicted to sorcery, in which Moses was their instructor...."[20] There

18. Strabo, *Geography* (Loeb), XVI, ll, 35-36; *contra*, Apuleius *Apologia* (London: Bell & Sons, 1888), p. 336, and Justin, *Philippine History*, cited in Cory, *Ancient Fragments* (1876 ed.), p. 80.

19. *Against Apion*, in *Works* (trans. T. Lodge; London, 1602), Bk. II, p. 790.

20. *A True Discourse* (ca. A.D. 180) by Celsus the Greek Platonist was one of the most profound, eloquent, and uncompromising attacks delivered against Christianity by the paganism of the ancient world. Although the original work was destroyed by church censorship, large fragments of it were preserved in Origen's refutation, *Against Celsus* (ca. 250), which was known to the Renaissance in both Greek and Latin versions. The quotations given in the text above are from Origen's refutation as translated into English in the Ante-Nicene Christian Library (ed. A. Roberts; Edinburgh, 1869), Bk. I, chaps. xxiii and xxvi. Origen likewise notes that a heavy assault upon Moses came from Egyptian writers, who alleged that his miracles "were wrought by sorcery, and not by divine power."—Bk. III, chap. v, p. 89. The underlying design of Celsus in derogating Moses is thus analyzed by Origen: Celsus "thinks that he will be able the more easily to establish the falsity of Christianity, if, by assailing its origin in Judaism, he can show that the latter also is untrue."—Bk. I, chap. xxii, p. 19. It is interesting to see Marlowe pursuing the same scheme. Marlowe may or may not

can be no doubt that others in the sixteenth century besides
Calvin knew of these pagan blasphemies, for we find Henry
Smith, in *Gods Arrow Against Atheists*, denying at some
length the views of Porphyry and Apion that the miracles
of Moses "were done by Art Magicke, and not by the
power of God," [21] and Mornay admitting that "some
Authors haue attributed those myracles to Magicke, and
othersome to naturall reasons." [22]

Nevertheless, one distinction must be made. Some of
these opponents of Moses seem to ascribe to him real magical powers. Marlowe's rationalism forbids him to do so. His
idea is, rather, that Moses, although an ignoramus by
comparison with Harriot, knew enough science to produce
optical illusions and other phenomena useful to his ambitions. Quite similarly, Marlowe once said in the hearing of
Kyd that "things esteemed to be donn by devine power
might haue aswell been don by observation of men." [23]
The latter phrase seems to mean the observation, by men,
of the laws of nature and application of such knowledge
to effect consequences hitherto unknown.

But to return to the Baines paper. Marlowe supports his
assertion that Moses was a juggler by two quotations from
Scripture and a generalization of his own, as follows:

> That it was an easy matter for Moyses being brought up in
> all the artes of the Egiptians to abuse the Jewes being a rude
> & grosse people.
> That Moyses made the Jewes to travell xl yeares in the

---

have read Origen directly, but it is safe to say that Origen, as an influential forefather of controversy, helped to determine the nature of
both the attack and the defence in Elizabethan theological dispute and in
that way inevitably had some indirect effect on Marlowe.

21. Henry Smith, *God's Arrow Against Atheists* (London, 1604),
p. 42; first published in 1593.
22. *Op. cit.*, chap. XXVI, p. 467.
23. Brooke, *Life*, p. 107.

wildernes, (which Jorney might haue bin done in less then one yeare) ere they Came to the promised land to thintent that those who were privy to most of his subtilties might perish and so an everlasting superstition Remain in the hartes of the people.

That the first beginning of Religioun was only to keep men in awe.

The first of these is based on Acts 7:21 and 22. I give the Geneva version: "And whē he was cast out, Pharos daughter took him up, & nourished him for her owne sonne. And Moses was learned in all the wisedome of the Egiptians, and was mightie in wordes and in deedes." Now the change from the Bible's "all the wisdom of the Egiptians" [24] to Marlowe's "all the artes of the Egiptians" may be only an accident, a slip in the reporting by Baines, but to the Renaissance mind it would embody all the difference between legitimate learning and the magical arts for which Egypt had long been notorious. [25] The substitution fits in with Marlowe's whole argument so neatly and is so typical of his deft irony that I cannot think it came from anyone but the dramatist. He says, in effect, "Of course Moses

24. The Bishops Bible has "al manner of wysedome of the Egyptians"; the Vulgate, "omni sapientia Aegyptiorum"; and the King James, "all the wisedome of the Egyptians."

25. Elizabethans would be likely to think immediately of Pharoah's magicians in Exodus. Celsus several times likens the miracles of Jesus to "the feats performed by those who have been taught by Egyptians" (Bk. I, chap. LXVIII, p. 475); and Origen says that this very text in Acts 7:22 does not mean that Moses acquired black lore in Egypt: "And in the Acts of the Apostles Stephen bears witness to the great learning of Moses.... For he says: 'And Moses was learned in all the wisdom of the Egyptians.' And therefore with respect to his miracles, it was suspected that he wrought them perhaps, not in virtue of his professing to come from God, but by means of his Egyptian knowledge, in which he was well versed. For the king, entertaining such a suspicion, summoned the Egyptian magicians, and wise men, and enchanters, who were found to be of no avail against the wisdom of Moses...."—Bk. III, chap. XLVI, p. 128.

was a juggler. Your own Bible says that he learned everything the Egyptians could teach him, and you know what
arts of illusion they were famous for. The Jews, poor devils
of slaves and herdsmen, had no chance with him." This
emphasis on the lack of education among the Jews was
frequent enough in the Renaissance, as is exemplified in
Gibbens' *Questions and Disputations:* "It is manifest hereby
that the Scripture applieth it selfe in a sort unto the rude-
nesse of the Iewes, to whom it was first directed." [26]

Marlowe's second argument from Scripture is clumsier.
According to the Pentateuch, the Jews first reached the
borders of Canaan within a relatively short time, but the
Lord in His wrath sent them back into the wilderness for
forty years in order that all the adults (save two) might
perish there for disobedience.[27] Marlowe brushes aside the
supernatural and calls on Machiavelism for the true explanation. Moses kept the Israelites in the desert because he
wished, by killing those who knew his secrets, to perpetuate
his power and the religion which sustained it.

The generalization follows naturally: "...the first beginning of Religioun was only to keep men in awe." In
other words, religions have always been invented by the
ambitious who have understood that the arm of man is a
far less terrifying instrument of power than the voice of a
god. No doubt this idea first glimmered in the mind of
some primeval savage annoyed by the dealings of the witch
doctor and the tribal chief. In Roman times, it received
moving expression in Lucretius' *De Rerum Natura.* And in
the sixteenth century it worried Hooker, Sidney, Mornay,
Calvin, Henry Smith, the writers of plays like *Selimus* and

26. Chap. III, p. 120.
27. Raleigh (*op. cit.*, Bk. II, chap. I, secs. iii and iv) estimates, on the
basis of pertinent Scriptural passages, that the first journey to Canaan
took slightly less than two years.

Life and Repentance of Mary Magdalene, and countless others.[28] Calvin, for example, declares that all men have an instinctive knowledge of God: "Wherefore it is most vayne which some doe say, that religion was deuised by the suttletie and craft of a few, by this policie to keepe the simple people in awe, whereas they them selues that procured other to worship God, beleeued nothing lesse than that there was any God at all." [29] Mornay states that Numa Pompilius originated the Roman religion "and under pretence, he bewitched the ignorant people with a thousand superstitions," and then continues: "Sceuola the Highpriest of the Romans... made three sortes of Gods: Poetical, worse than the worst men, Philosophical, whom they taught to haue bin men, howbeit y^t it was not good for the people to know it; and Ciuill, made by the Princes to hold their people in awe with...." [30] There is nothing unique, then, about Marlowe's assertion. One may even find Tacitus applying it explicitly to Moses: "To establish his influence over this people for all time, Moses introduced new religious practices, quite opposed to those of other religions." [31]

If Marlowe's onslaught on Moses is severe, that on Christ is savage. Besides the underlying accusation of quackery, there are express charges of bastardy, fornication, and

28. *Selimus* (ll. 335ff.) is quoted by Danchin and by Brooke (*Life,* p. 62). See *Life and Repentance of Mary Magdalene* (ed. F. I. Carpenter), ll. 500-11; Smith, *op. cit.,* p. 6. G. T. Buckley (*Atheism in the English Renaissance,* University of Chicago Press, 1932, pp. 75 and 89). cites Hooker, *Ecclesiastical Polity,* Bk. V, sec. 2, and Sidney's *Arcadia,* Book III, chap. x. In the latter, the temptress Cecropia derides "zeale of Deuotion, indeede the best bonde, which the most politicke wittes have found to holde mans witte in well doing.... So are these bugbeares of opinions brought by great Clearkes into the world.... Feare, and indeede, foolish feare, and fearfull ignorance, was the first inuenter of those conceates...."
29. Lib. I, chap. iii, fol. 4^v.
30. *Op. cit.,* chap. xxii, pp. 380-81.
31. *Histories* (Loeb), Bk. V, chaps. iii-iv.

homosexuality. Some admirers of Marlowe, unwilling to believe that the poet could have said such things, hold that his real words are here misrepresented. Others consider him guilty of something between gross violation of good taste and deep and final depravity. Both attitudes, I think, are unnecessary. In the course of the next few pages I hope to show that there is a high probability that Baines was reporting Marlowe quite accurately. For the moment, however, I am primarily concerned to show why the dramatist chose to make so scurrilous an attack.

It is true that his impiety might well have taken a more generous form. Christ and Moses could have been explained as self-deceivers, at worst, or as superlatively gifted men whose accomplishments had been magnified and teachings distorted by popular hallucination and the long working of rumor. But such moderation was not for the Elizabethans. The analogy of their defamation of Mohammed, for instance, is very revealing. A respectable divine like Henry Smith could write:

Mahomet himselfe was such a fleshly fellow, as though modest eares are loth to heare, yet because the filthinesse of this Prophet may not be concealed, I must utter it: He committed buggerie with an Asse, Bonfinius writeth it. Againe, he committed adulterie with another mans wife.... [p. 56] As Mahomets religion is defended by force of sword and fraude ...so likewise did it begin...and was established through wiles, deceit, subtiltie, and lies. For first hee hauing the falling sicknes, perswaded his wife and others, that it was the power of God, and the presence of the Angel Gabriel that caused him to fall downe. Sergius the hereticall Monk was at hand, and bare false witnesse to the same (saith Zonaras)....He had three companions all of a confederacie, to deuise and face out his lies with him. When hee perceiued that men gaue eare to him, hee fained that the Angell Gabriel had carried him to

Jerusalem, and thence to haue lifted him up to heauen, and there to haue learned his law. . . .[32]

How strangely parallel to what Marlowe says about the deserved crucifixion of Jesus is this comment on Mohammed by Mornay, surely one of the most temperate of men: "Whether he were a good man or no, let the people of Mecha (who woorshippe him at this day) iudge, which condemned him to death for his Robberies and murthers. And he himself in his Alcoran confesseth himself to bee a sinner, an Idolater, an adulterer, giuen to Lecherie, and subiect to women. . . ."[33] And of course the arraignment for sorcery often turns up: "The enuious Monke Sergius . . . picked foorth Mahomet, the most proud, arrogant, and insolent person of Arabia to take upō him to be a prophet, & by magick wrought such counterfeit miracles, as to this day a great part of the world are led wᵗ his error."[34]

All Elizabethan comment on Mohammed is in the same general vein. At the root of it lies the doctrine that every rival messiah is of the devil, and therefore a seat of congregated vices. This intolerance had been one of the strengths of Judaism, and, wrought into the fabric of the New Testament, it became a strength of Christianity in the days when the new faith had to conquer or die. The apostles denounced Simon and Elymas as deceivers and magicians because they tried to found religions of their own (Acts 8:9; 13:8). How badly fared the reputations of heresiarchs and apostates in the first centuries of the Christian era can be read in the pages of Eusebius' *Ecclesi-*

32. *Op. cit.*, pp. 55-56.
33. *Op. cit.*, chap. xxxiii, p. 624.
34. George Whetstone, *The Censure of a loyall Subject* (London, 1587), sig. D3ʳ. For similar Elizabethan opinions of Mohammed, read M. Hanmer, *The Baptizing of a Turke* (London, 1586?), sigs. B3ʳ, C7ʳ, D2ᵛ, and *The Mahumetane or Turkish Historie* (trans. R. Carr; London, 1600), fol. 1ff.

astical History, Irenaeus' *Against Heresies,* or Hippolytus' *Philosophumena.* Manes, Callistus, Marcus, Emperor Julian, and an infinity of others all seem to have been wizards, hypocrites, and degenerates, and to have met very unhappy deaths.[35] Coming down to more recent times, everyone remembers what the Catholics thought of Luther, what stories the Protestants circulated about the witchcraft and abominations of the popes, and what filth a bishop like John Bale could write about the Catholic saints.[36] Later on, the leaders of some of the more bizarre Puritan sects became victims of the same tradition. One must emphasize again that the men who wrote such abuse were reputable, excellent authors, most of them churchmen. It seems a little hard on Marlowe to require him to have more charity in his soul than did the ministers of God in his own century. The amenities of theological debate being what they were, Marlowe would see no reason for not adopting against Jesus the same tactics used by the Christians against their adversaries.

Let us go back to the details of the Baines memorandum. Marlowe makes three alternative assertions respecting the birth of Christ, all three calculated to impugn his divine origin. One is an obscene jest aimed at the annunciation: "... the Angell Gabriell was baud to the holy ghost, because he brought the salutation to Mary." As might be suspected similar ribaldries were not unknown in Elizabethan London. Thomas Lodge, in his *Wits Miserie, and the Worlds Madnesse,* is probably drawing a picture from life when he writes of the devil Derision who "neuer sitteth but in the chaire of Pestilence, his meerest profession is Atheisme: ... Christ his Sauior is a Carpenters sonne: Christians, Gali-

35. Socrates Scholasticus, *Ecclesiasticall Historie* (trans. M. Hanmer; London, 1585), Lib. I, chap. xvii, pp. 242-43; Eusebius (in same volume), Lib. III, chap. xxiii, p. 50; Irenaeus, *Against Heresies* (Ante-Nicene Library), Bk. I, chap. xiii.
36. *The actes of English votaryes* (London, 1546), *passim.*

leans in contempt: Nay such blasphemie uttereth he betwixt the Holy ghost and the blessed and Immaculate Virgine Marie, as my heart trembleth to thinke them." [37] But the humor of Marlowe's remark should not disguise for us the thoroughly serious place it has in the program of his argument.

Now, assuming the idea of a virgin birth to be fabulous and untenable and Jesus to have been born in the natural course of human kind, Marlowe's next contention is, "That Christ was a bastard and his mother dishonest." This slander had been spread by Jews, Mornay declares: "The Prophets haue told us that he [Christ] should be borne of a Virgin. The Gospell affirmeth Mary his mother to haue bin such a one; and yet the Iewes which haue come afterward, haue written that she was taken in adulterie." [38] Celsus introduces it in his *True Discourse* through a dialogue between Jesus and a Jew, in which the Jew

accuses Him of having 'invented his birth from a virgin', and upbraids Him with being 'born in a certain Jewish village, of a poor woman of the country, who . . . was turned out of doors by her husband, a carpenter by trade, because she was convicted of adultery; that after being driven away by her husband, and wandering about for a time, she disgracefully gave birth to Jesus, an illegitimate child, who having hired himself out as a servant in Egypt on account of his poverty, and having there acquired some miraculous powers, on which the Egyptians greatly pride themselves, returned to his own

37. Cited by Buckley, *op. cit.*, p. 87. Origen (Bk. VI, chap. LXXIII, p. 415), mentions some ridicule of the virgin birth by Celsus, but nothing exactly like Marlowe's.

38. *Op. cit.*, chap. xxx, p. 543. Cf. Smith, *op. cit.*, p. 48. The *Malleus Maleficarum*, famous witchcraft treatise by Institor and Sprenger (trans. M. Summers; Rodker, 1928, Pt. II, Ques. I, chap. XII), describes the practice of witches to "utter the filthiest words against the Purity of the Most Glorious Virgin MARY, casting the foulest aspersions on the Nativity of Our Saviour from Her inviolate womb."

country, highly elated on account of them, and by means of these proclaimed himself a god.[39]

Celsus later even designates the supposed father of Jesus, "a certain soldier named Panthera." It seems valid to conclude that Marlowe is drawing on this Jewish tradition.

His third alternative argument is that if Jesus was not illegitimate, at least he was merely the child of ordinary wedlock between Joseph and Mary: "... he was the sonne of a Carpenter and ... if the Jewes among whome he was borne did Crucify him theie best knew him and whence he Came." As previously Marlowe cited Scripture against Moses, so here he cites it against Christ. Two texts are appealed to. The first is the cry of the doubting Jews of Nazareth upon hearing Jesus preach: "Whence cōmeth this wisedome and great workes unto this man? Is not this the carpenters sonne? Is not his mother called Marie, and his brethren Iames & Ioses, and Simon and Iudas?" (Matthew 13:54-55). Later scoffers made the phrase a standard term of reproach. So at the time of the early Christian persecutions, "Libanius a singular Sophist, but an enimie to the truth, and a follower of Iulian [Apostata], looking and longing after his maisters victory in regard of his threates, came to a godly Schoolemaister ... in Antiocha, & scoffing at his religion scornfully asked him, Fabri filius quid nunc putas agit? What thinkest thou nowe doeth the Carpenters sonne?"[40] The other text used by Marlowe is, similarly, the denial by the Jews of Jerusalem that Jesus is the Christ:

Howbeit we know this man whence he is but when the Christ commeth, no man shal know whence he is.

---

39. Origen, Bk. I, chap. xxviii, p. 426, and chap. xxxii, p. 431.
40. W. Averell, *A meruailous combat of contrarieties* (London, 1588), sig. E4ᵛ. Notice especially the quotation from Lodge's *Wits Miserie* in the text, *supra*. And cf. Mornay's *A Treatise of the Church* (London, 1581), p. 52.

Then cried Iesus in the Temple as he taught, saying, Ye both know me & knowe whēcc I am: yet am I not come of my self, but he that sent me, is true, whom ye know not.[41]

Since both texts relate the incredulity of the Jews among whom Jesus lived, their combination is highly appropriate and can only be the result of conscious planning. Also striking is the fidelity with which the Baines note preserves the Biblical language. The inference is unmistakable that Baines is really transmitting the words of Marlowe, if not with absolute accuracy, then at least with substantial accuracy. The only other alternative is that Baines, or someone else unnamed, was clever enough to piece together the two texts into a damaging Scriptural argument and then diabolical enough to father it on Marlowe. In addition, the fabricator would have to achieve a mocking irony very like that displayed in Marlowe's works, and as a last stroke he would have to throw in some convincing references to the dramatist's acquaintances, Harriot, Cholmley, and Poole.[42] A theory like that cannot be taken seriously.

No, the argument is Marlowe's clearly enough, and if further proof be needed the next allegation of the Baines note will help to provide it: "That Crist deserved better to dy then Barrabas and that the Jewes made a good Choise, though Barrabas were both a thief and a murtherer." Here is continued the line of reasoning begun in the statement preceding. The Jews among whom Christ spent his life were the best judges not only of his real parentage but also of his crimes and deceptions. If they decided to crucify him instead of Barrabas, they knew what they were doing, "though Barrabas were both a thief and a murtherer." The exact words of this last clause are worth careful notice.

41. John 7:27-28. The Bishops' and King James Bibles have almost exactly the same words.
42. Brooke, *Life*, pp. 98, 99.

They disclose knowledge of a ticklish point in the harmonizing of the gospels. Barabbas is described by Matthew (27:16) only as "a notable prisoner called Barabbas"; by Mark (15:7) as "one named Barabbas, which was bound with his fellowes, that had made insurrection, who in the insurrection had committed murder"; by Luke (23:19) as Barabbas "Which for a certeine insurrection made in the citie, and murder was cast into prison"; [43] but in John (18:40) according to the Vulgate, Bishops' Bible, and King James Bible, the words simply are "This Barabbas was a robber" (*erat latro*). Now the Geneva translation renders John, "this Barabbas was a murtherer," evidently in order to avoid conflict with the other three gospels. It seems very much as if Marlowe knew and relished the differences. To him they would be one of those "Contrarieties oute of the Scripture" which he had drawn up to show to certain great men. At the risk of seeming superfine, I suggest that in the clause, "though Barrabas were both a thief and a murtherer," Marlowe puts the verb "were" into the subjunctive for a condition contrary to fact, and uses the word "both" to stress the contrasts between the gospels versions. The necessary presupposition for this view is that Baines is here transcribing Marlowe with minutest accuracy.

One further word as to Marlowe's argument that the Jews were in the best position to know the truth about Jesus. I have not seen these particular texts used elsewhere as Marlowe uses them. But, of course, the argument in its general tenor had long been employed by the Jews: "If Jesus (say they [Jews]) were the Christ; who should haue knowen and receiued him, rather than the great Sinagogue which was at that time? The obiection is very old.

43. All three of the foregoing quotations are given in the language of the Geneva Bible, but the Bishops', Vulgate, and King James versions are substantially the same.

...it is expressly sayd by the Prophetes, that when the Messias came unto them, they should be so blynde as not too knowe him, and so unthankeful as to despise him." [44]

Shameful in birth, shameful in death, and most shameful in life—such was Jesus according to Marlowe's indictment: "the woman of Samaria & her sister were whores & ... Christ knew them dishonestly.... St. John the Evangelist was bedfellow to Christ and leaned alwaies in his bosome ... he used him as the sinners of Sodoma."

The most that can be said for such charges is that they would not have been made but for certain Biblical passages:

The woman of Samaria answered, and said, I haue no husband. Iesus said unto her, Thou hast wel said, I haue no husband.

For thou hast had fiue husbands, and he whom thou now hast, is not thine husbãd: that saidest thou truely.

(John 4:17-18; Geneva)

Nowe there was one of his disciples, which leaned on Iesus bosome, whom Iesus loued.   (John 13:23; Geneva) [45]

In his libel on St. John, Marlowe's retention of the Scriptural phrase is again noteworthy. If his conclusions seem fantastic, it is well not to waste too much twentieth-century disgust on what is, after all, only too typical of sixteenth-century theological malice and ingenuity.

As in previous instances, Marlowe seems entitled to whatever credit for originality there may be in the elaboration of these particular points and the use of these particular

44. Mornay, *Trewnesse of the Christian Religion*, chap. xxxi, pp. 572-73.

45. Bishops' Bible: "There was one of Iesus disciples leaning on Iesus bosome (euen he) whom Iesus loued." Vulgate: "... unus qui recumbebat in sinu ipsius, is quem diligebat Ieschua." From earliest times, no one doubted that the allusion was to John the Evangelist himself. Marlowe has no Biblical authority for giving the woman of Samaria a sister.

texts, but the volume of similar abuse of Jesus among the pagan classics and the Jews is immense. It is so much like what was suffered by Moses and Mohammed that only a few representative examples need be offered. Celsus, for one, said that Christ lived "a most infamous life" and "was punished by the Jews for his crimes." [46] To Porphyry he was a "dead god, who was condemned by right-minded judges, and perished ignominiously by a violent death." [47] Lucian classified him among the impostors as "that Syrian adept from Palestine." [48] And the attitude of the Jews was thus described by Justin Martyr:

...you have sent chosen and ordained men throughout all the world to proclaim that a godless and lawless heresy had sprung from one Jesus, a Galilean deceiver, whom we crucified, but his disciples stole him by night from the tomb, where he was laid when unfastened from the cross, and now deceive men by asserting that he has risen from the dead and ascended to heaven. [49]

Marlowe is not reported as mentioning Christ's miracles or the resurrection, but what he would think of them is obvious.

The order of statements in the latter part of the Baines

46. Origen, Bk. VII, chap. LVI, p. 478, and Bk. II, chap. V, p. 7.

47. From Porphyry's early work, "On the Philosophy Derived from Oracles," cited in A. B. Hulen, *Porphyry's Work against the Christians* (Yale Studies in Religion, No. 1, 1933), p. 16.

48. *The Liar*, cited by Buckley, *op. cit.*, p. 7.

49. *Dialogue with Trypho* (Ante-Nicene Library), chap. CVIII, p. 235; also, Tertullian's *Against Marcion* in the same set, Bk. III, chap. VI, p. 130. In the Gospels the Pharisees accuse Christ of magic, and the same charge is refuted, for example, by Justin Martyr, *First Apology*, chap. XXX; the pseudo-Clementine *Recognitions*, Bk. I, chap. LVIII; and Mornay, *Trewnesse of the Christian Religion*, chap. XXX. Within Christianity itself many sorts of heretics expressed views upon Christ's divinity, from the Ebionites who believed him to be an ordinary man, to the Arians who thought him a subordinate part of God; but none of these was disrespectful of him. All were very widely known and discussed during the Renaissance.

note becomes harder to determine, but the next shafts seem directed not so much against Christ personally as against the ceremonies established by him and his church:

That if there be any god or good Religion, then it is in the papistes because the service of god is performed with more Cerimonies, as Elevation of the mass, organs, singing men, Shaven Crownes & cta. That all protestantes are Hypocriticall asses.

That if Christ would haue instituted the sacrament with more Ceremoniall Reverence it would haue bin had in more admiration, that it would haue bin much better administred in a Tobacco pipe.[50]

Paraphrased, the argument amounts to this: the only good religious ceremonies are those which keep the people most wonderstruck and submissive. Christ bungled the job by not surrounding his sacrament of the eucharist with more impressive decorations. Herein the Catholics have improved upon their master, and are far ahead of the Protestants, who hypocritically envy and condemn them on that account.

In other words, this is a new phase of the argument Marlowe had made before in connection with Moses, "the first beginning of Religioun was only to keep men in awe." There is a passage in Agrippa which helps to suggest this interpretation:

Of the members of Religion, the pompes of rites, and Ceremonies be not the least, in apparrell, in vessels, in lightes, in

50. Marlowe's word "instituted" in his phrase "instituted the sacrament" is used several times in the Communion Service of the *Book of Common Prayer* (see the prayer of consecration) and was customarily repeated by theologians, as by Adamo [pseud. for A. Mainardi] *An Anatomi . . . of the Mass* (Strassburg [?], 1556), fol. 112r: "As though Christ had instituted the sacramēt, to thentent that it should be bileued that he were in that host...." Four more instances of its use occur in Mainardi, fols. 109ᵛ, 119ʳ, 120ʳ, 153ᵛ. Similarly, Smith, *op. cit.*, p. 71; Mornay, *Treatise of the Church*, pp. 37, 109, 174. By "Elevation of the mass" is meant the lifting up of the Host by the priest during the mass.

belles, in organs, in singing, in encensinge, in sacrifices. . . . Numa Pompilius was the firste that commaunded ceremonies to the Romans, that under theire pretence or colour he might allure men to deuotion, faithe, iustice, and religion, and more easily gouerne the rude and fierce people, which had usurped the rule of the Realme with force and iniurie.[51]

Apparently, then, Marlowe shifted naturally from disparagement of Jesus as a pretender into the scornful charge that he was not even good enough at his business to know the psychology of religious deception. Thence flowed a discussion of the relative merits of Catholic and Protestant ritual. Marlowe's compliment to the "papistes," although a poisonously back-handed one, must have been particularly enraging to his Protestant auditors. Some of the bitterest English invective was expended on the idolatry and superstition of the Catholic mass. The whole episode serves well to show Marlowe's living concern in contemporary religious questions. Nowhere is his satire so double and triple edged.

Even more remarkable, but for a different reason, is his statement that holy communion "would haue bin much better administred in a Tobacco pipe." Why should Marlowe have chosen that particular comparison? Probably because of a general association of ideas between the Christian sacrament and the Indian use of tobacco for religious ceremonies. A vivid description of such ceremonies was given by Harriot in his book, *A briefe and true report of the newfoundland of Virginia*, published in 1588:

The Spaniards generally call it Tobacco. The leaues thereof being dried and brought into powder: they use to take the fume or smoke thereof by sucking it through pipes made of claie. . . .

51. Agrippa, *Of the Vanitie . . . of Artes and Sciences* (London, 1569), chap. LX, fol. 85[r].

This Uppówoc is of so precious estimation amongst thē, that they thinke their gods are maruelously delighted therwith: Wherupon sometime they make hallowed fires & cast some of the pouder therein for a sacrifice: being in a storme uppon the waters, to pacifie their gods, they cast some up into the aire and into the water . . . but all done with strange gestures, stamping, sometime dauncing, clapping of hands, holding up of hands, & staring up into the heauēs, uttering therewithal and chattering strange words & noises.[52]

Of course, this passage does not declare that tobacco pipes were used during the rites, but it shows how the idea of the Christian sacrament might bring into Marlowe's mind the thought of tobacco, which in turn would draw in the image of a pipe. If this theory is correct, we have here a uniquely intimate view of the swift workings of his consciousness. To be sure, since other books on America also had accounts of tobacco ceremonies,[53] we cannot say definitely that Marlowe was remembering either Harriot's conversation or his book. But Harriot's narrative on this subject seems to have been one of the best of its kind, and certainly it is the closest, most likely source of suggestion for the dramatist. In view of Marlowe's naming of Harriot earlier in the Baines note, it would be surprising if Harriot's book were not also in his thought here. At any rate, it seems difficult any longer to dismiss the tobacco pipe as a merely random irreverence. Marlowe used that comparison because he had in mind the religion of the Indians. And he was much too fine a satirist not to intend all the sardonic implications of a parallel between the rites of the dancing,

52. London, sig. C3.

53. Monardes, *Ioyfull Newes Out of the newe founde worlde* (trans. J. Frampton; London, 1577), Pt. 2, fol. 38; J. Acosta, *The Naturall and Morall Historie of the East and West Indies* (trans. E. G.; London, 1604), Lib. V, chap. xxvi, p. 404.

chattering savages of Virginia and those of the Christian Elizabethans.

The discussion of ceremonies then shades into two strictures on the Apostles:

That if he were put to write a new Religion, he would undertake both a more Exellent and Admirable methode and that all the new testament is filthily written.[54]

That all the apostles were fishermen and base fellowes neyther of wit nor worth, that Paull only had wit but he was a timerous fellow in bidding men to be subiect to magistrates against his Conscience.

Beside these statements may be put Kyd's averment that Marlowe esteemed "paul a Jugler." [55] The objectives here seem to be to damage both Jesus and the New Testament by discrediting those who published his teachings. The New Testament made no secret of the fact that most of the apostles were men of the humblest origin, and that some of them on occasion had denied or betrayed Jesus. This had therefore seemed a vulnerable point to antagonists like Celsus: "Jesus having gathered around him ten or eleven persons of notorious character, the very wickedest of tax-gatherers and sailors, fled in company with them from place to place, and obtained his living in a shameful and importunate manner." [56] Celsus also dwells on the treachery of the apostles, and reasons that if Jesus could not win more faithful, better educated followers than these he could not

54. With "more...Admirable methode" connect "would haue bin had in more admiration" in the comment on the sacrament, just analyzed.

55. Brooke, *Life*, p. 107.

56. Origen, Bk. I, chap. LXII, p. 466; also Bk. II, chap. XLV, p. 46. Highly interesting evidence of Renaissance study of Celsus comes in Mornay's reference to this opinion: "For whereas Celsus the Epicure obiecteth, that Jesus chose Publicanes and men of wicked conuersation to be his Disciples: euen therein peculiarly hath he shewed the effectualnes of his doctrine in the curing of mens soules."—*Trewnesse of the Christian Religion*, chap. XXX, p. 557.

have been much of a messiah. As far as Paul was concerned, Celsus was silent; Paul would make against his case. But Julian the Apostate had singled Paul out as the one "who surpassed all the magicians and charlatans of every place and every time." [57] Of Paul's "wit" (intelligence) there could be no denial by anyone who remembered the Bible stories of the many disputations he won, and Marlowe is careful to admit it expressly. In the opinion that Paul "was a timerous fellow in bidding men to be subject to magistrates against his Conscience" he is certainly relying on what Paul wrote in Romans 13:1 and 5:

> Let euerie soule be subiect unto the higher powers: for there is no power but of God: and the powers that be, are ordeined of God.
>
> Wherefore ye must be subiect, not because of wrath onely, but also for conscience sake. [58]

I confess to some difficulty in seeing how Marlowe knows that Paul is here acting against his conscience. A suggestion may be ventured, however: Marlowe means that Paul gave this bidding to his followers in order to ingratiate himself with the Roman authorities, although his conscience told him that if Christians always obeyed it they would sometimes have to violate the law of God. All Renaissance exegesis stipulated an exception to the command in such cases, but Paul makes no exception. [59] It is noteworthy to see

57. In his famous polemic against Christianity, *Against the Galileans* (*ca.* A.D. 363; trans. W. C. Wright for the Loeb Library, 1923), I, 341.

58. The Geneva Bible has an important marginal note to this verse: "...here he speaketh of ciuill Magistrates: so that antichrist and his cannot wrast this place to establish their tyrannie ouer the conscience." This Puritan interpretation explains why Marlowe used the phrase "subiect to magistrates."

59. E.g., Bishop Hooper "Annotations on Romans xiii" in *Later Writings of Bishop Hooper* (Parker Society, 1852) p. 102; and Henry Bullinger, *Decades* (Parker Society, 1849), Decade II, Sermon IX, pp. 390-91

Marlowe bringing in this text because it had great contemporary importance as a storm center in the struggles between civil and ecclesiastical power. It was always being cited by the dominant Catholics against the Huguenots in France, by the Protestants against the Catholic minority in England, and within the English church by the Anglicans against the Puritans, to justify maximum control of those bodies.

In speaking of the apostles Marlowe had also criticized the New Testament as "filthily written" and had offered to write a new religion according to a "more Excellent and Admirable methode" upon request. This is a cavil rather against literary style and organization than against subject matter,[60] the argument apparently being that from "fishermen and base fellowes" one could expect nothing better. It is an opinion which was shared by a considerable number of humanists, as Agrippa complains:

I see many waxe prowde in Humane learning and knowledge, that therefore they do despise and lothe, the Sacred and Canonicall Scriptures of the Holie Ghoste, as rude and rusticall, because they haue no ornamentes of woords, force of sillogismes, and affectate perswasions, nor the strange doctrine of the Philosophers.[61]

60. The French translation of Origen's *Against Celsus* published at Amsterdam in 1700 expresses Origen as saying that the apostles spread the gospel by divine aid only, "ni par la force de leur éloquence, ni par la netteté de leur Méthode, ni par les autres artifices de la Rhétorique & de la Dialectique, qu'on apprend dans les Ecoles des Grecs...."—Bk. I, p. 38. The English translation has, in place of "Méthode," "any orderly arrangement of their message"—Bk. I, chap. LXII. J. Anwick, *Meditations* (London, 1587), Epistle Dedicatory, contrasts "Method and ornamentes of arte" with "goodness in substaunce" of a book.

61. *Op. cit.*, sig. A4ʳ. For other excellent statements see Mornay, *Trewnesse of the Christian Religion*, chap. XXVI, pp. 452, 455; P. Viret, *The Worlde possessed with Devils* (London, 1583), Dial. 4, sig. D5; E. Bulkeley, *Answere to Ten friuolous...reasons* (London, 1588), p. 13.

And in so official a place as the authorized *Sermons* it is said that "the phrase of the Scripture is sometimes so homely, grosse, and playne, that it offendeth the fyne and delicate wittes of some courtiers." [62] One need scarcely go back into antiquity except to mention that Celsus and his contemporaries had no respect for the style of the Greek originals either.[63]

Omitting two items which do not deal with religion, we come to Baines's final allegation, that Marlowe "saieth likewise that he hath quoted a number of Contrarieties oute of the Scripture." The prevalence of this sort of analysis in Elizabethan times may be judged by the fact that Arthur Broke in 1563 wrote a whole book, *The Agreemente of Sondry Places of Scripture*, to prove that 107 cases of seeming contradiction in texts were only apparent and not real. His Epistle to the Reader runs:

There are also diuerse whiche (not caring for any religiō but rather wishing y^t al thing wer disordered, & y^t euery one shold do what semeth hī best) wickedly take certain scrapings of ye holy scriptures, and assone as they haue foūd in thē some litle shew of discord, they lay hand on y^t as if they had ouer come al, tending to no other end but to brīg ye word of god to be despised & hated. . . .

In like fashion, Nicholas Gibbens clarifies some two dozen places where "perhaps a Manichee or some blasphemous Atheist, will argue a contradiction in the Scripture." [64] And a great many other citations could be brought to show that the Elizabethans realized the acuteness of the danger. But it was a danger which had confronted the church ever since its earliest days, and the defense against it had engaged

---

62. *Certaine Sermons appointed by the Queenes Maiestie* . . . (London, 1587) II, sig. T5^b.
63. Origen, Bk. VI, chap. II, p. 337.
64. *Questions and Disputations*, p. 38.

some of the ablest champions of Christendom.[65] Probably most troublesome were discrepancies in the genealogies of Christ given by Matthew and Luke, and the varying accounts of the passion and resurrection. A long history might be written on this subject alone.

On leaving the Baines note, one has the sense that tantalizing secrets yet lie hidden there. But some things about it are now plain. Baines has given us a more faithful transcript of Marlowe's words than we have ever realized. No doubt it suffers from some omissions, some dislocations in the sequence of the statements reported, and possibly a few minor verbal misquotations. But through these obscurities appears the shape of an ordered argument. And as individual units the statements seem to be recorded with a high degree of accuracy. Almost every one refers to a definite Scriptural text; several unmistakably repeat the phraseology of the Bible. Such things do not happen by chance or by the malevolence of a Richard Baines.

I should not like to say that there are no light or careless touches in Marlowe's argument. Probably Marlowe himself would smile ironically to hear that said. But the predominant seriousness of his purpose is not to be mistaken. Marlowe has not only searched the Scriptures; he has also read many books and plucked from many orchards of the ancient and modern worlds. If specific books must be mentioned as influencing him, Mornay's *Trewnesse of the Christian Religion* and Origen's *Against Celsus* are likeliest to have done so,[66] but indebtedness to them cannot

65. Origen, Bk. VII, chap. xviii, p. 440; Tertullian, *Against Marcion*, Bk. IV, chap. i, p. 175; St. Augustine, *Reply to Faustus the Manichaean*, Bk. III, p. 152; Macarius Magnes, *Apocriticus* (ed. T. W. Crafer; New York: Macmillan, 1919), Bk. II, chaps. xii and xvii.

66. Buckley (*op. cit.*, chap. x), has suggested that Marlowe knew the anonymous work *De Tribus Impostoribus*, which assailed Moses, Christ, and Mohammed. Scholars are still debating whether the book we now

be absolutely proved. It is better to conclude generally that the thoughts of the ethnics, of the Jews, and of his own Elizabethan contemporaries all left their mark on him. Into these ideas he breathed the living reality of his convictions, and dared to utter them abroad at the risk of his career and his life that other men might share the truth. He became one of the spokesmen of a tendency. For free thought was stirring in England in a vague, unorganized way during the last fifty years of the century. Underneath the intonations of the orthodox writers, one can hear it rising, this mutter of revolutionary dissidence. For the most part it was scattered and anonymous. But in Marlowe we can see the quintessence of it drawn together and revealed. This is the unique historical importance of the Baines note, to which we have never sufficiently awakened. Of whom among the Elizabethans have we such another record? Not Raleigh, not the scientists, nor any of Marlowe's fellow dramatists, nor any other literary Englishman whose work we know. For revolutionary impact and scope it stands alone, an extraordinary document in the history of English free thought.

---

have under that title is not a late seventeenth-century production. I incline to think it is.

4. IN *TAMBURLAINE*

IN APPROACHING NOW THE IMMENSELY DIFFICULT PROB-
lem of the religious meaning of *Tamburlaine* we
must hold fast to these clear ideas about Marlowe's
crusade against Christianity, without at the same
time forgetting the limitations imposed upon its expression
by the necessity of tracing a particular historical narrative.

The first question to be met is whether the two parts of
Tamburlaine form, for purposes of interpretation, one
entity or two. The Prologue to Part II gives us Marlowe's
own statement:

> The general welcomes Tamburlaine receiv'd,
> When he arrived last upon our stage,
> Hath made our poet pen his second part,
> Where death cuts off the progress of his pomp,
> And murderous Fates throws all his triumphs down.
>
> (ll. 1-5)

That is, plainly, the second part was not originally con-
templated but was written as a result of the great popularity
of the first part. Hence the first part was designed as a
separate, self-subsisting play, and Marlowe's meaning in
it must be sought within its own borders, not imported
from the second part. Further confirmation, if any be
needed, comes from the fact that Marlowe exhausted his

historical sources in the first part, as he would not have done had he been planning a continuation. [1] This is not to say that the religion of each part may not be elucidated by a comparison with that of its companion piece, but simply that each part has its independent meaning, for which it is the primary authority. In effect, there are really two *Tamburlaine* plays, not one.

Religious ideas of the first play revolve around two conceptions uttered by Tamburlaine himself. The earlier and more significant one is that a law of nature commands him and all other men to seek regal power. The later is that in his conquest he is acting as the Scourge of God. In due course it will be necessary to see whether these two conceptions are contradictory. At present, however, an analysis of the idea of a law of nature requires all our attention.

It is essential to notice that the famous passage in which Tamburlaine states this idea is his reply to the bitter accusations of treachery urged against him by Cosroe, his ally and sovereign against whom he has rebelled and who lies dying before him. The circumstances call for a basic declaration of principle, and it is as such that Tamburlaine offers it:

> The thirst of reign and sweetness of a crown
> That caused the eldest son of heavenly Ops
> To thrust his doting father from his chair,
> And place himself in the imperial heaven,
> Moved me to manage arms against thy state.

1. Also worthy of mark is the absence in the closing scenes of Part I of any sign looking forward to a continuation. No further resistance is in sight for Tamburlaine: he and his generals settle down to the administration of their provinces. When Marlowe wrote the second play he had to invent a whole new batch of foes for him. Completely missing is anything in the nature of an epilogue promising new action, such as concludes *Selimus* and 2 *Henry IV*, or the internal forward and backward references which interconnect the plays of the *Henry VI* trilogy.

What better precedent than mighty Jove?
Nature that framed us of four elements,
Warring within our breasts for regiment,
Doth teach us all to have aspiring minds:
Our souls, whose faculties can comprehend
The wondrous architecture of the world:
And measure every wandering planet's course,
Still climbing after knowledge infinite,
And always moving as the restless spheres,
Wills us to wear ourselves and never rest,
Until we reach the ripest fruit of all,
That perfect bliss and sole felicity,
The sweet fruition of an earthly crown. (II, vii, 12-29)

Repetition of the doctrine in the next lines by all of Tamburlaine's lieutenants gives it emphasis as something common to the whole group which surrounds him. And it stands out the more because it comes early in the play and is the first attempt by any of the characters to formulate a real creed. Even Tamburlaine has hitherto merely said that he is the favorite of Jove and holds the Fates fast bound in iron chains—strong poetry, perhaps, but very vague religion.

Now the doctrine deserves all the prominence Marlowe gives it, for it is one of the most remarkable in the Renaissance. Precisely what is its content? Tamburlaine's revolt has a divine sanction in Jove's usurpation of the throne of his father Saturn. Desire for power, unchecked by morality, is characteristic of the deity. God is a God of Force. The same struggle for supremacy is ordained by Nature among the elements composing man's body. And his soul is a pure energy ranging the heavens insatiably for the knowledge and comprehension which are another kind of power. The very spheres themselves with their eternal motion illustrate a like energy. Therefore the struggle for power is the law of man's life and he must obey it by grasping unscrupulously at the supreme eminence of the throne. This is a true moral imperative, a higher ethics. Force is the nature of God, the constitution of the universe, and the law for mankind.

Tamburlaine here speaks like a prior incarnation of Nietzsche. Surely this is unique philosophy for the Renaissance. Just how amazing it is one does not realize until he begins to turn over in his mind various thinkers who suggest themselves for comparison. Bruno, Machiavelli, Raleigh, Montaigne, Lucretius have nothing like it. It is obviously completely outside the whole Christian development, patristic and medieval as well as Renaissance. Plato and Neoplatonism, Aristotle, the Stoics, Epicureans, and Sceptics of antiquity present few points of contact. Not until we arrive at the pre-Socratic physicists is there any real possibility of influence, and that highly dubious. This would come from the doctrine of Strife, enunciated in varying forms by Empedocles, Heraclitus, and Anaximander. Empedocles had spoken of Strife and Love as material substances operating upon the four elements, Strife separating them and Love combining them. As an allusion in *Hero and Leander* shows,[2] Marlowe knew this doctrine, but if he used it at all in the *Tamburlaine* passage he changed it radically by omitting Love altogether as a principle in the world. Also, as Aristotle points out in the *Metaphysics*,[3] Empedocles seems to have identified Strife with evil, Love with good, whereas Marlowe emphatically made Strife

2. Sestiad II, ll. 291-93:
>   She trembling strove; this strife of hers (like that
>   Which made the world) another world begat
>   Of unknown joy.
3. I, iv; III, iv; XII, x. All the fragments of Empedocles and Heraclitus are translated by J. Burnet, *Early Greek Philosophy* (3rd ed., London: A. & C. Black, Ltd., 1920), with an excellent analysis.

good. A few of the surviving fragments of Heraclitus, on the other hand, are much closer to Marlowe:

Homer was wrong in saying: 'Would that strife might perish from among gods and men!' He did not see that he was praying for the destruction of the universe; for, if his prayer were heard, all things would pass away....

(Frag. 43)

War is the father of all and the king of all; and some he has made gods and some men, some bond and some free.

(Frag. 44)

But when other fragments are joined to these, Heraclitus can be seen to have meant that Strife was a sort of tension necessary to a deeper harmony which obtains in the physical and moral world. Marlowe says nothing of this. And perhaps it would be difficult to prove that the fragments quoted above were available to him.[4] In sum, therefore, even if the germ of the *Tamburlaine* philosophy came direct from the early Greeks—a big if—it has undergone an enormous transformation.

Thus the doctrine as a whole possesses the most startling originality. Some of its parts, however, were familiar enough to the Renaissance mind. Inherited from the Greeks, the conception of the four elements as two pairs of contraries fighting with each other, fire against water, and earth against air, had passed into the groundwork of all physics and physiology. The Huguenot poet Du Bartas has this typical account of the human body:

And such a Warre our Bodies peace maintaines:
For, in our Flesh, our Bodies Earth remaines:

4. Apparently the details of Heraclitus' doctrines were not well known in the Renaissance. For instance, he had been but little quoted by Aristotle and Plato, and the account of his philosophy given by Diogenes Laertius was very sketchy.

Our vitall spirits, our Fire and Aire possesse:
And last, our Water, in our humours rests.
Nay, there's no part in all this Bulke of ours,
Where each of these not inter-mixe their powers,
Though't be apparant (and I needs must graunt)
That aye some one is most Predominant.

.   .   .   .

Not, that at all times, one same Element
In one same Body hath the Regiment:
But raigning in his turne, his subiects drawes
After his Lore: for still New Lords new Lawes.

.   .   .   .

So (or much like) the while one Element
Ouer the rest hath modest Gouernment:
While, in proportion, though un-equall yet,
With Soueraigne Humours Subiect Humours fit,
The Body's sound...
But if...
It Tirannizing, seeke to wrack the rest
It ruines soone the Prouince it possest.
Where soone appeares, through his proud usurpation,
Both outward change and inward alteration.[5]

Very striking is the way in which Marlowe has skipped over certain features of the theory, as that the warring elements must preserve a certain balance or proportion if the body is to remain healthy, and that one element must not "Tirannize" over the others. He has first isolated and then exalted the fact of the warfare.

An equally interesting method is to be observed in his description of the soul. Standing alone it is altogether orthodox, displaying certainly all of the beauty but none of the originality critics have been wont to attribute to it.

5. Du Bartas, *Deuine Weekes & Workes* (trans. J. Sylvester, 1605?), 1st Week, 2nd Day, pp. 33-40. See Aristotle, *Metaphysics*, IV, ii, 21; *Batman vppon Bartholome* (1582), Bk. X, cap. III, fol. 154ʳ. Spenser's *An Hymne in Honour of Love* (ll. 74-91) allegorizes this doctrine.

What is unorthodox is the use to which it is put. Another selection from Du Bartas is apposite:

> And, though our Soule liue as imprison'd here
> In our fraile flesh, or buried (as it were)
> In a darke Tombe; Yet at one flight she flies
> From Calpe t'Imaus, from the Earth to Skies;
> Much swifter then the Chariot of the Sunne
> Which in a Day about the world doth runne.
>
> .　　.　　.　　.　　.　　.　　.　　.
>
> By th' Aire steepe staires, she boldly climbs aloft
> To the Worlds Chambers; Heau'n she visites oft
> Stage after Stage: she marketh all the Spheares,
> And all th'harmonious, various course of theirs:
> With sure account, and certaine Compasses,
> She counts their Starres, she meates their distances,
> And differing paces; and as if she found
> No Subiect faire enough in all this Round,
> She mounts aboue the Worlds extreamest wall,
> Farre,· farre beyond all things corporeall;
> Where she beholds her Maker face to face....[6]

Clearly, the only real divergence of this conception from that of Tamburlaine comes in the final lines dealing with the highest object of the soul's search, where indeed the contrast is absolute. Exactly the same similarities and contrasts appear in this discussion in Calvin's *The Institution of Christian Religion*:

But the powers of the soule are farre from being enclosed in those exercises that serue the body. For what pertaineth it to the body, for a man to measure the skie, to gather the number of the starres, to learne the greatnesse of one, to know what space they be distant one from an other, with what swiftnesse or slownesse they go their courses, how many degrees they decline this way or that way?

6. First Week, 6th Day, pp. 219-20.

... Truely the manifold nimblenesse of the soule, by which it surueieth both heauen & earth, ioyneth things past with things to come ... also the ingeniousnes by which it inuēteth things incredible, & which is the mother of so many maruelous arts, are sure tokens of diuine nature in man.[7]

Evidently Marlowe's description is well within the Christian tradition until the sudden crescendo of blasphemy at the close.

We have here the key to the evolution of the Tamburlaine doctrine. Instead of being borrowed from any thinker ancient or modern, it was a new interpretation of phenomena selected from the common knowledge of the time. No one before Marlowe, we may say, had arranged the evidence in quite that way or drawn so drastic a conclusion from it. And what else is the essence of originality?

A comparison of the Du Bartas and Calvin quotations with Tamburlaine's speech draws our particular notice to its ending. Both in thought and in language it is a conscious and pointed denial of the Christian view that the *summum bonum* of man is the attainment of bliss in heaven. Tamburlaine's climactic words,

> That perfect bliss and sole felicity,
> The sweet fruition of an earthly crown,

are intended to contrast sharply with the words customarily used to express the Christian ideal. For example, the head-

7. Lib. I, cap. v, fols. 8ᵛ-9ʳ. Similarly, Palingenius, *Zodiake of life* (London, 1588), Bk. V, p. 82:

> But some perchaunce will seeke
> What Wisedome is to know, and sure the troth hereof to speake,
> Nought else but knowledge chiefe she is, by which the pured minde
> Who neither mortall waight doth presse, nor earthly thought can blind
> Doth scale and clime the skies aboue, and there in ayry place
> With God doth dwell, despising here, all things in mortall case....

And Mornay, *Trewnesse of the Christian Religion*, p. 101; La Primaudaye, *The French Academie* (London, 1586), chap. i, p. 25.

ing of chapter XIX of Mornay's *The Trewnesse of the Christian Religion* reads: "That the wysest of all ages agree that God is the utmost end and soueraine good, felicitie, or welfare of man." And Calvin's statement is that "all men be borne & do liue to this end, to know God...." [8] William Allen in his *A Defense and Declaration of the Catholike Churchies Doctrine* several times speaks of "the ioyfull fruition of heauens blisse" and "the fellowship of perpetuall fruition with the Angels." [9] So also in *Certaine Sermons appointed by the Queenes Maiestie* constant mention is made of "the fruition of his glorie." [10] These are only a few of innumerable instances. Tamburlaine's *earthly* crown is matched against the *heavenly* crown of the saints. [11] Otherwise there would be no point in his specification of "earthly." Accordingly we must read his doctrine as containing an implied challenge to the Christian system.

Does Tamburlaine's speech represent Marlowe's own belief? The question is beset with many and obvious difficulties, but it is a crucial one and an answer must be attempted. On the negative side there is the fact that the philosophy is eminently suitable to the Scythian conqueror and may therefore be merely a dramatic invention. On the affirmative, there are several strong considerations. Mar-

8. *Op. cit.*, fol. 4^r. For other expressions of this principle, the cornerstone of all Renaissance ethics, see L. Bryskett, *A Discourse of Civill Life* (London, 1606), p. 165; C. Valerius, *The Casket of Jewels* (London, 1571), chap. II; Vives, *De Tradendis Disciplinis*, chap. IV; Aquinas, *Summa Theologica*, I-II, Ques. iiff.

9. Antwerp, 1565, fols. 34^r, 57^v.

10. Vol. II, e.g. sigs. KK8^v, LLI^r. The same language is used by Morton, *A Treatise of the Nature of God* (London, 1599), p. 161; Thomas à Kempis, *Imitatio Christi*, Bk. I, chap. XV; John More, *A Lively Anatomie of Death* (London, 1596), fol. A2^v; Calvin, Lib. I, cap. XV, fol. 66^v, and Lib. III, cap. XXV, fol. 410^v.

11. Revelation 2:10: "be thou faithful unto death, and I will give thee a crown of life"; 1 Peter 5:4; James 1:12.

lowe was a largely subjective playwright, fond of bringing his own opinions into his works. This particular philosophy is given a definitely anti-Christian direction. Most significant of all, the ethical conclusions drawn in Tamburlaine's speech bear no small resemblance to those reported of Marlowe by Greene in his well known deathbed injunction in 1592:

Is it pestilent Machiuilian pollicie that thou hast studied? O punish follie! What are his rules but meere confused mockeries, able to extirpate in small time, the generation of mankinde. For if *Sic volo, sic iubeo*, hold in those that are able to command: and if it be lawfull *Fas et nefas* to doe any thing that is beneficall [i.e. to the individual ego], onely Tyrants should possesse the earth, and they striuing to exceede in tyranny, should each to other bee a slaughter man; till the mightiest outliving all, one stroke were left for Death, that in one age man's life should ende....[12]

Here, as in *Tamburlaine*, the moral code dissolves under the primacy of the will to power, *fas et nefas*, which replaces it as the law of conduct. Whereupon Greene aptly objects that the outcome of an unlimited war for supremacy by everyone can only be mutual extermination. The passage throughout is addressed to Marlowe as to a friend and seems to indicate that Greene knew his beliefs at first hand. As such it has great evidential value. Of course the doctrine it ascribes to Marlowe is brutal in its consequences,

12. *Groatsworth of Wit*, ed. Grosart, *Works of Robert Greene*, XII, 141. Greene's characterization of the view as Machiavellian, though it may be only a loose Elizabethan application of the term to anything considered wicked, may also mean that Marlowe did actually form his idea of the law of strife from a study of Machiavelli. If so, he misunderstood the Italian political thinker. Machiavelli recommended some types of unscrupulous dealing as a necessity of the times but always kept in view the ultimate good of the Italian people and recognized that Christian ethics provided a superior ideal, if men would only follow it.

but these seldom fill the purview of an ecstatic young poet in his twenties. All told, it seems quite likely that the Tamburlaine creed is what Marlowe himself believed.

We are now ready to set beside it the other important religious idea expressed by Tamburlaine in the first play, that he is the Scourge sent by God to chastise mankind. Let us notice first the much fainter emphasis given this latter conception. It does not appear until the middle of the third act, and then is inserted almost casually. As Theridamas is voicing his confidence in their victory over Bajazeth, Tamburlaine applauds him:

> Well said, Theridamas! speak in that mood;
> For Will and Shall best fitteth Tamburlaine,
> Whose smiling stars gives him assured hope
> Of martial triumph ere he meet his foes.
> I that am term'd the Scourge and Wrath of God,
> The only fear and terror of the world,
> Will first subdue the Turk, and then enlarge
> Those Christian captives which you keep as slaves,
> Burdening their bodies with your heavy chains,
> And feeding them with thin and slender fare,
> That naked row about the Terrene sea.... (III, iii, 40ff.)

Then follow ten lines more of incongruous indignation for the sufferings of Christians in the Turkish galleys. Taken in this context the Scourge of God idea looks like an opportunistic afterthought on Marlowe's part designed to rally some favor to his hero as a protector of Christians.[13]

13. This is the view of W. Thorp, "The Ethical Problem of *Tamburlaine*," *JEGP*, XXIX (1930), 385-89. Unlike Tamburlaine's philosophy of strife, his claim to be the Scourge of God is related by the western European narratives. As a rule, they simply include it among the incidents of his life without giving it either much space or an emphatically Christian coloring. Marlowe retains their practice in the former respect but not in the latter. Had he followed them in both he would have obviated, or at least minimized, the conflict between Tamburlaine's two creeds. But he felt that he needed the Christian coloring for reasons

It is quite out of character for Tamburlaine to have any such solicitude. Twice more in Part I the idea receives very incidental mention.[14] In no instance is it a statement of faith made in response to a direct challenge, as was the case with Tamburlaine's great apology in Act II, already discussed. By every test of emphasis it must be held subordinate to the sense of that apology wherever the two conflict.

Now as soon as we examine the Renaissance meaning of the Scourge of God it becomes clear that the two do conflict. The explanation that the great conquerors who ravaged the earth with war were ministers of God to punish the wicked and try the faith of the righteous was given everywhere in Christian literature. It was applied, for example, to the career of Mohammed:

... y° Church of Rome beganne to lift up her selfe in pride and abhomination, the Pope calling himselfe uniuersall Bishop. God was highly displeased with this wickednes, and suffered Mahomet to rise as a rod or scourge to whip his people.[15]

If Tamburlaine's designation of himself as God's Scourge is taken with its usual Christian connotations, it contradicts his views upon God and man as previously determined. For as against a god of merely naked power it opposes the Christian God of justice and mercy, and against a universal

---

of dramatic sympathy with his hero. Again, he might have achieved consistency by omitting the law of strife. But the subjective urge to inject his own philosophy was too strong.

14. In single lines, once by Tamburlaine at IV, ii, 32, and once by his enemies at IV, iii, 9. In neither case is any real point made of the reference. The bare use of the verb in the Prologue, "scourging kingdoms with his conquering sword," does not necessarily connect Tamburlaine with God.

15. Hanmer, *Baptizing of a Turke*, sig. El°. R. W. Battenhouse (*Marlowe's Tamburlaine*, Vanderbilt University Press, 1941, pp. 99ff.), has done a service in pointing out the Christian content of the Scourge of God. But for the reasons given *passim* in my text I must disagree completely with his view that Marlowe makes the concept unify and govern the entire meaning of both parts of *Tamburlaine*.

law of strife for mastery it sets the law of moral obligation. To be sure, Tamburlaine regards himself as privileged to commit any cruelty in his function as divine avenger, but under this theory what he punishes is sin against the moral order. Is it certain, however, that Marlowe intends the conception of Tamburlaine as Scourge to carry with it these Christian connotations? May not all of Tamburlaine's religious ideas be harmonized by simply amputating the Christian appendages and considering him as the servant of a deity who is Power without Justice and who punishes disobedience in man merely because disobedience is rebellion, regardless of fictions about right and wrong?

There is something attractive in this unification. In its favor is the argument that fully half the number of Tamburlaine's victims are not shown by the drama to be guilty of any vestige of sin or crime. What, for instance, is the fault of Mycetes, or the King of Arabia, or the virgins of Damascus? On the other hand, there are, I believe, insuperable objections to stripping the Scourge of God idea of all Christian meaning. It bore such a meaning to the Elizabethan audience, and Marlowe may be presumed not to have wished to violate it altogether. Moreover the circumstance that Tamburlaine first called himself the Scourge of God while promising to free Christians from the Turks would inevitably fix the term in a Christian atmosphere. And again, one suspects that Marlowe wished at times to win for his protagonist the greater sympathy and awe Elizabethans would naturally feel for the emissary of their own God.

There seems to be no legitimate way out of the conclusion that the inconsistency is there and must remain there. But this should not disturb us. Most early Elizabethan dramas were not minutely wrought masterpieces, each bit fashioned in clear-sighted relationship to every other bit.

Like most of his contemporaries, Marlowe was sometimes
perfectly content to achieve an immediate objective in one
passage without worrying about, or perhaps even noticing,
its intellectual incompatibility with certain effects reached
in other passages. A general impression of psychological
unity was all that mattered. Tamburlaine gives this impression because Marlowe never fails to stress his greatness with
relation to God. When Tamburlaine describes God as
Force and man as born to seize dominion, we feel the authority by which he sweeps forward to his ends. When
Tamburlaine aspires to the very throne of Heaven, we feel
the grandeur of his blasphemy. And when he visits the
wrath of God upon men, his figure dilates beyond mortal
form with the terror and universality of his mission. Thus
many individually jarring elements contribute to the larger
harmony of the characterization.

One further issue appertaining to the Scourge of God
notion remains to be dealt with. It is sometimes contended
that this notion always entailed for Elizabethans the villainy
of the person who acted as Scourge, and hence Marlowe's
use of it shows an intention that Tamburlaine, too, should
be regarded as a villain to whom due punishment is finally
meted out. But neither the premise nor the deduction can
be conceded, on several counts. Even strict Christian theory
did not condemn all scourges as wicked men.[16] And in
practice many a world conqueror who, like Alexander the

16. See H. Institor and J. Sprenger, *Malleus Maleficarum*, Pt. I, Ques.
15: "...the wicked are punished sometimes by the good and sometimes
by other wicked men. For as Gratianus says (XXIII, 5), sometimes God
punishes the wicked through those who are exercising their legitimate
power at His command;...And sometimes He punishes by His nations
being aroused, either by command or permission, but with no intention
of obeying God, but rather greedy for their own gain, and therefore
to their own damnation; as He now punishes His people by the
Turks...." See the chapter on politics and ethics, *infra*, for authorities
who regard the historical Tamburlaine favorably although calling him
the Scourge of God.

Great, had slaughtered his tens of thousands, was held in high popular esteem throughout Renaissance Europe. Specifically, many of those historians who recorded that Tamburlaine was known as the Scourge of God wrote very favorably of him in most respects and saw nowhere any sign of God's displeasure toward him. As far as Marlowe's protagonist is concerned, the manner of introducing him as the Scourge of God in a passage in which he resolves to crush an overbearing Turk and release his Christian slaves proves unmistakably that the title is meant to confer sympathy, not to take it away. Additionally, the whole dramatic emphasis through the manipulation of incident and speech is in Tamburlaine's favor, as I shall point out in the chapter on ethics. For all these reasons it is impossible to agree that Marlowe wishes us to interpret his hero as an evildoer pursued by the wrath of the God whose commands he executes.

On the contrary, if the outcome of Part I has any bearing on the sense of the play, it shows that Tamburlaine's religious ideas were admirable and right. Under their banner he marches to incomparable triumph. Zenocrate's warnings of defeat, which he overrides, are never fulfilled, and show only the more plainly how irresistible is his victory. Let us recall again that Part I was first written as an independent, definitive drama. It is there, on the summit, that Marlowe would have left his Tamburlaine had not the plaudits of the crowd called him to devise a sequel.

In that sequel he used over again the old religious themes and added some that were new. Both the law of strife and the Scourge of God doctrines reappear, but this time the latter is brought to the fore with full and frequent development. Act IV, scene i, is the key scene. As usual the context is important. The slothful son, Calyphas, has been idling in his tent while Tamburlaine and his other two sons defeat the army of the Turks. With his own hand Tamburlaine kills him as a deserter, and then makes this extraordinary address to the Deity:

> Here, Jove, receive his fainting soul again;
> A form not meet to give that subject essence
> Whose matter is the flesh of Tamburlaine,
> Wherein an incorporeal spirit moves,
> Made of the mould whereof thyself consists,
> Which makes me valiant, proud, ambitious,
> Ready to levy power against thy throne,
> That I might move the turning spheres of heaven;
> For earth and all this airy region
> Cannot contain the state of Tamburlaine.   (IV, i, 111-20)

Beneath the Aristotelian terminology of "form" and "essence," this is the same soul visualized by Tamburlaine in the first play as climbing after knowledge infinite, but climbing now after sovereign power infinite, even against the throne of God. And why is the soul thus valiant, proud, and ambitious? Because it partakes of the qualities of God. Consequently God himself must be of this nature. In other words, he is the God of Force we have encountered before, who, by creating man in his own mould, has given him a being which must fulfill itself by perpetual contest. Again it is fascinating to watch Marlowe using his favorite ironical device of perverting a Christian dogma. Genesis 1:26 declares that God made Adam in his image. The Christian exegesis of this text uniformly was that it meant that man's soul was created capable of an intellectuality and a moral integrity modeled upon God's own.[17] But Marlowe accepted the text in order to link a God of War with warrior man. And Tamburlaine's vaunt,

17. Gregory of Nyssa, "On the Making of Man" (*Nicene and Post-Nicene Fathers*, Vol. V), chap. xvi; Bullinger, *Decades*, Decade II, Sermon x, p. 394; Gibbens, p. 33.

> For earth and all this airy region
> Cannot contain the state of Tamburlaine,

is a fitting appropriation of words which the Bible reserves for God: "But will God indeed dwell on the earth? Behold, the heauen, and heauen of heauens cannot containe thee" (1 Kings 8:27).

Yet, after this furious challenge to the Deity, only a few lines later in the same scene Tamburlaine's retort to the curses of his captives is that his cruelties are a part of his mission on earth as the Scourge of God. Here occurs the most ample, specific, and eloquent statement of the doctrine in either of the two plays:

> Villains, these terrors and these tyrannies
> (If tyrannies war's justice ye repute),
> I execute, enjoin'd me from above,
> To scourge the pride of such as Heaven abhors:
> Nor am I made arch-monarch of the world,
> Crown'd and invested by the hand of Jove,
> For deeds of bounty and nobility;
> But since I exercise a greater name,
> The scourge of God and terror of the world,
> I must apply myself to fit those terms,
> In war, in blood, in death, in cruelty,
> And plague such peasants as resist in me
> The power of heaven's eternal majesty. (IV, i, 146-58)

The contradiction between the two doctrines is no greater, though more evident, here than in Part I, and troubled Marlowe as little. As we have remarked, they have this paramount effect in common, that they both serve to glorify Tamburlaine. Why Marlowe chose to lay much greater stress upon the Scourge of God idea in Part II by referring to it a dozen times and giving it such potent amplification as that above is somewhat difficult to say.

One may doubt that the expansion has much significance [18] except to show that as the dramatist's inspiration waned and he was harder put to it to keep the constant procession of victories from growing stale he resorted to emphasis upon Tamburlaine's unique connection with God in the form which would be most familiar and impressive to the audience. If we remember that the idea as Marlowe uses it implies not a moral denunciation but a justification of his hero, we cannot see its increase as a prelude to retribution in his death.

The problem of these death scenes may now be considered. Tamburlaine's last action before he is stricken with mortal illness is the burning of the Koran and renouncement of his faith in Mahomet. Immediate onset of his sickness at the end of the same scene some fifteen lines later has given ground for the opinion that it is God's vengeance for his blasphemy. But we must look closely at the text.

> *Tamb.* In vain, I see, men worship Mahomet:
> My sword hath sent millions of Turks to hell,
> Slew all his priests, his kinsmen and his friends,
> And yet I live untouched by Mahomet.
> There is a God, full of revenging wrath,
> From whom the thunder and the lightning breaks,
> Whose scourge I am, and him will I obey.
> So, Casane: fling them in the fire. [*They burn the books.*

18. One should notice that in Part II the claim that Tamburlaine is God's scourge is made exclusively by Tamburlaine, never by his enemies, and always as matter for self-praise or self-justification. See I, iv, 60-63; II, iv, 80; IV, i, 149, 200; IV, iii, 24, 99; V, i, 92, 184; V, iii, 248. Hence there is no dramatic leverage for the view of some critics that Marlowe uses the idea to condemn Tamburlaine. Marlowe's technique of exposition gives exactly the opposite result. And there are signs that, even so, he does not endow it with a precise religious significance. At I, iv, 60-63 Tamburlaine commands all three of his sons to become scourges of the earth. God doesn't seem to have much to say about it. Marlowe's use of the conception throughout is primarily dramatic and only secondarily religious.

Now, Mahomet, if thou have any power,
Come down thyself and work a miracle.
Thou art not worthy to be worshipped
That suffers flames of fire to burn the writ
Wherein the sum of thy religion rests.

   .   .   .   .   .   .

Well, soldiers, Mahomet remains in hell;
He cannot hear the voice of Tamburlaine:
Seek out another godhead to adore,
The God that sits in heaven, if any god,
For he is God alone, and none but he.   (V, i, 178-201)

Of course Tamburlaine has never been a Mohammedan in anything save name, and the episode has nothing to do with the rest of the scene in which it appears, dramatizing the siege of Babylon. Accordingly, it looks as if Marlowe inserted it simply as one final burst of religious pyrotechnics. From the Christian standpoint the general tenor of the speech is innocuous, even laudable. Tamburlaine does not here dare God out of his heaven, as is sometimes supposed, but rather dares Mahomet out of his hell, and proves to the content of all good Christians that that pagan personage has no stomach for a fight. He then gives his allegiance to a deity whose thunder and lightning suggest the Jehovah of the Old Testament, capping the Christian tendency of the pronouncement by stating that he serves him as a scourge.[19] It is inconceivable that on the whole this renunciation of a pagan god, hated by the Elizabethans, in favor of one who is at least approximately Christian could have been meant as a blasphemy deserving immediate re-

19. Note also that Tamburlaine's language accepting "The God that sits in heaven, if any god, / For he is God alone, and none but he" is Christian. The latter phrase comes from Deuteronomy 4:35: "...the Lord he is God, there is none else beside him"; and 32:39: "See now that I, even I, am he, and there is no god with me." For "sits in heaven" see the discussion of the Orcanes-Sigismund episode below.

tribution.[20] One qualification must be entered as to the "if" clause, "if any god," which I shall notice in a moment.

The suggestion is advanced that Marlowe intended a parallel between Tamburlaine's scoffing at Mahomet and the mocking challenge made by the Jews to Christ on Calvary that he prove his divinity by freeing himself from the cross: "If thou be the Son of God, come down from the cross." [21] Considering Marlowe's frequent sardonic mishandling of the Scriptures there is a good deal to be said for this view. But if he had any such comparison in mind it is deeply latent in the passage and is not expressed. In order to reach expression it would have had to employ language more closely equivalent to that of the Gospels. I do not believe that a parallel between Mahomet and Christ would spontaneously occur to even the most alert Elizabethan hearing Tamburlaine's defiance. After all, while denying Mahomet Tamburlaine affirms his loyalty to the true God. And surely in all periods of history heathen gods had often enough been dared by true believers, without thought of analogy to the jeers at Calvary. Hence we must return to the conclusion that the overt meaning of Tamburlaine's speech was not blasphemous and merited no retribution from the Christian standpoint. Whether it may have had a private meaning for Marlowe, not expressed in the actual words, is a different matter.

20. The typical Elizabethan attitude would be that of P. Giovio, *A shorte treatise upon the Turkes Chronicles* (trans. Ashton; 1546), fol. lxv[v], writing approvingly of the Sophy of Persia, who "called Mahomet in despite, a bondeman, and a vyle bowghte drudge. The bookes of his lawe whersoeuer he founde theym, as false heresies & diuilysh doctrine he brent them. Besyde thys he commaunded Mahomets temples to be throwen downe, and of them made stables and dogge kenels." Giovio's book was in the Cambridge libraries during Marlowe's college years and is considered one of the probable sources of his play. The passage given above may even have suggested the Koran-burning to him.

21. Matthew 27:40; Mark 15:30-2; Luke 23:35-7. The suggestion is that of Battenhouse, *op cit.*, pp. 173-74.

But one sly, venomous little phrase remains to perplex the issue, the "if" phrase in the lines,

> Seek out another godhead to adore;
> The God that sits in heaven, if any god,
> For he is God alone, and none but he.

The agnosticism it entailed was treated in Elizabethan times as one of the characteristic and dangerous forms of "atheism." So in the Cerne Abbas investigation of Raleigh and his friends, this question was asked of every witness:

Itm whome do you knowe, or have harde, that have argued, or spoken againste? or as doubtinge, the beinge of anye God? ...Or to sweare by god, addinge if there be a God, or such like....[22]

And the intimate bearing of the phrase upon Marlowe's own beliefs is clear from Baines's report that Marlowe said, "That if there be any god or any good Religion, then it is in the papistes because the service of god is performed with more Cerimonies...." What, then, shall be thought of its appearance in Tamburlaine's declaration? First, that it is inconsistent with all the rest of the speech, especially the lines, "There is a God, full of revenging wrath... Whose scourge I am...," which categorically aver the existence of God. Slipped in almost unaware, as it is, it is not of bulk or force sufficient to outweigh the Christian associations of the whole. Neither is it reconcilable with the rest of Tamburlaine's thinking, since it is the sole hint of agnosticism to be found there. What it seems to be is one of those badgering interpolations that Marlowe used in his war against Christianity. Probably in the Tambur-

---

22. See also Lyly's "Euphues and Atheos," wherein the unbeliever Atheos declares, "And in my iudgement if there be any God's it is the worlde wherein we lyue"; cited by Buckley, p. 73. Seneca's *Thyestes* (Loeb), 404-7, likewise has the parenthetical "si sunt tamen di."

laine speech it dropped from his pen by a sudden impulse, by an automatic association of ideas. I am aware that this type of explanation does little honor to Marlowe as an exact artisan, but, to my mind, it is all too easy to overrate him in this respect. His works are often shapeless with free impulse and ardent improvisation. We shall meet with the "if" phrase again before long.

The Koran-burning episode being what it is, to interpret the advent of disease as God's vengeance would be to signalize a triumph for Mahomet as against Tamburlaine's semi-Christian loyalty, which even Marlowe would hardly wish publicly to propose. Furthermore, no character in the play so interprets it. Tamburlaine merely announces, "But stay; I feel myself distempered suddenly," and it never occurs to him or to anyone else that there is any connection between his burning of the Koran and his illness. The technique of exposition habitual to Elizabethan drama would almost certainly have required Marlowe to make this connection expressly had he intended his audience to see one there. This he unmistakably did in the earlier episode of the punishment of King Sigismund by God for perjury, giving over a whole scene (II, iii) to statements by Orcanes, Gazellus, and Sigismund himself that the latter's death is the consequence of God's anger. From this field of dramatic technique comes, I think, the soundest solution of the problem. Marlowe made the illness follow close upon the abjuration because he considered that the time had arrived for ending the play, and wished to compress the remaining events. Such compression, often injurious to the logic of incident, is a familiar feature of Elizabethan drama.

We search Tamburlaine's death scene in vain for any sign that he is being visited by God's chastisement. There is no triumphant moralizing on the part of his enemies.

We hear great choric laments by his followers for the loss of so noble an instrument of heaven's will. All is sympathy, adoration, and grief. Tamburlaine himself renounces nothing of his past conquests or of the philosophy which prompted them, but mourns only that he cannot live to subdue the entire earth, and commends this task to his sons. And if we look for enlightenment to what is said about this scene in Marlowe's Prologue the result is the same. The words,

> Where death cuts off the progress of his pomp,
> And murderous Fates throws all his triumphs down,

state the simple fact of his death without moralizing comment. If anything, "murderous Fates" actually implies pity for Tamburlaine. This would not be the way to describe God's retributive justice. It is instructive to contrast the tone of this Prologue with that of the Prologue to the contemporaneous drama, *Selimus* (*ca.* 1591):

> Here shall you see the wicked sonne pursue
> His wretched father with remorslesse spight:
> And danted once, his force againe renue,
> Poyson his father, kill his friends in fight.
> You shall behold him character in bloud,
> The image of an unplacable King:
> And like a sea or high resurging floud,
> All obstant lets, downe with his fury fling.

When an Elizabethan playwright set out to condemn his villains he did not spare the adjectives. Marlowe himself was equally outspoken when he wished to denounce Faustus in the prologue and epilogue to his later play. His avoidance of this attitude in *Tamburlaine* was in accord with the view uniformly taken by the historical sources, that

Tamburlaine's death was quite normal and lacking in supernatural implications.[23]

In dying, Tamburlaine makes one great discovery: that
he himself is a human being not exempt from mutability.
And he stays the grief of his son Amyras with words which
show his own reconciliation to death:

> Let not thy love exceed thine honour, son,
> Nor bar thy mind that magnanimity
> That nobly must admit necessity.   (V, iii, 199-201)

It is tantalizing indeed that at this crucial juncture Tamburlaine should use a term capable of so wide a range of
philosophic meaning as the term "necessity." [24] Does he
intend it in the broad sense that there is an inexorable
purpose active in all things throughout the cosmos or in
the more limited sense that there are physical laws which
no one can avoid? The latter seems more likely. The whole

23. La Primaudaye (*French Academie,* chap xliv, p. 475) is representative: "This good successe (which is most to be maruelled at and very
rare) accompanied him always untill his death, in so much that he
ended his days amongst his children, as a peaceable gouernour of innumerable countries." Also Fortescue, *The Forest,* Bk. II, chap. xiv:
"...yet as a man in the ende, he paieth, the debte due unto nature...."
See the chapter on ethics, *infra.*

24. A full account of the various meanings would require a history of
philosophy. The term was widely current among the Greeks, and seems
usually to have indicated an absolute Fate controlling all things, as it
did for the Stoics. See E. Zeller, *Stoics, Epicureans, and Sceptics* (1870),
chap. vii; Burnet, *op. cit.,* p. 222. Aristotle has an elaborate discussion in
Metaphysics, V, v, and *Parts of Animals,* I, i, distinguishing a number
of possible meanings, many of them not involving a providential or
fatalistic purpose. His analysis of the difference between "absolute"
necessity and "conditional" necessity was taken into the Augustinian
controversy about free will, where "absolute" necessity became identified
with complete predestination, and "conditional" with God's foreknowl-
edge consistent with man's free power of choice. The controversy raged
intermittently for centuries and was revived in the Renaissance by
Calvin's doctrine of predestination. Chaucer's interest in the question,
following Boethius, is familiar. See *Nun's Priest Tale,* 3245 ff., *Troilus,*
iv, 953-1078, and Robinson's notes on them.

context is about physical death and nothing else. Theridamas' supplementary advice to Amyras immediately afterwards,

> My lord, you must obey his majesty,
> Since fate commands and proud necessity, (ll. 204-5)

introduces no more general meaning, although it concludes
that the death is fated. And probably the doctrine of necessity here is the same as that voiced earlier by Zenocrate as
she died:

> I fare, my lord, as other empresses,
> That, when this frail and transitory flesh
> Hath sucked the measure of that vital air
> That feeds the body with his dated health,
> Wanes with enforced and necessary change.
>
> (II, iv, 42-6)

Each man lives out his allotted span. All men must die. This
realization by Tamburlaine was rich with potentiality for
more humane principles in ethics and humility in religion.
But the potentiality was never actualized, for, as already
observed, no revolution was worked in his other ideas. He
expressly kept his philosophy of conquest and his belief
that he was the Scourge of God, and gave no sign of
abandoning the law of strife. What the ending of the play
leaves us with, then, is simply the conclusion that death
comes even to the mightiest. Tamburlaine's life is not condemned; it is praised; its magnificence was its goodness.
Nor are his religious tenets condemned. Holding them, he
lived splendid years and reached an end far happier than
any which most men suffer, a mighty king surrounded by
loving sons and friends. Only death came to cut off the
progress of his pomp, as it must finally for all men.

A word, in conclusion, upon the question of Tamburlaine's belief in a future life. At different times until the death scene he impartially visualized classical, Mohammedan, and Christian heavens and hells. The random and conflicting nature of these allusions tells us that they were mere currents of imagery ebbing and flowing in Marlowe's mind, possessing no serious religious significance. Tamburlaine's beautiful elegy on the reception of Zenocrate into heaven seems to have a purely musical and pictorial purpose. It is a Christian heaven, complete with crystal battlements, singing seraphim and cherubim, the river of life (Revelation 22:1), and God stretching out his arm in majesty. Marlowe wanted a gorgeous painting of the abodes of bliss, and got it even if he had to send a Mohammedan Zenocrate to a Christian heaven via a highly heterodox Tamburlaine. Such is the measure of Marlowe's opportunism. Significantly enough, when Tamburlaine himself is on his deathbed he says virtually nothing about an after life. Except for a fleeting reference to being rapt above the stars by Jove, his thoughts are on the future of his two sons. It is through them that he seems to expect his real immortality:

> But sons, this subject, not of force enough
> To hold the fiery spirit it contains,
> Must part, imparting his impressions
> By equal portions into both your breasts;
> My flesh, divided in your precious shapes,
> Shall still retain my spirit, though I die,
> And live in all your seeds immortally. (V, iii, 168-74)

Both his body and his soul will live on in the persons of his sons and their descendants. And this, in all probability, was close to Marlowe's own feeling about the matter. The man who ridiculed the "bugbeares" of the fear of hell could not have believed in hell himself, and if not in hell, then

surely not in heaven. For the Renaissance, the denial of
these two would practically mean denial of any personal
future life. There would remain the possibility of some
such merger of the soul in the Divine as was offered by
Platonism, or a Pythagorean metempsychosis. But Marlowe
nowhere gives any sign of accepting these solutions.

Enough has now been said about the issues touching
Tamburlaine himself, and it remains to comment on an
important episode in which he is not involved: the Orcanes-
Sigismund story that opens Part II. Pretty clearly this is
an outcome of Marlowe's anti-Christian prejudices, only
transparently disguised. With slight suggestion from the
Tamburlaine sources, the poet reaches out into an entirely
distinct period of Hungarian history for a narrative of
Christian bad faith which has no integral position in the
plot of his drama. The Christian King Sigismund, having
concluded a truce with the Mohammedan King Orcanes,
breaks it, on the jesuitical argument that no promise need
be kept to heathens and that God commands the act of
treachery for the advancement of the Christian cause. Fred-
erick even brings forward the Biblical analogy of

> Saul, Balaam and the rest,
> That would not kill and curse at God's command

and were punished by God for their mistaken mildness of
heart.[25] One can imagine with what wry relish Marlowe
sketches this portrait of the Christians and their God. Of
course, Marlowe redeems himself superficially by having
Orcanes appeal to Christ for vengeance and thereafter win
a victory over Sigismund, but even in this act of atonement

25. In her edition of the play Ellis-Fermor cites I Samuel 15 and
Numbers 22 and 23 and remarks that Marlowe's application of the
Balaam story here is inaccurate since Balaam obeyed God in refusing
to curse the tribes of Israel. It is hard to say whether the inaccuracy
was intentional or not.

lurk new sins. Orcanes reverts twice to the gibing little
"if" clause: "If there be a Christ, as Christians say"; [26] and
again, "If there be Christ, we shall have victory" (II, ii, 39
and 64). As a Mohammedan he should have no doubt of
the existence of Christ, for Islam accepts Christ as a mighty
prophet, a fact which must have been perfectly well known
to Marlowe as a student of divinity. And although Orcanes
attributes his final victory to the joint intervention of Mohammed and Christ, his follower Gazellus remarks, with
caustic rationalism,

> 'Tis but the fortune of the wars, my lord,
> Whose power is often prov'd [i.e. asserted to
> be] a miracle.[27]

We know that Marlowe ridiculed the divinity of Christ
and therefore that this is his own comment. Orcanes replies
that nevertheless he will give credit to Christ for his triumph; but the damage is done, the poison of negation has
already been injected. It is the same throughout the episode.
The ostensible purport is to vindicate the justice of Christ,
but in the course of doing so Marlowe has suggested the
hypocrisy of Christians, the cruelty of Jehovah, doubts as
to the existence of Christ, and scepticism of his miracles. It
is a skillful piece of sniping that he does. Naturally the unity
of dramatic impression suffers badly as a result. The notion

26. Contrast the words of Bonfinius, *Rerum Ungaricarum decades
tres*, Marlowe's probable source, as cited in Ellis-Fermor's edition of
Tamburlaine: "Nunc Christe, si Deus es (ut aiunt, et nos hallucinamur)
tuas measque hic injurias, te quaeso, ulciscere." Bonfinius' passage affirms
the existence of Christ; Marlowe's puts it into the conditional.

27. Marlowe's meaning for the word "prov'd" is the same as that in
the first statement reported of him by Baines: "That the Indians and
many Authors of antiquity haue assuredly writen of aboue 16 thousand
yeares agone wheras Adam is <said> proued to haue liued within 6
thowsand yeares." In both cases there may well be an ironic tinge in
"prov'd"—what proof!

that Marlowe is a carefully objective playwright is a chimera.

The indignant prayer of Orcanes contains one remarkably fine passage which has been much commented upon, and not always wisely. After invoking the aid of Christ, "if there be a Christ," he exclaims:

> Open, thou shining veil of Cynthia,
> And make a passage from th'imperial heaven,
> That he that sits on high and never sleeps,
> Nor in one place is circumscriptible,
> But everywhere fills every continent
> With strange infusion of his sacred vigour,
> May, in his endless power and purity,
> Behold and venge this traitor's perjury!
> Thou, Christ, that art esteem'd omnipotent,
> If thou wilt prove thyself a perfect God,
> Worthy the worship of all faithful hearts,
> Be now reveng'd upon this traitor's soul....
>
> (II, ii, 47-58)

Commentators have seen in these lines every sort of esoteric, subtle new doctrine. But the plain fact is that although the poetry here is extraordinary, the doctrine is not. The most orthodox Elizabethan Anglican could immediately subscribe to it.

At first sight it presents a surprising combination of conceptions of God as a being occupying one definite locality, the empyrean, and as a being not thus limited. But the Christian view of the Deity embraced both conceptions. The God who sat on a throne in heaven and watched mankind on the earth beneath with unsleeping eyes was a survival of primitive anthropomorphic religion which came into Christianity very early by way of the Old and New Testaments. On the other hand, God the uncircumscribed essence permeating and sustaining all things was the more refined conception of later thinkers. Both were in the Bible and could not be rejected. Both were useful: the cruder one for the ignorant, the nobler one for minds not so easily satisfied. In Elizabethan popular writings the need for a definite physical image of God and Heaven was too imperious to be denied, but in works on higher levels the position was always taken that God was "aboue measure, place, circumscription and magnitude," [28] a Being incorporeal and without dimensions. The only concession made by the theologians was that God's essence, although equally present everywhere, did indeed reveal itself most clearly in heaven.

Marlowe's actual language in the line, "That he that sits on high and never sleeps," is totally conventional. George Peele writes in *The Device of the Pageant borne before Woolstone Dixie:* "London, give thanks to him that sits on high. . . ." [29] Scriptural authority could be quoted from Psalms 80:1, describing God who "sitteth above the Cherubim," and Daniel 7:9, "I beheld till the thrones were cast down, and the Ancient of days did sit. . . ." But theologians vigorously explained that these words did not signify physical shape and position. Thus St. Augustine:

> . . . when it is said that God 'sitteth', the expression indicates not a posture of the members, but a judicial power, which that Majesty never fails to possess, as He is always awarding deserts as men deserve them. . . . [30]

28. A. Hyll, *The Defence of The Article* (London, 1592), fol. 2ʳ. Likewise Gregory Nazianzen, "The Second Theological Oration" (*Nicene & Post-Nicene Fathers*, Ser. 2, Vol. VIII), sec. x: God is incorporeal and without circumscription. And Calvin, *Institution*, Lib. III, cap. xx, fol. 372ʳ: ". . . he is not limited in any certain coast, but is spred abroade throughout all thinges." Also, Bullinger, *Decades*, Decade IV, Sermon III, pp. 141, 142; and an infinity of others.
29. *Works*, ed. Bullen, I, 78.
30. "On Faith and the Creed" (*Nicene and Post-Nicene Fathers*, Vol. III), chap. vii; *Confessions*, Bk. III, chap. vii, and Bk. V, chap. i.

Consequently, Marlowe cannot be supposed to have intended by this phrase a localizing of God. He is speaking only of God as a judge.

Similarly, the phrase "who never sleeps" was familiar to Elizabethans as describing God's power to see and chastise all the offenses of men. A character in the old play, *The Tide Tarrieth No Man*, declares:

> But God is not dead, neyther is he a sleepe,
> Although for a time his hand he doth hold:
> Yet doth he remember his little sheepe,
> And will reuenge the wrong done to his folde.[31]

And in the *Queens Reception at Norwich*, 1578: [32]

But he that neyther sleepes nor slackes such furies to correct,
Appointed me Debora for the Judge of his elect.

So that this other phrase of Marlowe's is designed to emphasize the inevitability of God's vengeance upon the traitorous Sigismund, and not God's materialization in heaven. There is no conflict whatever with the next line, "Nor in one place is circumscriptible."

The orthodoxy of what follows in the Orcanes passage may be seen from a comparison of it with a few standard Christian disquisitions upon God. In his *A Treatise of the Nature of God*, Morton says:

For as in time, so also in greatnesse God must bee knowne and acknowledged to be infinite, not inclosed or comprehended

---

Any other view would involve acceptance of the Anthropomorphite heresy, for which see Augustine, *De Videndo Deo*, quoted in Bullinger, Decade IV, Sermon III, p. 138. Socrates Scholasticus (*Ecclsiasticall Historie* [1585], Lib. VI, cap. VII, p. 365), describes this heresy and its beginnings in the fifth century A.D.

31. Tudor Facsimile ed., Vol. LVII, sig. f iii. See also Du Bartas, 1st Week, 7th Day, p. 235. Cf. Psalms 44:23: "Awake, why sleepest thou, O Lord? arise, cast us not off forever."

32. J. Nichols, *Progresses of Queen Elizabeth* (1788), Lib. IV, p. 15.

within any creature or place eyther in heauen or in earth, but filling all creatures, and all places both in heauen and earth, yea stretching and extending himselfe beyond the compasse of the world by infinite degrees, and that not onely by his power (his essence beeing in some set particular place) ... it is not so with God, who as in power, so also in his substance and essence is euery where, in al things and in all places. ...[33]

Here is Orcanes' uncircumscribed God, filling all things with mysterious power and essence. The very language is derived from Jeremiah 23:24: "... doe not I fill heauen and earth? saith the Lord." [34] Even the phrase, "Nor in one place is circumscriptible," had been foreshadowed by St. Augustine's "Deus solus inuisibilis, solus imensus, solus incircumscriptus, solus immutabilis, solus incorporeus." [35] And indeed almost any typical Christian treatment reads like a prose redaction of Marlowe's verse:

... [God is] greater than place, more infinite than capacity it selfe, uncapable of circumscription or commensurability ... by his essential presence, or coexistence more than penetrative, being so in both, in all things that are ... yet so as they cannot environ or encompasse him. [p. 49] ... Scripture teacheth. ... Doe not I fill heaven and earth? saith the Lord. Doth He fill heaven and earth by his power, or by his knowledge onely? Nay, but most properly and in the first place by his essentiall presence. For his Essence is infinitely powerfull, infinitely wise.[36]

33. P. 219.
34. Also Wisdom of Solomon, 1:7: "The Spirit of the Lord filleth the world."
35. Quoted marginally in John Proctor's *Fal of the Late Arrian* (1549), sig. F8ᵛ, the book of whose anti-Trinitarian argument Marlowe possessed a manuscript copy, as Kyd testified.
36. Thomas Jackson, *A Treatise of the Divine Essence and Attributes* (London, 1628), p. 45.

When we notice that the words of Orcanes under study are both preceded and succeeded by his prayer to Christ, it becomes further evident that the whole of his appeal is couched in intentionally Christian terms.[37] Now it is strange enough that Orcanes the Mohammedan should describe God like a Christian theologian in these lines, and about eight lines before drop in an "if" clause, "if there be a Christ, as Christians say," like an Elizabethan "atheist." However we have grown somewhat accustomed to these things in the play. But what is most surprising, in view of the Baines note and other testimonies, is that Marlowe in writing like a Christian theologian should write so magnificently. There is no question but that it is magnificent. And so we arrive at the realization that however bitterly Marlowe may have hated Christian dogma there were some elements in it, notably its teachings about God, which could enlist the highest fervor of his imagination. This truth should warn us not to oversimplify the problem of Marlowe's attitude toward the religion. His intellectual contempt was probably energized by a strong emotional repugnance, but also somewhere in the recesses of his spirit there survived a powerful imaginative loyalty which warred against them. It was the fact that the Faustus material gave scope to the conflict of these forces that allowed him there

37. In the ten lines preceding the invocation almost every phrase has a Biblical origin. The reference in "man Whose shape is figure of the highest God" is to Genesis 1:26: "And God said, Let us make man in our image, after our likeness." The accusation that Christians "in their deeds deny him for their Christ" echoes Titus 1:16: "They profess that they know God; but in works they deny him." Christ's having "the power of his [God's] outstretched arm" incorporates Exodus 7:5: "And the Egyptians shall know I am the Lord, when I stretch forth mine hand upon Egypt" with orthodox doctrine that Christ was the executive member of the Trinity in the creation and judgment of the world. "If he be jealous of his name and honour" is of course in the Commandments, Exodus 20:5: "...for I the Lord thy God am a jealous God...." Like his Faustus, Marlowe "profited in divinity," but not to the ends expected by his teachers.

to write his greatest play. In discussing it later we shall have more to say on this subject. But for the present we may reflect that it is small wonder if Marlowe's plays give such a confused religious impression. The playwright's nature, which he was constantly projecting into the drama, was itself in fundamental confusion.

Still, it is important to notice that the element of Christianity which inspires Marlowe in the Orcanes speech is not far removed from the conception of God as Force which we have previously attributed to him. We hear of God's "power" and "sacred vigor" infused in every continent, and of his vengeance. But where are divine love, tenderness, mercy? Nowhere in either *Tamburlaine* play are these more specifically Christian attributes of Deity given any stress. There was ample opportunity to do so had Marlowe wished, especially in the faith of Zenocrate. Yet she is made to speak little of God. Only in one minor respect is the prevailing sternness lightened. God is said by Tamburlaine to tune the music of the angel hosts to the souls of men, and appears thus as a source of the beautiful. We remember in like manner the scene of Part I in which Tamburlaine, apostrophizing the loveliness of Zenocrate, feels the beauty "With whose instinct the soul of man is touched" and of the "heavenly quintessence" of poetry, highest attainment of the wit of man. By these strokes a slightly Platonic tinge is given to God's nature, but it is scarcely perceptible in the awful lightning-stricken darkness of the primary effect. As we shall see, the same conception of God as power prevails in Marlowe's other plays in a way too impressive to be anything but a signature of his subjectivity.

This, surely, is the unity, and the only unity, underlying all the diversity of the religious attitudes in both *Tamburlaine* plays—that God is a god of thunder. And so per-

meating is the sense of the presence of this Being that in
the modern meaning they may be called the least atheistic
of plays. Through all his ragings against Heaven, his boasts
that he is a divinely commissioned Scourge or is imitating
a God of Strife, Tamburlaine is wrestling with God, from
whom he cannot escape. He must conquer God, or else
succeed in feeling that he stands in a special relation of
favor to Him. And so perhaps it was with Marlowe.

5. IN *FAUSTUS*

Fa*ustus* IS THE ONLY ONE OF MARLOWE'S PLAYS IN which the pivotal issue is strictly religious and the whole design rests upon Protestant doctrines. This issue, stated simply, is whether Faustus shall choose God or the evil delights of witchcraft. In the first scenes we witness the temptations which lead to his fall through the witch bargain, and in subsequent scenes his agonized struggle to escape damnation by repentance. Thus the drama is not primarily one of external action but of spiritual combat within the soul of one man, waged according to the laws of the Christian world order. Now this theme allows Marlowe congenial opportunities of blaspheming without fear of being called to account. Through Faustus he can utter strictures on prayer, on Hell, on the harshness of Christian dogma, and then cover them safely with the usual orthodox replies. But withal Marlowe never lets these iconoclastic sallies overthrow the Christian emphasis of the whole. Like a crucible whose walls contain a seething liquid, the Christian structure of the play stands firm around the eruptions of blasphemy, and does not break.

Faustus' state of mind in the early scenes is that of a man apt for reprobation. Most dangerously is he "swollen with cunning, of a self-conceit," to use the authoritative words of the Prologue. In his pride he thinks to emulate God by ruling the elements surrounding the earth and even to stretch above them to the revolving spheres and "all things that move between the quiet poles" of the globe of the universe. His curiosity does not admit the limits placed by God on man's proper knowledge but longs for strange philosophy and the possession of the whole of Nature's treasury. And like Tamburlaine he is also a fiery thirster after sovereignty, for he aspires to do feats of war and govern kingdoms.

To these sins of pride, curiosity, and ambition must be added outrageous blasphemy. Divinity he characterizes as harsh and contemptible. Specifically, his reason for thinking it harsh appears in his first soliloquy, wherein he weaves several texts from Scripture into a cruel syllogism: [1]

> 'Stipendium peccati mors est.' Ha! 'Stipendium,' etc.
> The reward of sin is death: that's hard.
> 'Si pecasse negamus, fallimur
> Et nulla est in nobis veritas.'
> If we say that we have no sin,
> We deceive ourselves, and there is no truth in us.
> Why, then, belike we must sin,
> And so consequently die:
> Ay, we must die an everlasting death.
> What doctrine call you this, Che sera, sera:
> What will be, shall be? Divinity, adieu!   (I, i, 39-49)

Faustus, in short, is appalled by the injustice of a dogma which consigns all men inevitably to damnation. As a matter of fact, from the standpoint of any orthodox Elizabethan, Faustus' conclusion is perfectly correct as far as it

---

1. The major and minor premises of the syllogism are texts from Romans 6:23 and First Epistle of St. John 1:8 respectively, as is indicated in the notes of F. S. Boas' edition of the play (1932).

goes. Because man's nature has been warped by original sin, man cannot possibly fulfill the mandates of God's law, and therefore in strict justice he must suffer damnation. But Faustus makes the fatal error of not going on to see that man, thus condemned by the letter of the law, is redeemed through the sacrifice of Christ if he will have faith in God's mercy and will repent of his sins. This doctrine, with the exact nature of Faustus' blindness, is very clearly set forth in Thomas Becon's *The Dialogue Between the Christian Knight and Satan,*[2] which even refutes the identical syllogism:

Satan. "Hear therefore how evil the matter goeth with thee, and in how great danger thou art. But I will set this matter before thee plainly in the form of a *syllogismus* that thou mayest perceive it the better.

He that filleth not perfectly the ten commandments cannot enter into life, but die the death everlasting....

Thou hast not perfectly kept the commandments of God: thou are not righteous: thou hast trangressed God's precepts.

Therefore it followeth necessarily, that thou shalt not live with Christ, but that thou shalt be damned for ever."

.   .   .   .

Knight. "I answer therefore unto thy argument on this manner. As concerning the major of the first proposition... I grant and deny not but that it is true.... But the minor and second proposition, which is that I fulfil not the commandments of God, that I am not righteous, by no means do I grant, but plainly affirm that it is false...."

Satan. "What meneth [needeth] the minor much probation? ask thy conscience... and in the epistle of John it is

2. *Works* (published by the Parker Society), pp. 626-28. Wide use of the syllogism as a form was made in Elizabethan religious controversy. See, for example, chap. v of W. Whitakers, *A Disputation on Holy Scripture,* likewise published by the Parker Society.

read: 'If we say we have no sin, we deceive ourselves, and
the truth is not in us':"

.   .   .   .

Knight. "As concerning these things, which thou hitherto
hast alleged out of the old and new testament, and reasoned
with me, all these things are the law or else belong unto the
law:...God hath set forth to sinful man two things: one is
the law, the other is the gospel. And I confess with all my
heart that the law is the word of my God; and according to
this former word, I mean the law, I do knowledge and confess
both frankly and with an open voice...that I am a sinner,
guilty of everlasting damnation....

But I know and also have another manner of obtaining
righteousness and fulfilling the law, which thou canst not cast
away from me. For God himself hath taught me this manner
and way in the gospel, even that I should believe in Christ,
which alone hath most perfectly fulfilled the law, and all
obedience for my sake. By this faith all my sins are forgiven
me, and the Holy Ghost is given to me, which purifieth my
heart, and beginneth to fulfil the law in me."

The matter is of utmost importance because Faustus' inability to repent in the later climactic scenes of the play
arises from this same failure to believe wholly and passionately in the mercy of God. Dwelling upon the vileness of
his sins and thinking that they can never be pardoned, he
despairs and is lost. Thus Marlowe has given to his story
an impressive psychological and theological continuity running from the first lines to the last. At the very outset of
the action Faustus is revealed as already well on the way
to the damnation which finally overwhelms him.

In becoming a witch Faustus formally renounces God
and gives himself over to the worship of the devil. Under
the monstrous shadow of this most mortal of all sins he
also commits lesser sins of voluptuousness. But, increas-

ingly as the years of his bargain expire, his pleasures are broken by convulsions of remorse. As we watch the futile agony of his struggle to repent, we are bound to ask, Is it possible for him to repent? Does Marlowe mean us to understand that he is predestined to eternal death and God denies him the power to repent? The answer given by the drama is unmistakable. Faustus has free will, free capacity to repent. It is his own fault that he does not, and so he goes to a condign doom. Thus the Good Angel begs him to believe that it is never too late for him to repent.[3] If the Evil Angel tells him that his chance is past, it is a lie designed to take away all hope and hence all power of action. Both Mephistophilis and Lucifer, who are in an excellent position to know, fear his thinking of God, and are obliged to terrorize him with threats. And just before the death scene the Old Man tries to persuade him that God is offering mercy if only he is willing to receive it:

> I see an angel hover o'er thy head,
> And, with a vial full of precious grace,
> Offers to pour the same into thy soul:
> Then call for mercy, and avoid despair.

> (V, i, 69-72)

These lines, indeed, sum up the theological meaning of the play. Coming from a character whose Christian faith even Mephistophilis admires, they make untenable any theory that Faustus' fall is predetermined in a Calvinistic sense.

3. This, of course, was the view of all Christian churches. See *Certaine Sermons appointed by the Queenes Maiestie* (1587), Vol. II, sigs. 114ʳ&ᵛ; Hyll, *The Defence of the Article*, fol. 19ʳ; John Nichols, *A declaration of the recantation of Iohn Nichols* (London, 1581), sig. 14ʳ. All three of the foregoing authorities, and numberless others, cite the case of Christ's forgiveness of the thief upon the cross, just as Faustus does in a moment of hope (IV, vA, 33). Many of them also emphasize that repentance can come at the very last hour of life. Perhaps that is why Marlowe undertakes in Faustus' final soliloquy to depict the thoughts of his closing hour, indicating that a possibility of salvation yet remains.

Catholic, Calvinist, and Lutheran all agreed that man, of his own nature, was too weak and corrupt to repent of his sins unless God chose to give him the grace [4] to do so. Calvin, however, taught that God gave grace only to those men whom, in his unsearchable wisdom, he had elected for salvation.[5] On the other hand, the Catholic church and the more moderate Protestants, whom Marlowe followed in this instance, declared that grace was obtainable by any man who really sought it, and that everyone was able to seek it. The steps by which it might be achieved were often codified, as in this excerpt from Thomas Morton's *Treatise of Repentance:*

"This way or ladder whereby we are to clime up to regeneration, hath foure steps, for so we will make a homely and familiar diuision of it.... The first step which is to be made by this carnal man now repenting, is to get the true knowledge of his owne estate, to wit, how sinfull and wretched he is in himselfe by nature, and at this present. The second step is humiliation or contrition, wrought in him by the due consideration of his own estate. The third, is a full purpose or resolution of mind to seeke for grace and regeneration. The fourth and last part, is the diligent using of the meanes appointed by God, for the obtaining of grace: the which meanes are three in number. The first is amendment of life: the second, the hearing of Gods word: the third is praier, or inuocation of the name of God." [6]

4. A succinct definition of grace is given by H. Bullinger, *Sermons* (trans. by H. I.; London, 1587), Decade IV, Sermon I, p. 529: "Grace is the fauour and goodnesse of the eternall Godhead, wherewith hee according to his incomprehensible goodnes doth gratis freely for Christ his sake embrace, call, iustifie and saue us mortall men."

5. *The Institution of Christian Religion*, Lib. III, cap. XXIV, fol. 407^r.

6. London, 1597, sig. A7^v. A very similar list is drawn up in *Certaine Sermons appointed by the Queenes Maiestie*, Vol. II, sigs. KK3^r-KK6^v. See also T. Becon, *Catechism* (Parker Society), Pt. I, "Of Repentance," pp. 11-12; and Thomas Hooker, *The Poore Doubting Christian* (London, 1638), p. 49.

The "contrition, prayer, repentance" which the Good Angel says are "means to bring thee unto heaven" are evidently parts of this well understood process of regeneration.[7]

The trouble with Faustus, then, is not that God withholds from him the grace necessary to repentance but that he himself refuses to make a real effort to accept it when it is offered. He lets himself be lured away by the embraces of Helen and by threats of physical torment from the demons. Thereby he earns the rebuke of the Old Man:

> Accursed Faustus, miserable man,
> That from thy soul exclud'st the grace of Heaven,
> And fliest the throne of his tribunal seat! (V, ii, 127-29)

He becomes one of those wilful men who resist grace, within the usual Protestant definition thus typically stated by Edward Bulkley in *An Apologie for Religion:*

"... you [Bulkley's Catholic opponent] write improperly and falsely in charging us, that we say all goodnes proceedeth so farre from grace, that it lieth not in mans power neither to haue it nor to refuse it, but of necessitie it must haue effect. Improperly you write, in putting, *hauing Gods grace,* in steede of *obtaining and getting it.* We say, it is in man to haue it, when God doth giue it, without which gift it is not in mans power to get it. But it is in man to resist it. For the grace of God offereth saluation to all, but it is resisted and reiected of many, in that their hard and stony harts will not admit it. The grace of God is offered to men, when his word is preached, and they be called to repentance; but it is with many, and

7. Also in favor of this view that Faustus is free to repent is the fact that Marlowe's source, the *English Faust Book,* implies that Faustus has this freedom (chap. xiii): "In this perplexitie lay this miserable Doctor Faustus, hauing quite forgot his faith in Christ, neuer falling to repentance truly, thereby to attaine the grace and holy spirit of God againe, the which would haue been able to haue resisted the strong assaults of Satahn... but he was in all his opinions doubtfull, without faith or hope, and so he continued."

namely you, as Zacharie saith: *They refused to hearken, and pulled away the shoulder, and stopped their eares, that they should not heare. Yea, they made their hearts as an Adamant stone, least they should heare the Law.* . . . I know no man that denieth, but such men doe resist the grace of God, which yet is receiued of them that are written in the booke of life, whose wils it reformeth. . . ." [8]

Against these many and powerful tokens that Faustus is free to repent, one line from the play is sometimes quoted to prove the opposite. In Act II, after the Bad Angel tempts him to despair by assuring him, "Faustus never shall repent," Faustus submits with the words "My heart is harden'd, I cannot repent" (II, ii, 18). But this line does not necessarily mean that God has hardened Faustus' heart; it may mean that Faustus has hardened it himself by repeated offenses. The hardening of the heart of a sinner is an expression found time and again in Scripture, especially in Exodus, where Pharaoh's obstinacy against Moses is in question. [9] For Calvinists these texts meant that the initiative in the process of hardening came from God. [10] But for other Protestants, as also for Catholics, they meant something different, which Henry Bullinger's exegesis illustrates:

"In the same sense, GOD is said to harden man. For when the Lorde calleth man, and hee resisteth, making himselfe unworthie of the kingdom of heauen, he doth then permit him unto himselfe: that is, hee leaueth man unto his owne corrupt nature, according unto which the hart of man is

8. Edward Bulkley, *An Apologie for Religion* (London, 1602), p. 123.
9. E.g. Exodus 4:21: "And the Lord said unto Moses, When thou goest to return into Egypt, see that thou do all those wonders before Pharaoh, which I have put in thine hand: but I will harden his heart, that he shall not let the people go." Also Exodus 7:3 and 13; 8:15 and 32; Psalms 95:8, etc.
10. Calvin, Lib. II, cap. IV, fol. 116ʳ; John Knox, *An Answer to . . . an Anabaptist* (1560), *passim*.

stonie, which is mollified and made tractable by the onely
grace of GOD: therefore the withdrawing of Gods grace is
the hardening of mannes hart: and when wee are left unto
our selues, then are we hardened." ¹¹

For the sake of consistency with the other indications in
the play, Faustus' words should be given this meaning. But
even if they be taken to imply that Faustus thinks himself
predestined to eternal death, they are no more than the
outcries of a tormented spirit, showing his efforts to evade
responsibility but not intended by Marlowe to overthrow
the plain doctrine of the whole drama.

   Another, but less important, question which is sometimes
raised is whether Faustus ever temporarily repents and then
relapses. Properly speaking, he never repents at all. He
takes the first step to repentance, which is conviction of
sin, but never advances to the requisite faith in God's mercy
through Christ. True faith, like that of the Old Man, is
steadfast in all adversity, not to be deflected by pain or
lust as are Faustus' momentary impulses to call upon Christ.
At root, Faustus does not genuinely believe he can be saved.
And, as we have already seen, the reason why he does not
believe is that he does not try hard enough to do so. Hence
he feels only the waverings of remorse and the horrors of
despair. His last soliloquy, especially, is a magnificent study
of despair as the theologians of all Christian sects pictured
it. So Calvin writes graphically describing this state:

   11. *Sermons,* Decade III, Sermon x, p. 492. To the same effect are
Bulkley, *op. cit.,* p. 159, and P. Moulin, *The Anatomy of Arminianisme*
(London, 1620), chapters under the heading "Of the prouidence of
God." In the old play, *The Conflict of Conscience* (ed. Dodsley, Vol.
VI), where the situation is remarkably like that in *Faustus,* the despond-
ent sinner, Philologus, declares, "I am secluded clean from grace, my
heart is hardened quite" (V, v, p. 127). In the end Philologus repents
and is saved in time, but whether he freely co-operates in the process
or whether all is determined by God is not clear from the exposition.

...we ought chiefely to fasten our thought upon this, howe wretched a thinge it is to be estranged from the fellowshippe of God: and not that onely, but also to feele the maiesty of God so bent against thee, that thou canst not escape but be fast strained of it....For first his displeasure is like a most violent fier, with touchinge whereof all thinges are deuoured and swallowed up. Then, all creatures do serue him to execute his iudgement, that they to whom the Lord shall so shew his wrath, shal fele the heauen, earth, sea, and beastes, as it were with cruell indignation enflamed against them and armed to their destruction....Wherefore the unhappy consciences do finde no rest, from being vexed and tossed with a terrible whirlewinde, from feeling themselues to be torne in peeces by God beinge angirly bent against them, from being pearced and launced with deadly stinges, from trembling at the lighteninge of God, and beinge broosed with the weight of his hand: so that it is much more ease to enter into al the bottomles depthes and deuoringe pittes, than to stande one moment in those terrours.[12]

And the Faustus soliloquy is likewise illuminated by *Ane Treatise of Conscience* of the Scottish theologian, Alexander Hume:

...hee that hes the feeling of his awin sinne, and of the wrath of God aganis his sinne, in the highest degrie; that man sall see nathing but the angrie face of God, burning like a consuming fire against him, and sal think na uther thing, but that the Lord in his just judgment has castin him away, out from his presence & kingdon: Quhilk of al torments, that man can suffer in this life, is the gretest.[13]

Thus Faustus' dreadful vision of the face of the Almighty in anger and his frenzy to find somewhere, anywhere, a

12. Lib. III, cap. xxv, fol. 419ʳ.
13. Alexander Hume, *Ane Treatise of Conscience* (Edinburgh, 1594), pp. 35-6.

place of escape are elements of this tradition.[14] And at the
end the Christian sense of the play is confirmed by the
Epilogue as by a solemn seal.

Within this framework, which it has voluntarily imposed
upon itself, the spirit of Marlowe's iconoclasm struggles
fitfully to burst free. For example, when the two angels
prompt Faustus,

> *Faustus.* Contrition, prayer, repentance—what of these?
> *Good Ang.* O, they are means to bring thee unto heaven!
> *Bad Ang.* Rather illusions, fruits of lunacy,
> That make them foolish that do use them most,
>
> (II, i, 17-20)

we know that the Good Angel is doctrinally right. But we
also know that the Bad Angel is speaking for Marlowe
himself, who, according to Thomas Kyd, used to "gybe at
praiers" and to "iest at the devine scriptures." What the
Bad Angel does is to treat prayer and repentance as phenomena of abnormal psychology having no connection
with religious truth. These things, he says, are the inven-
tions of brainsick men, who are likely to make others as
brainsick as themselves. A rationalistic explanation like this
was entirely characteristic of Marlowe, and was not unknown to other Elizabethans. It was, for instance, condemned by Alexander Hume in these terms:

This kinde of trouble that proceids from the Conscience,
seemis sa strange & difficil to natural and worldly men, that
they can hardly consaue it, but takes it euer up wrang: and
estiems those persons that are so troubled, either to be furious,
lunatick, or fantastick: either els to haue taken sum appre-
hension, melancholie, or vaine conceit: ...[15]

14. Suggestions for some of these details were forthcoming from the
English Faust Book, chap. LIX-LXIII, which was itself a faithful reflection
of long Christian usage
15. *Op. cit.,* p. 36.

Again, Faustus' insistence that "Hell's a fable" recalls the statement of Richard Baines that Marlowe "perswades men to Atheism willing them not to be afeared of bugbeares and hobgoblins." And so with other sallies by Faustus, the Bad Angel, or Mephistophilis against the Christian scheme.[16]

There is also a class of what might be called silent protests against the official Christianity of the play. Theologically speaking, Helen of Troy is only a fleshly wanton who decoys Faustus from the way of salvation. Yet Faustus' passion for her glows with some of Marlowe's most transcendent poetry. She is a symbol of the ideal of beauty of pagan Greece, well loved by Marlowe. In like manner, all the lucubrations, the discontents, the giant ambitions of Faustus in the first act are authoritatively condemned as evil because they denote his approaching fall. Yet the verse is exultant and the ideas and emotions are the same as those which animate Tamburlaine, Barabas, and the rest of Marlowe's great creations, and hence in all probability animated the poet himself.

Nevertheless, an important qualification must be added. It is an error to suppose that the highest poetry of the play is limited to the passages of rebellion. Surely there has seldom been more noble expression of the sense of failure and the pain of everlasting banishment from God than that of the lost demon, Mephistophilis:

> Why, this is hell, nor am I out of it:
> Think'st thou that I, that saw the face of God,
> And tasted the eternal joys of heaven,
> Am not tormented with ten thousand hells,
> In being depriv'd of everlasting bliss?

16. E.g. Faustus' malicious perversion of Christ's dying words, "Consummatum est," to the signing of his bargain with Mephistophilis (II, i, 74) is typical Marlovian gibing. And the derision of divinity in Act I is quite of a piece with Marlowe's commentaries on Scripture as reported by Baines and others.

> O, Faustus, leave these frivolous demands,
> Which strikes a terror to my fainting soul.
>
> (I, iii, 78-84)

Scarcely less eloquent are his later words:

> Hell hath no limits, nor is circumscrib'd
> In one self place; but where we are is hell,
> And where hell is, there must we ever be: ...
>
> (II, i, 122-24)

Any rounded analysis of Marlowe's reactions to Christianity must emphatically record that this thought of hell as exile from God is able to touch deep places in his soul.

Nor is it true, as some scholars say, that Marlowe's conception of hell is singular, unheard of, and un-Christian. Deprivation of the sight of God's face was always considered the chief punishment suffered by devils.[17] As the anonymous writer of the addition to the 1665 version of Reginald Scot's *A Discourse concerning Devils and Spirits* declares:

> ... the infinite source of their misery is in themselves, and is continually before them, so that they can never enjoy any rest, being absent from the presence of God: which torment is greater to them, then all the tortures of this world combin'd together.[18]

Again, the notion that the damned spirits carried hell within themselves in all their wanderings is a familiar doctrine,

---

17. Heaven's bliss consisted mainly in the vision of God's face. Matthew 18:10: "...in heaven their angels do always behold the face of my Father which is in heaven." But Bullinger cautions against too literal an interpretation of this perception: "To be short, we shall see God face to face, we shall be filled with the companie of God, and yet be neuer wearie of him. And the face of God is not that countenance that appeareth in us, but is the most delectable reuealing and inioying of God, which no mortall tongue can worthily declare."—*Sermons*, Decade I, Sermon ix.

18. Bk. II, chap. 1, p. 493.

later exemplified in Milton's Satan. An explanation of it is
given by St. Thomas Aquinas:

...a twofold place of punishment is due to the demons: one,
by reason of their sin: and this is hell; and another, in order
that they may tempt men; and thus the darksome atmosphere
is their due place of punishment.... although the demons
are not actually bound within the fire of hell while they are
in this dark atmosphere, nevertheless their punishment is none
the less; because they know that such confinement is in store
for them. Hence it is said in the gloss upon Jas. iii. 6: 'They
carry the fire of hell with them wherever they go.' [19]

This, in all probability is Marlowe's meaning—that hell is
both a state of mind and a locality. Nothing that Mephistophilis says need imply that mental torment is the *only*
punishment suffered by the damned. And, manifestly, all
through the drama there is a considerable traffic of demons
to and from a definitely situated hell, which Faustus himself
visits, and to which he is eventually haled away. In short,
the devils are in hell when they wander about the earth to
tempt mankind; they are also in hell when tossing on muck-
forks the burning bodies of the reprobate. But even if Marlowe can be taken to mean in the Mephistophilis speeches
that hell is exclusively mental, he would still have behind
him the authority of such great, if unorthodox, Christian
intellectuals as Abelard and John Scotus Eriugena.[20] Upon

19. *Summa Theologica* (trans. Eng. Dominican Fathers), I-II, Ques.
lxiv, Art. 4. Likewise *Batman uppon Bartholome*, Lib. II, cap. xx, fol.
11^v: "and therefore because they [devils] trespasse continuallye where-
soeuer they goe, they beare alwaie with them their pain, as saith
Gregorie."

20. A. C. McGiffert (*A History of Christian Thought*, Scribner's,
1933, II, 181), says of John Scotus: "For one thing he read the future
life in exclusively spiritual terms. Heaven and hell are not places but
states of mind"; and of Abelard (II, 219) that in his *Dialogus inter
philosophum, Judaeum et Christianum* "Heaven...is communion with
God and hell is separation from him." Gregory of Nyssa, "On the Soul

any view, what is most significant for our purposes is that refined Christian thought proves capable of inspiring Marlowe to some of his most superb poetry.

Throughout the play a certain conception of God, much like that in *Tamburlaine*, is discernible. The Deity is a symbol of power, of creative energy, and of retribution. He is "heaven's great architect." The heavens in their beauty remind Faustus of "God who made the world." To be a magician and to control the storms of the air is to be a demigod, and Faustus half thinks himself capable of godhead, as does Tamburlaine. Then later in the speeches of Mephistophilis already quoted, God is a blinding and ineffable vision, loss of which is the most poignant of all pain. Finally, God is a wrathful presence who is always with Faustus and never lets him go. Offset against this totality of power and fear, the few indications of heavenly mercy are scarcely noticed. Neither Faustus nor any other character in the play so speaks of God as to make us really feel that he is a being who can love men and be loved by them. We are never persuaded that God is truly a Father who looks with tenderness on his erring children of the earth. This lack was in no way necessary to the plot. Rather, since the same thing is true in all of Marlowe's plays, it seems to come from some coldness in the poet's own religious temperament.

In so far as Marlowe's anti-Christian bias is concerned, the play allows us to draw some further conclusions of great interest. The magnificent dramatizations of Christian ideas in some of the speeches of Mephistophilis and Faustus, especially the closing soliloquy, suggest that however scornfully Marlowe rejected the system intellectually, it still had a powerful hold of some sort on his imagination and emo-

a nd he Resurrection" (*Nicene and Post-Nicene Fathers of the Christian Church*, V, 443) doubts that Hell is a specific place.

tions. After all, he had been reared in an Elizabethan house-hold and had attended Elizabethan schools in which religious instruction must have been hammered into him continually during the most susceptible years of his life. He grew to despise and hate all this, I believe, and to struggle against it as a creature of man's fear of the unknown and the dark. And yet, it would appear, there came to him afterwards moments when the ingrained creed sought to take possession of him again, moments when he almost felt that his life had failed of its highest consummation, and an indefinable sense of estrangement lay cold upon him. Then in the dim, uncontrollable regions of the mind would wait the persuasion of guilt, the ancient terror of God's anger. The course of Marlowe's life and of his plays does not indicate that he ever allowed these elements in his nature to dominate him. On the contrary, one may well believe that in order to suppress them he resorted the more strenu-ously to his ironical mockery. But they were there, and out of them grew his greatest drama, with all its revealing emotional contradictions. Almost everywhere we look in Marlowe's works we find them present. However desperate his desire to be free, he was bound to Christianity by the surest of chains—hatred mingled with reluctant longing, and fascination much akin to fear.

6. IN *THE JEW OF MALTA*
AND OTHER PLAYS

T*he Jew of Malta* IS THE THIRD SUCCESSIVE PLAY in which the plot chosen by Marlowe lends itself naturally to criticism of Christian life and principles. As in *Faustus* the doctrinal framework is orthodox. Ferneze is the official voice of Christianity in the drama, defending the confiscation of the Jew's wealth and denouncing him at the end for his many crimes. The voice, however, is a most apathetic one, through which sounds always the sardonic laughter of Barabas, irrepressible and triumphant.

One method of attack widely used in the play is to set off the doctrines of Judaism against those of Christianity in such a way as to equalize the two. For instance, Katherine warns Mathias not to talk to Barabas: "Converse not with him; he is cast off from heaven" (II, iii, 159). But Barabas in the same scene is even more outspoken in his contempt of Lodowick:

> *Lod.* Whither walk'st thou, Barabas?
> *Bara.* No further: 'tis a custom held with us,
> That when we speak with Gentiles like to you,
> We turn into the air to purge ourselves;
> For unto us the promise doth belong.
>
> (II, iii, 44-8)

Does the Christian disdain to walk with the Jew? The Jew no less disdains to walk with the Christian. Does the Christian think himself the sole possessor of God's promise? So does the Jew. Has the Christian his authority in the New Testament? The Jew has his in the Old (e.g. Genesis 12 and 17). Inevitably the effect of this kind of juxtaposition of creeds is to question the absolute of Christianity and reduce everything to relativity.

These conflicting claims of the two religions were, of course, often set forth in contemporary literature. John Foxe in his *Sermon preached at the Christening of a certaine Jew*[1] objects that the Jews

being otherwise a people most abhorred of God, & men...
would neuerthelesse most arrogantly vaunt them selues to bee
more esteemed, and more precious in the sight of God, then
all other nations, people and tongues: and that they were his
only darlings, and therefore could not by any meanes be
defrauded of the power of his promise. ...

And Christian preemption of the promise is illustrated in a similar comment on the Jews in John Rogers' *Displaying of ... the Familie of Loue:*[2]

For so much as they blaspheme Christ the sonne of God, and
denie his Godhed, and resurrection, they haue no part nor
fellowship with us of the promise of God, touching Christ
our Lord, neither are partakers of his mercie. ...

All such pronouncements declare, of course, one-sidedly against the Jews. Marlowe, on the contrary, allows Barabas ample liberty to have his say unopposed, and emphasizes the contentions of Judaism not only in the passage quoted

1. London, 1578, fol. cl^v. Also, Mornay, *A Treatise of the Church*, p. 154.
2. Fol. E6^r.

but also in such other statements by Barabas as "These are blessings promised to the Jews" (I, i, 103) and

> In spite of these swine-eating Christians,
> Unchosen nation, never circumcis'd....[3]
>
> (II, iii, 7ff)

It is one thing to give an occasional airing to the Jewish point of view by way of a realistic drawing of character, as Shakespeare does with Shylock, and quite another thing to afford it frequent, powerful, and often uncontested expression, as Marlowe does through his hero.

Contrasts of doctrine are again brought to the fore in Barabas' plots against Lodowick:

> This offspring of Cain, this Jebusite,
> That never tasted of the Passover,
> Nor e'er shall see the land of Canaan,
> Nor our Messias that is yet to come;
> This gentle maggot, Lodowick, I mean,
> Must be deluded: ...
> It's no sin to deceive a Christian;
> For they themselves hold it a principle,
> Faith is not to be held with heretics:
> But all are heretics that are not Jews;
> This follows well....   (II, iii, 302-14)

Scorn of Christian for Jew reaches no such pitch in the drama as that here achieved by Barabas for the Christian who knows nothing of the sacred Hebrew ceremonies and will never enter the promised land. The syllogism in the closing lines is a particularly neat bit of Marlovian logic.

---

3. See also "Becomes it Jews to be so credulous?" (I, ii, 360); "O thou that with a fiery pillar ledd'st..." (II, i, 12ff); "He is not of the seed of Abraham" (II, iii, 231), etc. Marlowe's meaning in giving Barabas so many quotations from the book of Job (see the notes in Bennett's edition, *passim*) is not clear. It scarcely seems possible that he intends to suggest a prolonged parallel between the sufferings of the two men.

Its major premise is the notorious Catholic doctrine that promises made to heretics need not be kept. This is imputed to the French Catholic League by the Huguenots, for example:

The counsell of Constance (say they) commandeth us to keepe no faith with the enemies of the faith: by which decree, Iohn Hus and Hierome of Prague were condemned to death, and the Cardinall S. Iulian was sent as legate into Hungarie, to breake the treatie of peace made with the Turkes...as if God had not shewed the error of that decree, by the tragicall effects ensuing....[4]

And Philip of Spain was charged with reliance upon it in treacherously attacking England:

...no maruell, if they obserue no solemnities in warres against us, whom they hold for heretikes, hauing already determined, that faith and promise is not to be performed unto heretikes (Concil. constant.).[5]

Marlowe so introduced the doctrine in 2 *Tamburlaine*, it will be remembered, as to call shame on the Christians who employed it. Here in *The Jew of Malta*, as in the earlier play, he says nothing about a Catholic origin, but attributes the odious principle to all Christians. Then he makes one

4. *The Contre-Guyse* (London, 1589), fol. E4ᵛ. The doctrine was supposed to have originated with the Council of Constance in 1415 to justify its burning of John Hus as a heretic in spite of the safe-conduct given him by the Emperor Sigismund. See J. H. Wylie, *The Council of Constance to the Death of John Hus* (London, 1900), p. 183. See also R. Crompton, *A short declaration of the ende of Traytors* (London, 1587), fol. C4ᵛ, attributing the doctrine to Mary of Scotland; and Bulkley, *An Apologie for Religion*, p. 146, commenting on the part it played in the Christian defeat at the battle of Varna, the very episode dramatized by Marlowe in 2 *Tamburlaine*. *The Troublesome Raigne of King Iohn*, a play written soon after *Tamburlaine*, likewise puts it into the mouth of a Cardinal. See Pt. I, p. 255 of Hazlitt's edition.

5. M. Sutcliffe, *The Practice, Proceedings, and Lawe of armes* (London, 1593), p. 10. See likewise A. Marten, *An Exhortation* (London, 1588), fol. C1ʳ.

of his deft substitutions in the minor premise of the syllogism: "But all are heretics that are not Jews." [6] Christians may consider Jews heretics, but the latter know who the real heretics are. Ergo, faith is not to be kept with Christians. It does indeed follow well. The whole zest of the play is in these covert sallies.

In Barabas' derision of the "fruits" of Christianity the drama enters widely into the field of moral criticism. Not that Barabas as a man has any right to criticize on such grounds, considering his own record; but as puppet for the ventriloquist Marlowe he assumes the right:

> Rather had I, a Jew, be hated thus,
> Than pitied in a Christian poverty:
> For I can see no fruits in all their faith,
> But malice, falsehood, and excessive pride,
> Which methinks fits not their profession.
>
> (I, i, 112-16)

"By their fruits ye shall know them," Christ had said; and St. Paul, "But the fruit of the Spirit is love, joy, peace, long-suffering, gentleness, goodness, faith, meekness, temperance. . . ." [7] Barabas knew Christians by their fruits, and they proved most bitter to the taste. Later he returns to the subject in a more specific connection:

> Lod. No doubt your soul shall reap the fruit of it.
> Bara. Ay, but, my lord, the harvest is far off:
> And yet I know the prayers of those nuns
> And holy friars, having money for their pains,
> Are wondrous;—and indeed do no man good;   [Aside

6. Cf. also his words to Abigail in I, ii, 346-47: "I charge thee on my blessing that thou leave/ These devils and their damned heresy!"

7. Matthew 7:20; Galatians 5:22-23. Also Ephesians 5:9: "For the fruit of the Spirit is in all goodness and righteousness and truth"; Philippians 1:11: "Being filled with the fruits of righteousness, which are by Jesus Christ. . . ." These ideas are of course endlessly discussed in Elizabethan treatises. Cf. A Conference containing a Conflict had with Sata (London, 1577), fol. A4ᵛ; and Rogers, op. cit., fol. A₃ʳ.

And, seeing they are not idle, but still doing,
'Tis likely they in time may reap some fruit,
I mean, in fulness of perfection.   (II, iii, 78-85)

Such phrases as "doing," "fruits," and "fulness," spoken
of monks and nuns, had perfectly obvious meanings for a
Protestant audience. So had the prayers which might be
bought for pence. But the whole extent of Marlowe's derision is not understandable save in the light of Kyd's report
that the poet was wont "to gibe at prayers" and the remark
of the Bad Angel in *Faustus* that "contrition, prayer, repentance" are illusions, "fruits of lunacy."

Similar ridicule occurs in the scene of Abigail's mock
conversion to Christianity, engineered between her and
Barabas so that she may get access to the jewels hidden in
the nunnery. The Friars, outrageous hypocrites themselves,
welcome her with churchly language:

Friar Jac. No doubt, brother, but this proceedeth of the spirit.
Friar Bar. Ay, and of a moving spirit too, brother....

.   .   .   .

Friar Jac. Hinder her not, thou man of little faith,
For she has mortified herself.
Bara. How! mortified!   (I, ii, 326ff.)

The technical meanings are clarified by P. Boquine, *A Defence of the Olde, and True profession of Christianitie:*
"No man commeth to Christ of himselfe, but called by God,
and moued by his Spirite"; [8] and H. Bullinger's *Decades:*

... when we say that penitents do mortify the old man, and
are renewed by the Spirit, or spiritually, we say nothing else
but that to all penitents the affections, senses or lusts of the
flesh... are not only suspected, but also convicted of
impiety....[9]

8. London, n. d., p. 56; also p. 126.
9. Decade IV, Sermon II, p. 104.

These sacred ideas are put into the mouths of two "religious caterpillars" as comments on a feigned conversion, and are subjected to mockery by a villainous Jew. Marlowe is enjoying almost a debauch of religious satire. The play is full of such instances. To be sure, most of them are cast in a specifically Catholic setting, which would help to render them digestible to Elizabethan playgoers, but since often the attitudes satirized are common to both Protestantism and Catholicism, the satire flies beyond the immediate setting to strike all Christianity. Especially in the first part of the drama there is little to show that Malta is a Catholic community. The ridicule is couched in general terms against all Christians.

Perhaps the scene of most forthright assault is that in which the Governor and Council of Malta expropriate Barabas' goods in order to pay the tribute money to the Turks (I, ii, 37-160). Notable, first, is the fact that Marlowe brings the whole question of confiscation to a sharp issue and makes it the occasion of a full-dress argument lasting well over a hundred lines. It was a question which, from the Christian point of view, might more expediently have been slurred over. For the issue was not whether the Jews of the island should pay their fair proportion of the tax but whether they should pay the whole of it. Marlowe makes this very clear:

> *Bara.* Are strangers with your tribute to be tax'd?
> *Sec. Knight.* Have strangers leave with us to
>   get their wealth?
> Then let them with us contribute.
> *Bara.* How! equally?
> *Fern.* No, Jew, like infidels;
> For through our sufferance of your hateful lives,
> Who stand accursed in the sight of heaven,
> These taxes and afflictions are befall'n,

> And therefore thus we are determined;
> Read there the articles of our decrees.   (I, ii, 58-67)

These articles provide that "the tribute-money of the Turks shall all be levied amongst the Jews," each to pay one half of his estate upon penalty of being forced to turn Christian and lose all his goods. The issue, in short, is put not on a political or economic but solely on a religious basis. To which Barabas has the poignant retort, several times repeated, "Is theft the ground of your religion?"; "What, bring you Scripture to confirm your wrongs?/Preach me not out of my possessions." Ferneze's answer is significant:

> No, Jew; we take particularly thine,
> To save the ruin of a multitude:
> And better one want for a common good,
> Than many perish for a private man: ...
>   (I, ii, 97-100)

It is no real answer, because payment of a fair share of the tax commensurate with their wealth would not cause the people of Malta to "perish." Marlowe had too logical a mind to intend this shift as anything but specious. In the second place, the answer rests on a text in John 11:49-50 relating the decision of a council of the chief priests and Pharisees to kill Jesus:

And one of them, named Caiaphas, being the high priest that same year, said unto them, Ye know nothing at all,
Nor consider that it is expedient for us, that one man should die for the people, and that the whole nation perish not.

Ferneze, in effect, puts Barabas in the place of Christ! The fine irony of this reversal was certainly not lost on the Marlowe who devised the mockeries of the Baines note.

The Governor continues with his argument from Scripture:

If your first curse fall heavy on thy head,
And make thee poor and scorn'd of all the world,
'Tis not our fault, but thy inherent sin.   (I, ii, 108-10)

Now this is a perfectly orthodox point. It is given in typical
form in Mornay's *Trewnesse of the Christian Religion:*

He [Christ] was deliuered by them [Jews] into the hands
of the Gentyles; and they themselues were scattered abroade
into the whole world, to bee a skorning stocke to all Nations.
Of these things and many other like doe the Rabbines com-
plaine in their Histories, and the more they speake of them,
the more doe they confesse Gods Iudgment upon themselues.
For what els are all these things, but the execution of this
their owne sentence upon themselues, *his blud be upon us &*
upon our Children? [10]

But, used by Ferneze under the particular circumstances,
it sounds, and was meant to sound, like sheerest hypocrisy:
" 'Tis not our fault if we have to take your goods, Barabas;
we really can't help ourselves, because you were born such
a rascal."

In reply, Barabas quotes Proverbs (10:2: "Righteousness
delivereth from death," and 12:28: "In the way of righteousness is life"): [11]

But say the tribe that I descended of
Were all in general cast away for sin,
Shall I be tried by their transgression?
The man that dealeth righteously shall live.
And which of you can charge me otherwise?
(I, ii, 114-18)

No man, says Barabas, ought to be chargeable with the
crimes of his ancestors. This plea for individual responsi-

10. P. 570. Likewise Viret, *The Worlde possessed with Deuils*, fol.
C2ᵛ; Foxe, *op. cit.*, fol. B4ᵛ.
11. Cited in Bennett's edition of the play, p. 54. The idea is frequent
in the Old Testament.

bility was not one, of course, which an Elizabethan divine could accept as exonerating a Jew from the stigma of tribal guilt. But it was one which appealed strongly to a native sense of justice in many an Elizabethan. Marlowe has so phrased Barabas' contention as to suggest a parallel to the theological doctrine of original sin, holding that every person born on the earth is so corrupted by the sin of Adam that he is inherently evil. Sermons and treatises galore in the period bear witness to the labors of the preachers to convince the ordinary man, against his sense of reason and justice, that he was evil because Adam had sinned thousands of years before.[12] Even in the Renaissance this doctrine, a survival from primitive conceptions of collective guilt, had begun to melt away under a new conception of individual accountability, prevalent today. Barabas' reply reads like a forerunner of the change. It is Marlowe's nearest comment on the doctrine of original sin.

Of course, Barabas lays himself open to retort by claiming that he himself lives righteously, and the Governor takes full advantage of the opening (ll. 119-21). But he has made his main point by insisting that he has rights as an individual. If as an individual he has committed offenses, he can be brought to a proper public trial; but now his goods are being taken by fiat of the council merely on the ground that he is a member of an outcast religion. Barabas points up the injustice of it by saying, finally, that the Christians might as well kill him as take away his means of livelihood. Marlowe gives Ferneze only the weakest of defences:

> No, Barabas; to stain our hands with blood
> Is far from us and our profession.

12. For example, T. Morton, *A Treatise of the Nature of God* (London, 1599), pp. 185-88; Bullinger, *Decades*, Decade III, Sermon x, p. 389; Mornay, *Trewnesse of the Christian Religion*, p. 205.

The Governor and his crew finally walk off stage to the accompaniment of the Jew's bitter satire:

> Ay, policy! that's their profession,
> And not simplicity, as they suggest   (ll. 161-62)

It would be naive to suppose, on the basis of what has been said above, that the Elizabethan spectator would side with Barabas in the debate. "Curse him; he's a Jew!" Besides, he had already been shown in the first scene as an unscrupulous knave, and was at that very moment perpetrating a deceit on the Governor. But Marlowe, unlike his audience, seems very clearly to side with his knave, weighting the issue in his favor from the first, putting him ever on the offensive, planting cant arguments against him, sharpening his replies, and leaving him the effective last word.

All that Barabas says in this scene, and much that he says in other scenes, is in harmony with what we know of Marlowe's views. Not that he has any personal sympathy for Jews, as far as one can tell. The warmth of human understanding that went into the making of Shylock is almost totally absent in Barabas. Marlowe is not a defender of Jews; he is an attacker of Christians. Shakespeare, perhaps, is neither, but a loving observer of men. *The Merchant of Venice* is primarily a clash of people of different creeds, *The Jew of Malta* a clash of the abstract creeds themselves. In the former play the devil occasionally cites Scripture for his purpose, but in the latter he cites much more of it, and the devil who cites it is not a Jew but a Christian. For the other devil becomes an angel of light as a messenger of religious satire.

The mood of the next play, *Edward II*, is entirely different. After *Dido* it is Marlowe's only drama which does not in one way or another stigmatize Christianity, and in which, as a matter of fact, religious questions are relegated to a quite minor role. Its chief attention is directed elsewhere, into the realm of political conflict. Religion appears almost solely in the farewells of the defeated as they go to their deaths. These evince scorn of the world and expectation of bliss in heaven, all in the best tradition of Christian handbooks on holy dying and *de contemptu mundi*.

For example, the Earl of Warwick, never previously noted for devoutness, exclaims when sentenced to the block: "'Tis but temporal that thou canst inflict. ... Farewell, vain world" (III, iii, 57-64). The remaining barons take their parting in the same spirit. When it is the turn of Edward's favorites to die, Baldock, who used to deride "such formal toys," adjures Spencer junior:

> Make for a new life, man; throw up thy eyes
> And heart and hand to heaven's immortal throne,
> Pay nature's debt with cheerful countenance;
> Reduce we all our lessons unto this,
> To die, sweet Spencer, therefore live we all;
> Spencer, all live to die, and rise to fall.   (IV, vi, 106-11)

Compare, typically, John More's *A Lively Anatomie of Death*:

Remember that we are borne to dye, and dye to liue: If this once were beaten into our braines, we would not so much deceiue ourselues.[13]

Edward himself, however, is chief speaker for this type of meditation. Defeated in war and pursued by his enemies, he yearns for the contemplative life of the cloister. And taking a last leave of his friends, he reflects: "Well, that shall be, shall be: part we must!" (IV, vi, 94). This

13. Fol. B2ᵛ.

statement of belief in predestination is to be compared with the "che sera, sera" of Faustus' opening soliloquy. Faustus the individualist, strong in the consciousness of his own powers, rejects the doctrine contemptuously. Edward in disaster finds it something of a refuge. Yet in the later swift alterations of his anguish at surrender of his crown he cannot always hold steady in this assurance, but calls upon God now to rain vengeance on the usurpers, now to make him

> despise this transitory pomp
> And sit for aye enthronized in heaven!   (V, i, 107-9)

The abdication scene is a struggle, almost as remarkable in its way as Faustus' agonized search for repentance, between Edward's wish to believe that the world is vain, and his stubborn longing to keep the glittering crown which is chief symbol of that vanity. During the closing scenes in the dungeon—scenes of physical exhaustion, disillusionment, and fear—the pangs of his earthly loss return spasmodically to conflict with his thoughts of heaven. Sensing that Lightborn is the bringer of death, he asks a moment's respite for prayer:

> Yet stay awhile; forbear thy bloody hand,
> And let me see the stroke before it comes,
> That even then when I shall lose my life,
> My mind may be more steadfast on my God.
>   (V, v, 74-7)

But in that moment his mind reverts to earth:

> Know that I am a king: O at that name
> I feel a hell of grief! Where is my crown?

Only as the stroke of death descends does he cry at last, "Assist me, sweet God, and receive my soul!" It is a noble essay in the psychology of devotion that Marlowe has written. The vacillations in religious achievement are shown with deepest understanding and solemnity. Thus the return is, although in lesser degree, to the attitudes dominant in *Faustus*.

Mortimer's beautiful and famous goodbye, spoken as he goes to the gallows, might possibly be judged to have some faint tinge of unorthodoxy:

> Farewell, fair queen; weep not for Mortimer,
> That scorns the world, and, as a traveller,
> Goes to discover countries yet unknown. (V, vi, 64-6)

This seems to suggest an after life in countries other than the "known" regions of heaven and hell. But the language is ambiguous and accords well enough with some Christian speculation. *Cardanus Comfort*, sometimes cited as source for Hamlet's "undiscovered country from whose bourne/ No traveller returns," has this expression:

Therefore Socrates was wont to say, that death might be resembled eyther to sound sleape, a long iorney, or destruction.... But if thou compare deathe to longe travaile and that the soule beyng let lose from prison of the bodye seeth al thinges and walketh euery where. Then what can be considered moore happye....[14]

Cardan's book takes a Christian viewpoint throughout.

The only remaining religious matter in the play is the conflict between Edward and the Cardinal on the issue of Gaveston's banishment. Threats by the Cardinal to excommunicate Edward and release his subjects from their allegiance were introduced by Marlowe, without warrant from Holinshed's *Chronicles*, as a parallel to the Pope's bulls against Queen Elizabeth similarly encouraging rebel-

---

14. London, 1576, Bk. II, fol. 26ʳ. Also Viret, *The Worlde possessed with Deuils*, fol. A4.

lion.[15] The appeal, of course, is to English hatred of Catholicism, and specifically of the papacy.

As against this one topical incident in *Edward II*, the whole theme of Marlowe's last play, *The Massacre at Paris*, is topical, embracing the wars of religion between Catholic and Huguenot in France from the St. Bartholomew massacre in 1572 until the assassination of Henry III in 1589. Marlowe's account is based with considerable fidelity on the Protestant pamphlets of the time, both French and English.[16] Its interpretations of character as well as episode are, consequently, those current among the Protestants. Considering the sympathies of English playgoers, this was inevitable. Hence the drama throws all favor towards Navarre as the pious, righteous leader of the Huguenots and all obloquy towards his adversary Guise as head of the Catholic League. Guise is said to be in alliance with the king of Spain and the Pope, as well as with the hated and notorious Queen Mother. King Henry wavers between the two parties until he is driven into the arms of Navarre by Guise's ambitions for the throne.

Upon this background of intrigue and butchery Marlowe projects a number of more specifically religious issues.

15. Cf. P. Stubbs, *The Intended Treason of Doctor Parrie* (London, 1585), fol. A2ᵛ; Marten, *An Exhortation*, fol. B1.

16. See Kocher, "François Hotman and Marlowe's *Massacre at Paris*," *PMLA*, VI (1941), 349-68, discussing Hotman's *De Furoribus Gallicis* (1573), as the source of the first six scenes of Marlowe's play. The later scenes appear not to have any one source but to be compiled from the general pamphlet literature. Among those pamphlets closest to the play are: *La Vie et Faits Notables De Henry de Valois* (Paris, 1589); *Le Martire Des Deux Freres* (Paris? 1589); *Les Meurs...De Henry de Valois* (Paris, 1589), Colynet, *The True History of the Ciuil Warres of France* (London, 1591); *An Historicall Collection* (London, 1598); *Les Cruautez Sanguinaires...* (Paris? 1589); M. Hurault, *Anti-Sixtus* (London, 1590); *A discourse upon the present estate of France* (London, 1588); *Martine Mar-Sixtus* (London, 1591); *The Brutish Thunderbolt* (London, 1586.) I shall publish a further article on this subject in *MLQ* later in 1946.

The Catholic doctrine of invocation of the saints is several
times held up to scorn, especially when Mountsorrell
murders the Protestant Seroune:

> *Ser.* O Christ, my Saviour!
> *Mount.* Christ, villain!
> Why, darest thou presume to call on Christ,
> Without the intercession of some saint?
> Sanctus Jacobus, he's my saint; pray to him.
> *Ser.* O, let me pray unto my God![17]
>
> (sc. v, ll. 79-84)

So is the Catholic idolatry in the use of the crucifix.[18] And
the issue regarding the mass is raised when the dying Guise
cries: "Vive la messe! " (sc. xviii, l. 86). Elizabethan hatred
of relics prompts Navarre's resolve

> To beat the papal monarch from our lands,
> And keep those relics from our countries' coasts.
>
> (sc. xv, ll. 16-17)

Nor would the play be complete, naturally, without the
usual attacks on the "fat Franciscan friars" who will aid
Guise, or the seminary at Rheims where English Catholics
received training for secret missionary work to be done in
the home country. Monasticism takes its most bitter baiting,
however, in the scene of the Friar's resolution to kill the
king because "the deed is meritorious" (sc. xx, l. 29). The
idea that a Catholic might acquire merit in heaven by as-
sassinating an enemy of the church was highly obnoxious

17. Also sc. xxi, l. 34. The doctrine is not quite accurately stated in
sc. v, ll. 78-84: Catholicism did not obligate the believer to call upon
God through the intercession of a saint, but merely permitted him to
do so. See Smith, *Gods Arrow Against Atheists*, p. 86; and Mornay,
A Treatise of the Church, p. 270.

18. Sc. v, l. 29 deals with the kissing of the crucifix. Also sc. v, l. 52.
The Catholic viewpoint is explained by J. Martiall, *A Treatyse of the
Crosse* (Antwerp, 1564), fols. 123ᵛ and 141ʳ.

to Protestants, particularly since it was thought to be used as justification for plots against Elizabeth herself.[19]

Not enough is made, in the drama, of Guise's references to the Protestants as "heretics"[20] to produce an effect of relativity comparable to that achieved by more emphatic measures in *The Jew of Malta*, as already discussed. Similarly, his contempt of all religion as a "word of such a simple sound" (sc. ii, l. 68), while reminiscent of the Machiavelli Prologue and the "bugbeares and hobgoblins" of the Baines note, is too momentary a flash of Marlovian lightning to make any difference in the blatant anti-Catholicism of the drama as a whole. The play is journeyman's work in every particular, and not least so in its religious aspect.

So much can be said without derogating in the slightest from Marlowe's truly great achievement as a poet and satirist of religion in the bulk of his drama. His struggle with Christianity was, indeed, one of the purest fountains of his literary inspiration. It was the occasion of his greatest play, and of many of the greatest passages in his lesser dramas. The depth of theological learning it evoked is astonishing. I do not think it too much to say that Marlowe's plays show both a more extensive and a more profound knowledge of Christian doctrine than those of any other Elizabethan playwright, including Chapman. There are whole scenes in which scarcely a line does not contain some allusion to the Bible or to didactic and controversial literature. The present study has been able only to hint at some of the chief features of this learning. Yet the mass of it is wielded with almost effortless ease, neither superficial nor heavy. Whether serious or comic, whether in grandeur

19. See footnotes in Bennett's edition, p. 246. Also the *Contre-League* (London, 1589), p. 52; and *An Advertisement from a French Gentleman* (London, 1585), p. 51.

20. E.g., sc. ii, l. 94; iv, 20; v, 3, 66; viii, 2.

of reflection or malice of satire, it has become like a native possession of the poet's mind, something capable of the most spontaneous utterance. One wishes to guard against undue eulogy, but the eulogy is in fact long overdue. Marlowe has not had his rights either as scholar or satirist of religion. In both provinces his gifts are of the highest order.

We should disabuse ourselves of the notion that he is a minor figure standing undistinguished under the aegis of Shakespeare. He is a giant in his own right, with thews, bones, and brain of his own, inferior to none in many of his qualities, and superior to all in a few. Even more emphatically, we should stop thinking of him as merely an *enfant terrible,* an Elizabethan bad boy engaged in pranks which he himself did not take seriously. The sheer intellectual labor involved, the width of reading and research, continued during and after his Cambridge days, the significance and splendor of the results in his writing, the persistence of his efforts both in and out of the drama to make himself a prophet of the new irreligion, and not least the grave dangers to which he exposed himself thereby, all forbid so superficial an estimate. On the contrary, religion was the one thing in the world that Marlowe took most seriously. The biographical evidence harmonizes with that of his plays to make it plain that, out of conscious, rational disbelief overlying unconscious need and fear, controversy about religion was the ruling passion of his soul.

7. WITCHCRAFT

ITCHCRAFT HAD FOR MARLOWE THE FASCINA-
tion possessed by any subject closely related
to divinity. Additionally it had, one supposes,
an imaginative appeal of a very strong kind
in its own right. Besides a gamut of wonders stirring to any
poet, it offered stuff peculiarly adapted for the working of
those dreams of transcendent power so native to Marlowe.
Thus he could accept witchcraft imaginatively because it
gave outlet to certain qualities deep-seated in his nature,
while at the same time rejecting it rationally because it did
not satisfy his mind.

That he rejected it intellectually seems certain, on the
basis of some of his sayings about religion. He who could
not accept the miracles of God could scarcely accept the
minor marvels of witchcraft. He who held that all religion
was but a device of policy to keep the populace in subjec-
tion could not credit the bugbears and hobgoblins of that
conception of hell which, by its threats of punishment, was
the chief instrument of terror. No hell; therefore no devils.
No devils; therefore no witches. For a witch, as William
Perkins says,[1]

1. William Perkins, *A discourse of the damned art of witchcraft*
(Cambridge, 1608), p. 167. Thomas Cooper (*The mystery of witchcraft*,

is a Magician, who either by open or secret league, wittingly and willingly consenteth to use the aide and assistance of the Deuill, in the working of wonders.

The whole basis of the theory of Renaissance witchcraft is religious. It goes back, in the last analysis, to certain Biblical passages like that dealing with the Witch of Endor. Marlowe would make short work of this kind of argument, as we well know. We can imagine also the burst of laughter with which he would greet another kind of argument for the superstition, citation of the testimony of eye-witnesses who had seen a covey of witches riding the air on broomsticks or had chanced on the orgies of the Sabbat in the wilds of some forest, where Satan himself presided in the shape of a huge goat. The road to witchcraft was not through Marlowe's intellect, but a road did exist.

His earliest reference to the subject is Iarbas' description of the storm in Act IV of *Dido* as having been the work of "some fell enchantress," forming clouds, hail, and lightning. This seems to draw on classical views of sorcery, whose exponent was usually a woman skilled in making tempests. However, Achates' opinion, "I think it was the devil's revelling night," introduces, anachronistically, the Christian idea of a witches' Sabbat. It is Marlowe's only allusion to these ceremonies.

Our chief interest, however, centers in his use of witchcraft theory as a foundation for the whole meaning of

---

London, 1617, p. 177), adopts this phrasing. In orthodox treatises on witchcraft, whose theory Marlowe adopts for the purposes of his drama, no clear distinction is made between a "conjurer," "black magician," "white magician," "enchanter," etc. All are customarily lumped together under the condemnatory term "witch." Accordingly in this chapter I use "witch" to include anyone who performs supernatural acts by demonic agency. For an opposing view, the reader may be referred to R. H. West's excellent book, *The Invisible World* (University of Georgia Press, 1939), especially chapter 1.

Faustus, and particularly for the character of Faustus himself. This character is in part the product of Marlowe's creative genius working upon the materials afforded him by the English translation of the German *Faustbuch*.[2] But it is also in important respects the product of Marlowe's own wide familiarity with Renaissance, medieval, and classical ideas about witchcraft. An examination of the play will reveal that, since Faustus is a witch, Marlowe has endowed him with much of the motive and behavior commonly believed to be typical of those who had signed the compact with Hell. Not that Faustus is merely a conventional portrait of a witch, of course. So high, imperious, and passionate a figure does not abide final classification. But many of his thoughts and actions are unmistakably those of the witch of European tradition; and they are not to be found in the *EFB*. The demonstration of this fact in the remainder of this chapter will put us in possession of information both as to Marlowe's learning and as to the right interpretation of his greatest dramatic achievement.

I. THE GIFTS OF MAGIC

We have first to consider the motives which impel Faustus to enter upon the crime of sorcery. One of the chief of these is the desire for power to control the grand forces of Nature. And here the witch basis of his characterization is seen to be clearly and importantly operative. For although we must rule out of consideration some of the desired powers, like that of producing winds, tempests, lightning, which are mentioned specifically in the *EFB* and hence can show nothing as to Marlowe's own familiarity

2. Hereafter referred to as *EFB*. References are to the later edition by W. J. Thoms in *Early English Prose Romances* (London, 1858), Vol. III. It varies from the edition of 1592 only in minor details, none of them significant for our purpose.

with witchcraft-learning, Faustus covets other powers not there mentioned which were widely believed to be possessed by witches.

Such, for instance, is the power "to make the moon drop from her sphere" (I, iii, 40). As A. W. Ward has pointed out,[3] in Roman literature enchanters were credited with the skill to draw the moon from heaven. There are examples in Virgil (*Eclogues*, viii. 69), Horace (*Epodes*, v. 45-46), Apuleius, Ovid, Lucan, Tibullus, and others. I should like to add that the same thought is very frequently repeated in Renaissance works. Reginald Scot declares: "And concerning this matter Cardanus saith, that at everie eclipse they were woont to thinke, that witches pulled downe the sunne and moone from heaven." [4] Bodin says: "... Hippocrate au liure de morbo sacro, deteste les Sorciers, qui se vantoyent de son temps d'attirer la Lune...." [5] In Lyly's *Endymion* (Act I, sc. iv) we find the witch Dipsas boasting, "I can darken the Sunne by my skil, and remooue the Moone out of her course;..." It is scarcely possible, however, that Marlowe, with his thoroughgoing knowledge of the original classical sources, did not get the idea straight from them.

From the classics likewise seems to come inspiration for others of Faustus' ambitions to change the face of nature— to "make swift Rhine circle fair Wittenberg" (I, i, 90), "make ... the ocean to overwhelm the world" (I, iii, 41), "dry the sea" (I, i, 145). These are characteristic Marlovian enthusiasms whose real originality everyone will wish to

3. In a note in his edition of *Faustus* (Oxford, 1878), p. 149. I shall take pleasure in citing Ward's excellent notes from time to time.

4. Reginald Scot, *The discoverie of witchcraft* (ed. B. Nicholson, 1886), Bk. XII, chap. xv, p. 203. Scot reverts to the idea twice more: Bk. I, chap. iv, p. 8, and Bk. XII, chap. iv, p. 177.

5. "Refutation des opinions de Iean Wier," p. 409 (bound in with his *De la demonomanie des sorciers*, Anvers, 1593).

defend. It does no wrong to his genius, nevertheless, to say that his conception of what a witch may do through demons takes its temper from beliefs already existing. The might of the classical sorceress is well described in the words of Medea in Seneca's *Medea*:

I have driven the seas back to their lowest depths, and the Ocean, his tides outdone, has sent his crushing waves farther into the land. . . . Phasis has turned his swift waters backward to their source, and Hister, divided into many mouths, has checked his boisterous streams and flowed sluggishly in all his beds. The waves have roared, the mad sea swelled, though the winds were still . . . [trans. F. Miller (Loeb Library), ll. 755-66].

Similar powers are given by Ovid to Medea in the *Metamorphoses* (vii. 199-207), a work intimately known and greatly loved by Marlowe, as hundreds of footnotes to his plays and poems testify:

. . . when I have willed it, the streams have run back to their fountain-heads, while the banks wondered; I lay the swollen, and stir up the calm seas by my spell. . . . Thee also, Luna, do I draw from the sky . . . [trans. F. Miller (Loeb)].

These passages and others like them from the Roman writers are referred to, sometimes at great length, by many Renaissance witch treatises; [6] but it is impossible to doubt that Marlowe, if he used them at all, went direct to the originals. That he did use them seems quite probable. Faustus' grandiose schemes for manipulating rivers, seas, and hills savor strongly of these classical texts, and Mar-

6. See H. Boguet, *An examen of witches* (trans. of the *Discours des sorciers*, ed. M. Summers; London, 1929), chap. xxvi, pp. 77ff.; M. del Rio, *Disquisitionum magicarum libri sex* (Venetiis, 1640), Bk. II, Ques. 9; J. Bodin, *De la demonomanie des sorciers* (1593), Bk. I, chap. v, p. 92. Ward has mentioned some of the classical passages but has not developed the comparison here intended.

lowe is, beyond all question, deeply read in the works from which these texts come. Moreover, as in the quotation from Ovid just given, they appear in the originals side by side with that other dream of drawing the moon from its sphere, which Marlowe pretty certainly got from the classics. A conclusion of general indebtedness naturally follows. Marlowe, of course, gives the older ideas new poetic value, as well as a modern geographical application.

Faustus wishes to dry the sea in order to extract treasure from the wrecked ships at its bottom. This seems to be not an altogether new piece of imagination. Del Rio writes: "Melidenses Indos inuenio solitos merces, quarum iactum fecerunt, conari incantationib. e pelagi fundo extrahere, quo eventu nescio. Lege Castannedam, lib. 1 Histor. Indica c. 30."[7] Eight of the forms for conjuration set forth in the *Verus Jesuitarum libellus*[8] call for the bringing of gold "ex abysso maris" by a demon. The following is one example:

Ego N. servus Dei, voco, cito, exorcizo te, O Spiritus! per sanctos apostolos et discipulos Dei...et per sanctissima et terribilissima verba: Aphriel, Diefriel...compare coram me in pulcra, affabili, et humana forma, et affer mihi (ex abysso maris) N. milliones optimi auri et expensibilis ubique monetae Hispanicae sine ullo tumultu, damno corporis et animae....

Also quite pertinent is Boccaccio's account[9] of a sorcerer named Theban who invokes a god "that hast also giuen power to my verses to drie up the seas, that I at my plesure might search the botome therof...."

Furthermore, the magical power "to slay mine enemies

7. Bk. II, Ques. 12, p. 113.
8. Reproduced in *Das Kloster*, ed. J. Scheible (Stuttgart, 1846), II, 836ff. The *Libellus* was published in Paris in 1508.
9. Fol. Dv^r, Ques. IV, of *Thirteene most pleasaunt and delectable questions* (London, 1587).

and to aid my friends" (I, iii, 98), asked of Mephistophilis by Faustus, is quite ordinarily offered by the Devil to the witch initiate. We have the testimony of Remy that Satan allures the prospective witch "by providing drugs to poison those upon whom a man wishes to be avenged, or to heal those to whom a man owes a debt of gratitude." [10] Bartolommeo della Spina says likewise that the Tempter promises witches "quod vindicari & in hostes suos retorquere possent iniurias, quas alio modo repellere non valent. ..." [11]

According to popular belief, a witch had power not only to slay his enemies, God permitting, but to practise against the life of kings. This idea is probably embodied in Faustus' lines:

> The Emperor shall not live but by my leave,
> Nor any potentate of Germany.   (I, iii, 112-13)

One has only to turn over the pages of Kittredge and Notestein to encounter many instances of the Elizabethan belief that kings were vulnerable to magic. The safety of Elizabeth herself was much feared for. Notestein relates the great precautions taken by her councilors to protect her, and details several trials of conjurors suspected of attempting her life. [12] In particular there was the affair at

10. N. Remy, *Demonolatry* (Lyons, 1595; Eng. trans. ed. M. Summers, London, 1930), Bk. I, chap. 1, p. 1.
11. *De strigibus* (Coloniae: Apud M. Cholinum, 1581), chap. xxv, p. 160. A. Roberts (*A treatise of witchcraft*, London, 1616, p. 27), says that witches stipulate for means to "helpe and hurt at their pleasure, and others like unto these."
12. W. Notestein, *A history of witchcraft in England from 1558 to 1718* (Washington, 1911), pp. 24-28. At p. 24: "Elizabeth had hardly mounted her throne when her councillors began to suspect the use of sorcery and conjuration against her life. As a result they instituted the most painstaking inquiries into all reported cases of the sort, especially in and about London and the neighboring counties. Every Catholic was suspected." A poem by J. Aske, *Elizabetha triumphans* (1588; repr. J.

Abingdon in 1578-79, in which four women, accused of making waxen images against the queen and two of her councilors, were hanged amid great public excitement.[13] Deriding the vulgar credulity on this point, Scot remarks that, if witches had such powers,

No prince should be able to reigne or live in the land. For (as Danoeus saith) that one Martine a witch killed the emperour of Germanie with witchcraft: so would our witches (if they could) destroie all our magistrates.[14]

As to things military, Faustus will have his spirits invent "stranger engines for the brunt of war" and bring him coin with which to levy soldiers to drive out the Prince of Parma (I, i, 93-95). Ward notes many legends of the exploits of wizards in war.[15] A passage from Del Rio is also worth recording:

Mihi dubium non est posse magicē per Daemones ... praestigijs, & industria varia, qua (ut & robore) plus cunctis mortalibus pollent, & urbes obsidione liberare ... & expugnandas

---

Nichols' *Elizabeth*, II, 555), shows the current popular distrust of Catholic magic: "This Pope doth send Magitians to her land, / To seeke her death, by that their devillish arte." Statements constantly turn up in the chronicles and witch treatises that other sovereigns were attacked by sorcerers: Edward II, Edward III, Henry V, Henry VI, Richard III, and Queen Mary of England, King Duffus of Scotland, Charles IX of France. It was commonly rumored that the death of Ferdinand, Earl of Derby, in 1594 was due to witchcraft.

13. G. L. Kittredge (*Witchcraft in Old and New England*, Cambridge, Mass., 1929, pp. 87-88), relates the incident and quotes a statement by Ben Jonson (*The Masque of Queens*) that he remembered its happening in his youth.

14. Bk. III, chap. xiv, p. 49.

15. P. 134. See also F. Hutchinson, *An historical essay concerning witchcraft* (London, 1720), chap. ii, p. 34: "1563. The King of Sweden carried four Witches with him in his Wars against the Danes. Scot l. 3 c. 15." The *Malleus maleficarum* gravely inquires: "... if a prince ... employ such a wizard as we have described for the destruction of some castle in a just war ... is his whole army to be considered as protectors and patrons of that wizard?"—Part II, Ques. 1, chap. xvi, p. 152.

praebere, & in praelijs victoriae causam esse, nō desunt ex-
empla, nec ratio expugnat....[16]

He argues, however, that God rarely permits Satan to give
money to his devotees: "Impijs etiam hac ratione diabolus
pecuniam, belli neruum, suppeditaret, quare facile pios
opprimerent, nisi Deus miraculo nouo subueniret." [17] In
chapter VI of the prose *Historie of Fryer Bacon*,[18] Bacon
does indeed invent some extraordinary instruments for capturing a town in France, and imagines many more.

Where knowledge is concerned, Faustus will require his
demons to "read me strange philosophy, / And tell the
secrets of all foreign kings" (I, i, 87-88), and later asks a
book "wherein I might see all plants, herbs and trees
that grow upon the earth" (II, i, 165ff.). This sort of information is exactly what is possessed by many of the
demon princes whom Reginald Scot, drawing upon Wier's
Pseudomonarchia daemonum, and through him upon the
fable world of medieval demonology, is able to charac-
terize with a quite domestic intimacy. "Astaroth...an-
swereth trulie to matters present, past, and to come, and
also of all secrets.... He maketh a man woonderfull
learned in the liberall sciences...." "Buer...absolutelie
teacheth philosophie morall and naturall, and also logicke,
and the vertue of herbes...." [19] Again, we read in the
Daemonologie of James I that Satan

... will oblish himselfe to teach them artes and sciences, which
he may easelie doe, being so learned a knaue as he is: To carrie

16. Bk. II, Ques. 12, p. 107.
17. *Ibid.*, p. 112.
18. Reprinted in Thoms's *Early English prose romances*. It is in chap.
v of this work that Bacon proposes to wall England about with brass,
an idea adpted by Marlowe (I, i, 89). He must have been acquainted
with the tradition on which the story rests, possibly with the prose
work itself. Indebtedness to Greene's play on this theme seems unlikely.
19. These descriptions occur in Scot at Bk. XV, chap. II, p. 319, and
chap. I, p. 315, respectively.

them newes from anie parte of the worlde ... to reueale to
them the secretes of anie persons, so being they bee once
spoken, for the thought none knowes but God.... [Bk. I,
chap. VI, p. 21; ed. G. B. Harrison].

In the last chapter of the prose *Historie of Fryer Bacon*
Bacon says: "I likewise have found out the secrets of trees,
plants and stones, with their several uses." [20]

Some additional and more particular texts can be brought
to show that English writers believed a witch could ascer-
tain through her familiars the secret counsel of Kings.
Thus Thomas Cooper:

The presence of Sathan and the euill Angels, in most places,
and communicating their knowledge together, wherethrough
they are acquainted with the secret consultations of Princes,
may giue also furtherance to this knowledge of things to
come.... [21]

When Valdes is picturing to Faustus the delights of
magic, he promises that they shall be attended by spirits in
the shapes of lions, Almaine rutters, Lapland giants, and
beautiful women (I, i, 125-30). The lion forms may have
been inspired by parts of the *EFB* wherein devils appear as
various kinds of beasts, although not lions specifically; but,
if not, there is abundant precedent for the idea: some of
Reginald Scot's demon potentates, for instance, rise up in
that form. [22] The giants are probably Laplanders because,

20. Thomas Cooper (p. 129) states that Satan is "exquisitely skilfull
in the knowledge of naturall things, as of ... vertues of plants, rootes,
hearbs, etc...."
21. P. 130. Also Perkins, *op. cit.*, pp. 59-60, and J. Cotta, *The triall of
witch-craft* (London, 1616), p. 117. Cotta explains it as Satan's imitation
of the prophet Elisha, who divined the hidden plans of the king of
Syria (II Kings 6:12).
22. "Marbas, alias Barbas is a great president and appeareth in the
forme of a mightie lion...."—Bk. XV, chap. II, p. 314. Roberts, p. 31:
"...sometime he [Satan] sheweth himselfe in the forme of foure-footed
beastes, foules, creeping things, roaring as a Lyon, skipping like a
Goat...."

as Ward notes,[23] Lapland was commonly regarded as the home of witches. Some lines from the play *Look about you* bear out the point:

> Then nyne times like the northern Laplanders,
> He backward circled the sacred Font,
>
> .   .   .   .
>
> And so turn'd witch, for Gloster is a witch.
>
> (sc. xiv, ll. 2125-30)

The advantages of assuming the bodies of lovely women were well known to malign spirits. The Tempter, says Remy, "fabricates some fair and delectable body and offers it for a man's enjoyment." [24] Lavater, extracting the essence of many a medieval legend, gives authority for three of the different forms imagined by Marlowe:

> We read that many spirites haue appeared unto certaine Hermites and Monkes in the shape of a woman, alluring and intising them to filthie lust. They appeare also in the fourme of brute beastes. . . . At one time some hath beene seene riding on horsebacke, or going on foote. . . .[25]

In the background of this part of our subject lies the wild region of tales of the succubi and incubi, demons taking on sex in order to have intercourse with men and women.

Thus far we have spoken of specific powers envisioned or bargained for by Faustus, and have traced their origins to the witchcraft tradition. It remains to suggest that not merely in these particulars but in the whole general conception of Faustus' motives, Marlowe is vitally influenced by witch lore. Faustus is animated by longing for wealth,

23. P. 137. Roberts (p. 20), refers to the magicians of Lapland and other northern countries. See also M. Summers, *The geography of witchcraft* (London, 1927), chap. I, p. 8.

24. Bk. I, chap. I, p. I.

25. L. Lavater, *Of Ghostes and spirites* (London, 1572; reprinted Oxford University Press, 1929), Pt. I, chap. XIX, p. 92.

honor, knowledge of hidden things, pleasure, imperial sway, godhead. So, according to prevalent belief, were the men and women who turned witch. Del Rio writes:

Velle in illis prodigiosis effectibus imitari, est animi prorsus superbi, & stulti, & violentis, ambientisque Dei similitudinem in omnipotentia, aut omni scientia. tales imitantur Diabolum, qui similis esse voluit altissimo.[26]

Cooper declares that Satan works by "Puffing them [witches] up with conceit of extraordinary skill in Natures secrets, & so with a vain imaginatiō to be as gods, through such rare knowledge and great power...."[27] Danaeus has this apposite description:

Other some there be, who being borne away w fonde vanitie of a proude mynde, whyle they are not able to containe themselues within the compas of mans understanding & capacitie, doo yeelde themselues vassals to Satan, being desierous to know thinges to come, & to foretel them to other: or els ambitiously desiering easely and with smal trauayle to dooe those thinges which other cannot. By which meanes, many both of the honourable, and learned sorte, are seduced by satan, as certen noble men & women of worship & honour, and many schollars....[28]

Renaissance treatises on witchcraft are abundantly sown with similar expressions. I have not space for a detailed comparison of the *EFB* with Marlowe's play on this question of Faustus' motives, but I think it is a fair summary to say that the *EFB*'s treatment is quite bare and that Marlowe has enormously amplified the whole subject. What

26. Bk. II, Ques. 4, p. 77. See also Bodin, *De la demonomanie*, Bk. I, chap. vi, p. 99, and Boguet, chap. viii, p. 32.
27. P. 9.
28. *A dialogue of witches* (London, 1587), Eii[v], chap. ii. See also Institor and Sprenger, *Malleus maleficarum*, Introduction to Pt. III, p. 203; T. Potts, *The wonderfull discouerie of witches* (London, 1613; reprinted by G. B. Harrison, London, 1929), p. 22.

Marlowe adds is very much closer to the content of the excerpts from Danaeus, Cooper, and Del Rio just given than to anything in the *EFB*. In fact, it is sufficiently close, as it seems to me, to justify the conclusion that Marlowe was genuinely influenced by the custom of the witch tractates. Of course, aspirations to power, wealth, and knowledge are the very stuff of Marlowe's personality, voiced by all of his great characters. But if there is a general correspondence between Faustus' hopes and those by which Satan is usually thought to beguile wizards; if, in addition, there is a correspondence between these temptations in some particulars; and if, finally, Marlowe used witch lore (not drawn from the *EFB*) in other parts of his play, there would seem to be good reason for thinking that the shape Marlowe gives to the character of Faustus in the scenes of his exultant anticipation owes something to the psychological analysis made by writers on witchcraft. Here, then, is excellent illustration of the relation between Marlowe's subjectivity and his learning. The characterization of Faustus is due exclusively neither to Marlowe's witch-learning nor to his projection of his own traits into the drama. The two currents flow together and reinforce each other.

II. THE INCANTATION

As Faustus is largely a witch in motive, so is he in conduct. Thus his *modus operandi* when he first conjures up Mephistophilis has abundant precedent in treatises on and popular superstitions about black magic. Here, as elsewhere, Marlowe can be shown to display considerable acquaintance with Renaissance, and possibly classical, learning. It will be the easier to do so because the *EFB* (chap. ii) contains very little that could possibly be held to have served as Marlowe's original.

One who could practice magic, Cornelius tells Faustus, must be

> grounded in astrology,
> Enrich'd with tongues, well seen in minerals.[29]
>
> (I, i, 139-40)

These are no mere haphazard pronouncements. "Of all operations in occult science there is not one that is not rooted in astrology"—so runs Morley's paraphrase of a portion of chapter LIII of Book II of Agrippa's *De occulta philosophia*.[30] The reason is that the wizard operates by drawing down the powers of the heavenly bodies and using them to compel the rising of spirits. This he does by inscribing in his circle the proper symbols ("Figures of every adjunct to the heavens, / And characters of signs and erring stars," as Faustus calls them, I, iii, 11-12) which represent the various heavenly objects and incorporate their virtue. He must know the symbols, which ones to use, and the proper time and manner of their use—all depending upon the science of astrology. The theory is thus explained by Bodin in an attack on the Florentine Academy:

... les nouueaux Academiques ont posé ceste maxime, qu'il faut coupler & lier le ciel & la terre, les puissances celestes & terrestres, & conioindre les uns auec les autres, pour attirer la puissance diuine, par les moyens elementaires, & celestes. Voila l'hypothese de Procle, Iamblique, Porphyre, & autres Academiques. Sur laquelle hypothese on peut dire que le maistre en l'art Diabolique ... [Pico della Mirandola] a fondé toutes les

---

29. As possible sources must be noticed passages in the *EFB*, chap. 1, saying that Faustus "accompanied himself with divers that were seen in those devilish arts, and that had the Chaldean, Persian, Hebrew, Arabian, and Greek Tongues" and that he "named himself an astrologian." Remark, however, that Marlowe goes farther, making languages and astrology *prerequisites* for magic.

30. H. Morley, *The life of Henry Cornelius Agrippa* (London, 1856), I, 184.

sorceleries & inuocations des Diables.... Car il compose des
caracteres, qu'il dict propres aux Demons de chacune planette,
lesquels characteres il veut estre grauez au metal propre à
chacune planette, à l'heure qu'elles sont en leur exaltation ou
maison auec une conioinction amiable, & veut alors qu'on ayt
aussi la plante, la pierre, & l'animal propre à chacune planette,
& de tout cela qu'ō face un sacrifice à la Planette, & quelques-
fois l'image de la Planette...." [31]

Furthermore, he must be "Enrich'd with tongues" because spirits are invoked not only in Latin but also in
Greek and Hebrew. Thus Greek and Hebrew letters are
written within the magical circle, especially the Hebrew,[32]
which are used to spell out one or more of the seventy-two
different forms of the mystic name Jehovah (Faustus
writes, "Jehovah's name, / Forward and backward anagrammatiz'd"), possessed of extraordinary potency over
demons. The necessity that the magician be "well seen in
minerals" is recognized by Boissard: "...metallorum
naturas, loca, & nomina: in quibus oportet multùm versatum
esse...." [33] But the reason for this requirement is rather

31. Bk. I, chap. III, p. 60. See likewise Thorndike, *A history of magic
and experimental science*, II, 258.
32. A look at the diagrams culled from ancient books of magic by
Scheible (*Das Kloster*, III, esp. pp. 288, 330) will convince anyone.
Agrippa, *De occulta philosophia* (*Opera*, Vol. I, Lugduni, n.d.), Bk. I,
chap. LXXIV, p. 117: "Hebraeas literas compertum à sapientibus omnùm
esse efficacissimus, quia habent similitudinem maximam cum coelestibus,
& mundo. Caeterarum verò linguarum literas tantam efficaciam non
habere, quia ab illis remotius distant." M. Conway (*Demonology and
devil-lore*, New York, 1879, II, 334), summarizes the contents of the
early Raven book printed at Dresden in 1501, saying that the magician
must "mark a circle on parchment with a dove's blood; within this
circle write in Latin the names of the four quarters of the heaven;
write around it the Hebrew letters of God's name, and beneath it
write Sadan; and standing in this circle he must repeat the ninety-first
Psalm. In addition, there are seals in red and black, various Hebrew,
Greek, and Latin words, chiefly such as contain the letters Q, W, X,
Y, Z...."
33. J. Boissard, *De magia*, in the *Tractatus posthumus* (Oppenheimii
Typis Hieronymi Galleri, n.d.), p. 27.

hard to fix. Perhaps it is that the magician needs this knowledge in his alchemical experiments, alchemy being considered as closely related to magic.[34] Perhaps it is that the efficacy of charms often depends on their being engraved on the right sort of substance, as in the quotation from Bodin just given.

For the actual process of conjuring Faustus is advised to carry with him "wise Bacon's and Albanus' works, / The Hebrew Psalter and New Testament." Bacon and Abano, reputed magicians, will supply the formulas for incantation, which will include recitations from the Psalter and New Testament. Ward's note[35] citing Reginald Scot and Morley's Agrippa upon the use of the Psalms and the Gospel of John for invoking devils can be supplemented by statements in Bodin and others.[36]

Before Faustus begins to summon the fiends, he has "pray'd and sacrific'd to them" (I, iii, 7). Their appetite for such acts of homage was often mentioned in the Renaissance. Binsfeld explains it as Satan's desire to ape God:

34. P. Binsfeldio, *Commentarius in titulum codicis lib. ix de maleficis et mathematicis* (bound in the same volume with his *De confessionibus*, H. Bock, 1605), Ques. v, concl. 9, p. 479: "Alchimistae ut plurimum etiam sunt invocatores Daemonum, ut plurimum Alchimia saepè sit coniuncta cum magia."

35. P. 141.

36. Bodin, Bk. I, chap. iii, p. 56: "Et le protecteur des Sorciers, apres auoir mis les cercles & caracteres detestables (que ie ne mettray point) por trouuer les tresors, il escript qu'il faut en foissoiant dire les Psalmes, De profundis, Deus misereatur nostri etc.... & lire la Messe....Et pour faire autres meschancetez, que ie n'escriray point, ils disent le Psalme cent & huictièsme." G. Gifford, *A dialogue concerning witches* (London, 1593; repr. Shak. Assn. Fac., Oxford University Press, 1931), sig. F2ᵛ: "Such an one is haunted with a fayrie, or a spirit: he must learne a charme compounded of some straunge speaches, and the names of God intermingled, or weare some part of S. Johns Gospell or such like...." The spurious fourth book of Agrippa's *De occulta philosophia* (p. 440) recommends the use in magic of "versiculus in Psalmis vel aliqua parte Sacrarum literarum." See also Thorndike, II, 858; Perkins, p. 146. These ideas are ubiquitous.

"Hinc summoperè desiderat adorari, quod diuinae maie-
stati competit.... Ex eadē caussa Daemones sacrificia
expetunt." [37] James I on incantation: "Two principall
thinges cannot well in that errand be wanted: holie-water
(whereby the Deuill mockes the Papistes) and some present
of a liuing thing unto him" (Bk. I, chap. v, p. 17). Francis
Coxe:

... whē the spirite is once come before the circle, he forthe
with demaundeth the exsorciste a sacrifice, whiche moste
commenlye is a pece of waxe cōsecrated, or hallowed after
their owne order (for they haue certayn bokes, called bokes
of consecration) or els it is a chickē, a lapwing, or some
liuinge creatur, whiche when he hath receyued: then doeth
he fulfill the mynd of the exsorcist, for oneles he hath it, he
will neither doe, neither speake any thinge. Of this testifieth
bacon in his boke of Necromancie.... [38]

After the circle has been drawn, the divine Name, the
appropriate astrological symbols, and the "breviated names
of holy Saints" are written in. Agrippa tells us why
Jehovah's names are of supreme virtue in magic:

Deus ipse licet sit unitissimus, sortitur tamen diversa nomina,
non quae diversas ejus essentias aut deitates exponant, sed
quasdam proprietates ab eo emanantes, per quae nomina, in

37. *Tractatus de confessionibus maleficorum et sagarum*, Dubium IV,
16, Praeludium, p. 178. Sacrifice could mean simply worship, but in
Marlowe's phrase "pray'd and sacrific'd" it seems to imply something
other than prayer: to wit, a blood sacrifice.
38. *A short treatise declaringe the detestable wickednesse of
magicall sciences* ... (London, 1561), sig. B1ᵛ. The allusion to Bacon will
be noticed. See likewise Bodin, Bk. II, chap. III, p. 162: "Nous auons
dict de ceux qui inuoquent les malins esprits à leur ayde ... & qui font
les inuocations par ceremonies, sacrifices, & paroles propres à cela...."
Kittredge (p. 94) gathers some English cases, especially one in 1590 in
which a dead cock was seized with other paraphernalia for conjuring
in a field near London. J. Nyder's *Formicarius* (Bk. V, chap. IV) has a
like case. See also Thorndike, II, 320. M. Murray, *The Witchcult in
Western Europe* (Oxford, 1921), gives a full discussion.

nos, & ea quae creata sunt, multa beneficia, & diversa munera, velut per carnales quasdam distillant [Bk. III, chap. XI, p. 272].

Marlowe need not have known Agrippa, however; the writing of the divine names is called for by almost every recipe in magic. Scot speaks of "the holy Names of God written all about" the circle (Bk. XV, chap. I, p. 473). Del Rio (Bk. II, Ques. 5, p. 80) condemns sorcerers for employing "aliqua nomina Dei incognitae significationis. . . ." The spurious Book IV of the *De occulta philosophia*, a conventional treatise on black magic, says: "In circulo autem ipso inscribenda sunt divina nomina generalia, & quae nobis defensionem praestant: & eum iis nomina divina, quae praesunt huic planetae, atque oficiis ipsius spiritus . . ." (p. 450). In *Faustus* Jehovah's name is said to be anagrammatized because all of the seventy-two names of God are variations (i.e., anagrams) of one mystic Name, formed by the transpositions of its component letters.[39]

Saints' names were apparently not so generally used as the other methods of command, possibly because Protestant sorcerers loyally scorned them. But there are instances. Consider, for example, the terrible compulsion suffered by any unlucky demon invoked like this:

Ego N. servus Dei, voco, cito, exorcizo te, o Spiritus! per sanctos apostolos et discipulos Dei, per sanctos Evangelistas, sanctum Matthaeum, sanctum Marcum, sanctum Lucam, sanctum Johannem, et per tres sanctos viros: Sadrach, Mesach et Abednego, et per omnes sanctos Patriarchas, Prophetas, et Confessores Sacerdotes, et Levitas, et per castitatem omnium virginum sanctarum, et per sancta et terribilissima verba: Aphriel, Diefriel . . . compare coram me. . . .[40]

39. Ward (p. 145) quotes as to the seventy-two names that "denotant semper Nomen Dei sive legantur a principio, fine, vel a dextris aut sinistris, suntque ingentis virtutis."

40. From the *Verus Jesuitarum libellus*, p. 837, previously cited. Most of the other formulas for incantation there offered similarly invoke the

I have not been able to find, however, that these saints'
names were ever abbreviated, if that is what Marlowe
means by the word "breviated." Or does he perhaps mean
"breviaried"?

The first part of the Latin invocation spoken by Faustus
seems to be largely of Marlowe's invention. It bears no
particular resemblance to the invocations of the classical
hags Medea (Ovid, *Met.*, vii. 192-219) and Erictho (Lucan,
Pharsalia, vi. 695-749) except in the fact that it is a frank
salutation and appeal to the infernal powers. This, however,
is worth remarking. Erictho calls upon the Furies, Hell
and its rulers, Chaos, Hecate, the Fates; on the other hand,
some Renaissance magical books like the *Elementa magica*
of Petri de Abano and Book IV of the *De occulta philosophia* try to make the whole process of conjuring seem a
rite of holiness. As Bodin (Bk. I, p. 56) puts it, "la plus
forte sorcelerie prend un beau voile de pieté." The magician
cleanses himself by fasting and prayer to God for nine days
before the act of magic. When the time for conjuration
arrives, he consecrates the circle and all his instruments
(see the quotation from Francis Coxe above). If he prays,
it is to God, and he never salutes the fiends but wields
against them the adverse power of holy names. Theoreti-
cally, the wizard is still on the side of the angels. Marlowe
casts aside this pretense and makes the ceremony a dedication to Satan from the beginning. He is thus falling in with
the classical tradition and with the orthodox Renaissance

saints. Ward (p. 146) notes that the elect souls of the blest formed part
of one of the hierarchies of the heavenly system to which appeal was
made in magic. Petri de Abano's *Elementa magica* (bound in Pars I of
the *Opera* of Cornelius Agrippa, pp. 455-77) has a complete recital for
conjuring, which runs, in part: "... & per hagios & sedem Adonay, &
per ô Theos, iscyros athanatos, paracletus: & per haec tria secreta
nomina, Agla, On, Tetragrammaton, adjuro contestor..." (p. 461). See
also Kittredge, p. 199, and Del Rio, Bk. I, chap. iv, Ques. 1, p. 29.

theological doctrine that any kind of conjuring is a worship of the Devil. No attempt is made to show Faustus as engaged in justifiable operations of white magic. Indeed, such an attempt would be out of keeping with the whole tone of the play. We may note in this connection that Faustus addresses the spirits of fire, air, and water because they are fiends, inhabiting these elements after their fall from Heaven.[41]

The phrase "quid tumeraris?" of the quartos, emended by textual critics to "quid tu moraris?" (correctly, as the subsequent quotations will show), is usually believed to have sprung from the *EFB*: "Faustus vexed at his spirit's so long tarrying, used his charms, with full purpose not to depart before he had his intent..." (chap. ii). It can be proved, however, that magicians expected trouble with recalcitrant spirits and customarily incorporated in their spells a phrase similar to this.

Cito, cito, cito, non morare: sed perfice meum postulatum! Veni, veni, veni! Quid tardaris tamdiu? Festina adventare: nam jubet te Adonai + Schadai + Rex regum + El + Ali....[42]

Venite ergo in nomine Adonay Zebaoth, Adonay Amioram, venite venite quid tardatis: festinate, imperat vobis Adonay Rex regum, El, Aty, Titiep....[43]

Et tunc paulisper quiescat, respiciendo circum circa, si spiritus aliquis compareat. Qui si tardaverit, reiteret invocationem, ut supra, usque tres vices. Et si pertinax non comparuerit incipiat

---

41. The usual classification of evil spirits is sixfold: (genus) igneum, aereum, terrestre, aquaticum, subterraneum, lucifugum.–Guazzo, *Compendium maleficarum*, Bk. I, chap. xix, p. 129; Del Rio, Bk. II, Ques. 27, sec. 2, pp. 213-18. Some writers like Agrippa (Bk. III, chap. xvi, p. 288) accept Marlowe's fourfold division.

42. From the *Verus Jesuitarum libellus*, p. 845.

43. Petri de Abano, p. 461.

conjurare potestate divina, ... reiterando per tres vices, de fortioribus in fortiores, objurgationibus, contumeliis. ... [44]

Because they represent general counsel and general formulas for all magicians, these quotations are the more adequate to show how widespread is the belief in the probable delay of the demon summoned. One should also notice that in the first two of the quotations the point about the delay is cast in the form of a question (quid tardaris?) as it is in *Faustus*, a form not at all necessarily intimated by the *EFB*.

In all the quotations the enchanter overrides the reluctance of the spirit by managing against him the names and power of God. Faustus does somewhat the same thing in citing Mephistophilis by Jehovah, Gehenna, the sign of the cross, and holy water. He is resorting to what Agrippa calls the third and most potent means to bind spirits to obedience:

Tertium vinculum ipsum est ex mundo intellectuali atq; divino, quod Religione perficitur: ut puta cum adjuramus per Sacramenta, per miracula, per divina nomina, per sacra signacula, & caetera religionis mysteria: quare hoc vinculum omnium supremum est [Bk. III, chap. XXIII].

But note again that this idea is not confined to Agrippa. The use of holy water and the sign of the cross in conjuration has widespread authority. So Bodin: "... en toutes Sorcelleries, & communications detestables des Sorciers, à

---

44. From the directions to conjurors given in *De occulta philosophia*, Bk. IV, p. 451. In the play called *John of Bordeaux* (*ca.* 1590-94; Malone reprints), Bacon asks the trembling spirit Astro, who is hesitating to appear, "quid moraris?" (l. 657). Medea in Greene's *Alphonsus of Aragon* calls the ghost of Calchas: "I charge thee come; all lingring set aside" (III, ii, 863). H. Logeman (*Faustus-notes*, University of Ghent, 1898, p. 32) remarks that Schröer cites from Scheible's *Kloster*, V, 1157, the formula: "Cito, cito, cito veni nec morare velis."

chacun mot il y a une croix, & à tous propos Iesus Christ, & la Trinité & l'eau beniste."[45] Reginald Scot:

> The reason that Magitians give for Circles and their Institution, is, That so much ground being blessed and consecrated by holy Words, hath a secret force to expel all evil Spirits from the bounds thereof; and being sprinkled with holy water, which hath been blessed by the Master, the ground is purified from all uncleanness... [Bk. XV, chap. 1, p. 472].

Del Rio declares it vicious magic "si adhibeantur certi characteres, aut figurae aliae, praeter signum crucis, ..."[46] A quotation from James I last given above also mentions holy water as essential in the ritual. It would seem, however, that the cross and blessed water were more normally employed in the preparation of the circle than in the actual invocation, contrary to Marlowe's usage.

We come now to one of the most interesting and persuasive evidences of Marlowe's debt to witchcraft theory. It is another example of his employment of orthodox views of theologians. Faustus learns from Mephistophilis that the latter was not compelled to appear by Faustus' conjuring speeches: he came of his own free will because, hearing these blasphemies, he had good hope to get Faustus' soul (I, iii, 48-56). The *EFB* has absolutely nothing on this point. But the better treatises on witchcraft are full of it. Guazzo: "Et sciendum est doemones non coactè, sed spontè accurrere ad hoc faciendum [making a pact], quia graui odio hominem prosequuntur..." (*Compendium maleficarum*, Bk. I, chap. vii, p. 33); Del Rio: "...dęmones ab hominibus cogi nequeunt, ut id faciant: sponte ergo daemones accurrunt: Dęmones autem graui hominem odio prosequuntur, quare nec putandi gratis accurrere, sed

---

45. "Refutation des opinions de Iean Wier," p. 459.
46. Bk. II, Ques. 5, p. 80. See Del Rio also at Bk. I, chap. IV, Ques. 1, p. 29.

vicissim aliquod operae suae precium stipulari" (Bk. II, Ques. 4, p. 72); James I:

> ... it is no power inherent in the circles, or in the holiness of the names of God blasphemouslie used: nor in whatsoeuer rites or ceremonies at that time used, that either can raise any infernall spirit, nor yet limitat him perforce within or without these circles. For it is he onelie, the father of all lyes, who hauing first of all prescribed that forme of doing, feining himselfe to be commanded and restreined thereby, wil be loath to passe the boundes of these injunctiones; ... that he may haue the better commoditie thereafter, to deceive them in the end with a trick once for all; I meane the euerlasting perdition of their soul & body.[47]

The doctrine of voluntary ascent, then, is well established in witchcraft theory. The remainder of the *Faustus* passage seems to be Marlowe's own elaboration of it. Fundamentally, of course, these authorities contradict those cited above in the discussion of Faustus' black rites, Agrippa among them, who hold that there is a real, effective force in magical words and symbols. In this split in Renaissance opinion, Marlowe deliberately sides with the church against the believers in white magic.

III. THE WITCH COMPACT

Since the terms of the written covenant come almost verbatim from the *EFB*, only some supporting lines need be noticed under this head.

Besides denying the Christian religion, Faustus affirmatively dedicates himself to Beelzebub as his sole God

---

47. Bk. I, chap. v, pp. 16-17. The same doctrine is announced in Gifford, sig. F4ʳ; Binsfeld, *Tractatus de confessionibus maleficorum*, sec. 9; Remy, Book II, chap. ix, p. 128. Thorndike (II, 849), calls it a "familiar theological conclusion."

(I, iii, 57-60). The Devil often makes this requirement of witches. Danaeus says:

Wherefore he [Satan] cōmaundeth them to forswere God theyr creator & al his power, promising perpetually to obey and worship him, . . . that they shall acknowledge him for their god, cal upō him, pray to him, & trust in him. Then biddeth he thē that they fall down & worship him. . . .[48]

And Boguet: ". . . he makes them abandon their share in Paradise and promise that they will, on the contrary, for ever hold him as their sole master and be always faithful to him" (chap. xxi, p. 59). The citations given above as to Faustus' prayer to devils before his incantation are also applicable here.

At another time Faustus promises to build to Beelzebub

an altar and a church,
And offer lukewarm blood of new-born babes.

(II, i, 13-14)

This is a queer mingling of classical or Hebrew methods of sacrifice with the widely circulated Renaissance superstition that witches were especially eager to kill unbaptized infants.[49] Renaissance witches do not erect altars and churches to the Devil: they worship him by night in the wilder fastnesses of the open country. On the other hand, they specialize in slaying babies. Binsfeld:

48. Sig. Ei^v (chap. ii). See also E. Fairfax, *Daemonologia*, ed. W. Grainge (1882), p. 41. Perkins, p. 184: ". . . they giue themselues unto Satan as their god . . ."; Cooper, p. 68.

49. Of the witch Erictho, Lucan writes (*Pharsalia*, vi. 557-58): ". . . she pierces the pregnant womb and delivers the child by an unnatural birth, in order to place it on the fiery altar. . . ." Horace's sorceress Canidia (*Epodes*, v) starves a young boy to death—not an infant. But these are isolated texts, and in view of the much more highly developed form taken by the doctrine in the Renaissance, Marlowe is probably relying on contemporary theories.

...pro certo habendum est, quod Dẹmones feruntur delectari sanguine humano. 26q. 5. c. Nec mirum. Sic omni tempore suos cultores solicitauerunt ad effundendum sanguinem, & ad immolandum homines. Psal. 105 [p. 642].

....Quod autem Daemon maximè insidietur infantibus nec-dum baptizatis, id accidit ex inuidia maxima. Inuidet enim illis aeternam foelicitatem, quam ipse amisit: & infantes, si Baptismo abluerentur, consequerentur [*Comment.*, Lex VI, Ques. 2, p. 645].

Bodin:

...le plus meschant meurtre entre les animaulx c'est de l'homme, & entre les hommes d'un enfant innocent, & les plus aggreable à satan, comme celuy que nous auons dict des sorcieres, qui reçoiuent les enfans, & les offrent au Diable, & soudain les font mourir, au parauant qu'on les ait presentez à Dieu....⁵⁰

The probability, therefore, is that when Faustus speaks of sacrificing newborn babes he means to kill unbaptized children as the offering most acceptable to Lucifer.

Later, after he has offended Lucifer by wishing to repent, he vows:

> Never to name God, or to pray to him,
> To burn his Scriptures, slay his ministers
> And make my spirits pull his churches down.
>
> (II, ii, 100-2)

There is much testimony that foul spirits abhor the name of God. Boguet declares:

50. Bk. II, chap. VIII, p. 222. Equally pointed statements will be found in Guazzo, Bk. II, chap. III, p. 152; Nyder, *Formicarius*, Bk. V, chap. III; Boguet, chap. XXXI, p. 89; Remy, Bk. II, chap. III; *Malleus malef.*, Part II, Ques. I, chap. XIII, p. 141; Jonson's *Masque of Queens* and his notes thereto; H. Holland, *A treatise against witchcraft* (Cambridge, 1590), sig. F2ʳ.

He [Satan] makes these wretched creatures [witches at the Sabbat] repeat their renunciation of God, Chrism, and Baptism, and renew the solemn oath they have taken never to speak of God, the Virgin Mary, or the Saints except in the ways of mockery and derision ... [chap. XXI, p. 59].

Bodin: "Ie ne doubte point, que les malins esprits n'ayent en horreur ce sacré nom, & qu'ils ne fuyent soudain quand ils oyent prononcer Iehouah." [51]

As for the burning of Scripture, slaying of ministers, and leveling of churches, the Devil's hatred for the things of religion was a normal enough part of witch tradition. Guazzo, citing Grillandus, says that when one becomes a witch

oportuit primo abnegare baptismum, & omnia Christianae fidei documenta relinquere. ... Deinde Ecclesiastica Sacramenta cuncta proijcere, pedibusquè propriis conculcare crucem, & imagines B. Mariae Virg. & aliorum sanctorum ... [Bk. I, chap. VII, p. 35].

Del Rio remarks:

... docet enim Diuus Antonius, apud Athanasiū, cunctis Daemonib. hostile odium in homines esse grauius in Christianos, atrocissimum in religiosos, & virgines Deodicatas: singulos tamen, non nisi, quātum Deus permittit, nocere [Bk. II, Ques. 27, sec. 2, p. 223].

51. Bk. II, chap. II, p. 134. The witchcraft manuals are thick with stories of travelers who stumble by chance upon the Sabbat orgies of the witches and disperse them by pronouncing the name of God (e.g., Bodin, Bk. II, chap. IV, p. 167). In the play, *The birth of Merlin*, the Devil warns Joan: "Thou must not speak of goodness nor of heaven, / If I confer with thee" (III, i, 206-7). H. L. Stephen (*State trials*, London, 1899, I, 222), records the testimony of the father of two bewitched children at the trial of the Suffolk witches in 1665: "... this deponent hath demanded of them, what is the cause they cannot pronounce those words [Lord or Jesus]: they reply and say, that Amy Duny [one of the accused] saith, I must not use that name."

There are, of course, all sorts of tales in the *Malleus*, Bodin, Nyder, and others of how evil spirits vex the monasteries, but their assaults seldom kill the monks and nuns.

For the pulling down of churches we have Macbeth's injunction to the witches:

> ... answer me:
> Though you untie the winds and let them fight
> Against the churches.   (*Macbeth*, IV, i, 51-53)

Kittredge has several instances of Elizabethan popular belief in the idea. Particularly, the destruction of St. Paul's steeple by lightning in 1561 was sometimes explained in this way.[52] Remy likewise says:

> More than once we have seen the images of Saints broken and cast down in their shrines by lightning, believed to have been directed against them by some Demon. For nowhere do the Demons more love to perpetrate their iniquities than where their hideousness is enhanced and intensified by contempt.[53]

In their extreme statement, nevertheless, Faustus' promises are greater than the conventional witch can perform. Marlowe is standing upon accepted folk notions, but reaching higher.

As his share in the agreement, Lucifer is to receive Faustus' soul wherewith to "Enlarge his kingdom" (II, i, 40). Satan always has this aim in increasing the number of witches, we are told by many writers. James I says:

52. Kittredge, pp. 155ff. He says: "It is only natural that the Prince of the Powers of the Air should manifest his hatred of God by attacking churches" (p. 155). Cotta, p. 29: "Speede in his Chronicle...within the time of Henry the 4. doth make mention of the apparition of the Divell in the habite of a Minorite Fryer at Danbury Church in Essex, with such thundring, lightning, tempests, & fire-bals, that the vault of the Church brake, and halfe the Chancell was carried away."

53. Bk. III, chap. III, p. 145. According to Bodin, some witches "avoient paction expresse avec Satan de rompre les bras & les cuisses des Crucifix...."—*Refutation*, p. 456.

For as the meanes are diuerse, which allures them to these unlawfull artes of seruing of the Deuill; so by diuerse waies use they their practises, answering to these meanes, which first the Deuill used as instrumentes in them; though al tending to one end: To wit, the enlargeing of Sathans tyrannie, and crossing of the propagation of the Kingdome of Christ... [Bk. II, chap. III, p. 34].

Mason says that Satan pretends to be controlled by magicians, "but it is onely to this end, that he may thereby the more strengthen them and enlarge his owne kingdome, by bringing into, & detaining men in this wicked errour...."[54] The idea, in this very phrasing, is quite common.

IV. THE CONSEQUENCES

Most of the incidents of Faustus' twenty-four years of questionable "voluptuousness"—dealings with the Pope, the Emperor, the horse-courser, the Duke of Vanholt, and Helen of Troy—need not detain us. They contain witchcraft material plentifully, but it is all imported without change from the *EFB*. The same is true, for the most part, of Faustus' several efforts to repent, frustrated by the threats of the devils. Marlowe's fiends, however, are somewhat more resourceful than those of the *EFB:* they entice Faustus to suicide when he shows a disposition to repent (II, ii, 19-25, and V, i, 64-67). The books on witchcraft teach that Satan habitually thus tempts witches, particularly when he fears to lose them, since their self-slaughter damns them irrevocably. Remy writes:

That as an End to a Life of every Crime and Impiety, the Demon insistently urges and impels his Subjects to kill themselves with their own Hand, especially when he sees that there

54. J. Mason, *The anatomie of sorcerie* (London, 1612), p. 44.

is imminent Danger of their being Suspected. But God in his Goodness and Mercy often thwarts this cruel Scheme.... [Bk. III, the heading of chap. VI].

Guazzo says: "Post multas impietates à Maleficis patratas, Daemon tandem conatur eos ad interitum per ipsorummet manus inducere." [55] Faustus' tormentors are only following a customary technique.

Turning now to the last scene, we meet with one or two very interesting possible reminiscences of Marlowe's reading. Faustus in despair says to the students, "The serpent that tempted Eve may be saved, but not Faustus ..." (V, ii, 41-43). The *EFB* has merely: "... but even as Cain, he also said, that his sins were greater than God was able to forgive ... (chap. LXII, p. 298). But the *Malleus maleficarum* (Part I, Ques. 17, p. 82) comes considerably nearer Marlowe in this statement, which it makes the subject of a full chapter of discussion: "So heinous are the crimes of witches that they exceed even the sins and the fall of the bad Angels; and if this be true of their guilt, how should it not also be true of their punishments in hell?" Reginald Scot (Bk. III, chap. XVIII, p. 55) repeats the statement: "Yea, M. Mal. writeth, that A witches sinne is the sinne against the Holie-ghost; to wit, irremissible: yea further, that it is greater than the sinne of the angels that fell." He proceeds with his characteristic humor to make fun of it. Insofar as the *Malleus* implies that a witch cannot be forgiven if he repents, it is against prevalent theory, as exemplified in the authorities cited earlier in this section. This prevalent view is, as we know, fundamental to Marlowe's conception of the play. Farther on in the same scene, Faustus cries: "... I would weep! but the devil draws in

55. Heading of Bk. II, chap. XIX. Other authorities: Boguet, chap. XLV; Bodin, *De la Demonomanie*, Bk. III, chap. VI, p. 311; Roberts, p. 15; James I, *Demonologie*, Bk. II, chap. VI, p. 51.

my tears.... Oh, he stays my tongue! I would lift up my hands; but see, they hold them, they hold them" (V, ii, 57-61). It is not sacrilege against these moving lines to point out that certain widely circulated superstitions are here embodied and transfigured.

An unrepentant witch cannot weep; no tenet of the witchcraft creed is more universal than this. So strong was this belief that inability to shed tears was often held to create a presumption that an accused person was a witch. The *Malleus maleficarum* recommends that a judge

take note whether she is able to shed tears when standing in his presence, or when being tortured. For we are taught both by the words of worthy men of old and by our own experience that this is a most certain sign, and it has been found that even if she be urged and exhorted by solemn conjurations to shed tears, if she be a witch she will not be able to weep: although she will assume a tearful aspect and smear her cheeks and eyes with spittle to make it appear that she is weeping; wherefore she must be closely watched by the attendants [Part III, Ques. 15, p. 227].

James I: "No not so much as their eyes are able to shed teares (thretten and torture them as ye please) while first they repent (God not permitting them to dissemble their obstinacie in so horrible a crime) . . ." (Bk. III, chap. vi, p. 81). Boguet interprets the cause of this phenomenon as does Faustus:

In conclusion, it is probable that the reason for the inability of witches to shed tears is that tears are chiefly proper to penitents for washing and cleansing their sins . . . and therefore they cannot be welcome to the Enemy of our salvation, who consequently prevents them as much as he can [chap. xl, p. 122].

The binding of Faustus' tongue and hands by devils invisibly present certainly owes something to Renaissance and earlier demon lore. Some typical quotations will be of interest. Guazzo says that Satan "Potest impedire multum linguae, manuum, crurium, retinendo in venis spiritus vitales" (Bk. I, chap. IV, p. 19). Binsfeld thus describes Satan's method of preventing an arrested witch from confessing: "Tertium modum taciturnitatem inducendi considerare possumus, per assistentiam demonis interius in faucibus & ore malefici, & eum impedientis ne possit loqui" (*Comment.*, Lex VII, Ques. 1, p. 676). Here is an account from the *Sadducismus debellatus* of the behavior of a possessed woman: "And when any desired her to cry to the Lord Jesus for help, her Teeth were instantly set close, her Eyes twisted almost round, and she was thrown upon the Floor...."[56] Similarly, from Boguet:

... if they tried to get her to kiss the Cross, she held her hands out to prevent anyone from approaching her ... and if they tried to get her to take the Cross in her hands to sign herself with it, she was at once deprived of all use in her arms and hands, so that she could not even take hold of it [chap. LIII, p. 175].

Several of these quotations match the situation in *Faustus* in that they illustrate the Enemy's efforts to retain those who are trying to slip from his grasp.

The burning of magical books (*Faustus*, V, ii, 194: "I'll burn my books") was the usual way of renouncing the black art. The heading of the last chapter of the prose *Historie of Fryer Bacon* runs: "Howe Fryer Bacon burnt his books of Magick, and gave himselfe to the study of Divinity only." Kittredge[57] quotes from a confession by one Hugh Draper accused of sorcery in 1561, "y^t longe since he so misliked his science that he burned all his

---

56. London, 1698, p. 10.
57. Note 86 to chap. XVI (p. 555). Consult also Bodin, *De la Demonomanie*, Bk. IV, chap. v, p. 387; Guazzo, Bk. III, p. 379.

bookes." These are but a few of many citable authorities. The Epilogue charges Faustus with an unlawful curiosity to know secrets intended by God to remain hidden. This condemnation of those engaged in any species of occult searching is very frequent, of course, and is quite ordinarily applied to witches. Binsfeld: "Quarta caussa dispositiua ad maleficia est Curiositas, quae his portentis illuditur per Daemonum fallacias, quando id imprudenter appetit scire, quod ei nulla ratione competit inuestigare..." (*De confessionibus*, Dubium IV, p. 165). Remy: "Some of these [witches] owe their fall to their persistent and over-curious temerity in inquiring into and weighing with their native reason those things which necessarily transcend the understanding of all the senses" (p. v of the Dedication).[58]

To turn now to some conclusions. The total pressure of this evidence is such as to require the inference that Marlowe's knowledge of witch tradition was one of the decisive factors in the shaping of the play. Taking the Faustus of the prose history, who is a witch, Marlowe has infused the reach and lift characteristic of his own great spirit but has worked fairly consistently within the outline supplied him by prevalent witch theory. Neither the dramatist's basic conception of his hero's character, therefore, nor his intention in many particular passages can be rightly understood save with reference to that body of belief. From it come suggestions for the pride, ambition, curiosity, and other qualities which estrange Faustus from God, as well as many of his specific cravings for supernatural power. From it come likewise the minutiae of the incantation

58. See excellent statements by Perkins (p. 11) and Cooper (p. 49). The latter says that the sin of curiositie which causes "search after knowledge and hidden Mysteries" is itself caused by "selfe conceit" (cf. *Faustus*, opening chorus, 1. 20, describing Faustus as "swoln with cunning, of a self-conceit").

scene, a ceremony in black magic. So also with the theory underlying the relationship between Faustus and the demons. Like the conventional witch, he cannot actually control them by his magic. But they, in turn, cannot control him save by suggestion. In order to keep his soul they must play upon the despair which he already feels, dinning it in that he cannot repent, tempting him to suicide, feeding him the opiate of voluptuousness, and threatening to tear him to pieces. In accordance with witch theory, he never loses the power to repent, if he will but determine to exercise it. But, like all witches, he is vigilantly guarded during his last hours by fiends who bind tongue, hands, and tears striving for prayer, and rend his heart for naming of his Christ. These influences from the superstition reinforce and blend with ideas deriving from the *EFB* and from Marlowe's own subjectivity.

The witchcraft theory expounded by the drama is quite orthodox. No intrusion of the author's rationalism is allowed to sap its imaginative validity. Nor is there any recourse, as far as I can see, to a theory of white magic like that presented in the occult science of Cornelius Agrippa.[59] The church recognized no such distinction between white and black magic as that which Agrippa tried to establish. In the church's view all magic was black magic, involving traffic with demons and damning its practitioner. Marlowe's play maintains a thoroughly orthodox basis in theology, ethics, and astronomy; it makes no departure from consistency in its witchcraft theory. Certainly the *EFB* does not authorize any such departure. It stigmatizes Faustus' practice as evil throughout. And all the indications in the play itself point in the same direction. The Prologue decisively brands Faustus' magic as "a devilish exercise" and

59. Argument to the contrary is ably made by West, *The Invisible World*, chap. VII and *passim*.

"cursed necromancy," that is, clearly, the black art, not the white. Cornelius and Valdes are described by the two scholars as exercising

> that damned art
> For which they two are infamous through the world.

Before the incantation, Faustus has "pray'd and sacrific'd" to devils. These details, and many others like them, would build up in the minds of the Elizabethan audience an over-whelming conception of Faustus as a supplicant to the infernal powers rather than a seeker after affinity with the benign occult energies of the universe. It is true that a few details of his incantation can be found in Agrippa's *De occulta philosophia,* as previously shown, but since the same details are common to many treatises on black magic and witchcraft, the fact is meaningless. Marlowe's play would successfully pass the scrutiny of such orthodox writers on witchcraft as Bodin and Binsfeld.

Marlowe's familiarity with the subject was, one judges, extensive although not necessarily profound. What he knows seems to consist of that sediment—part inchoate impression, part precise recollection—which remains in the mind after ample reading in a congenial field. That books and not oral transmission are the main channel of his information is indicated by the presence of many learned elements too complex and dignified for the common tradition of the tongue. No specific witchcraft texts can be pointed to as Marlowe's sources. We can decide with assurance, however, that he got the bulk of his materials rather from classical and Continental originals (either directly through writers like Bodin or indirectly through those English authors, like Scot, who are really commentators on the witch lore of the Continent) than from the native English superstition. All records prove that, where

witchcraft is concerned, the domestic product is, fortu-
nately for England, a meager and unimaginative thing beside the deadly luxuriance of the foreign growth. Only
from abroad could Marlowe have received inspiration for
Faustus' dreams of the miracles of magic and for the incantation scene. It goes without saying that he uses his
originals not in the manner of a dusty scholarship but with
the bold and sovereign hand of the poet.

The significance of these observations for an interpretation of the nature of Marlowe's mind and art is considerable. We have watched the primary force of his
subjectivity pulling into the play, by a kind of magnetic
energy, those details of learning which it can most har-
moniously inhabit. Yet these details are at the same time
perfectly synchronized with the intellectual and imaginative content of the drama as a totality. The fusion is complete. The result is a play both erudite and intensely
subjective. More and more, as we come to know Marlowe
better, we must conceive of him as a dramatist who com-
bines, translates, intensifies, and breathes personal meaning
into the common materials of his age, less and less as a poet-
god creating his flaming worlds out of nothing. To compare
great things with greater, we are reminded of Milton, and
discern something of the same power of gathering and
assimilation at the basis of Marlowe's genius.

III

SECULAR THOUGHT

8. POLITICS AND ETHICS

ARLOWE'S STRUGGLE AGAINST CHRISTIANITY, both in the outer world and within himself, was bound to have the most profound effects on the whole remainder of his thinking. In the sixteenth century, religion was, of course, the groundwork of all political and moral theory. God had ordained for the constitution and operation of human society certain principles, some of them explicit in the Bible, others implicit in the law of nature. These were the determinants of public and private justice. Now take away a belief in Christianity, as happened in the poet's mind, and room was at once opened for all manner of unusual philosophical development.

The first signs appear in *Dido*. In general the play is too literal a rendering of the *Aeneid* to be significant, but one passage immediately stands out:

> *Dido.* Fair sister Anna, lead my lover forth,
> And, seated on my jennet, let him ride,
> As Dido's husband, through the Punic streets;
> And will my guard, with Mauritanian darts
> To wait upon him as their sovereign lord.
> *Anna.* What if the citizens repine thereat?
> *Dido.* Those that dislike what Dido gives in charge,

Command my guard to slay for their offence.
Shall vulgar peasants storm at what I do?
The ground is mine that gives them sustenance,
The air wherein they breathe, the water, fire,
All that they have, their lands, their goods, their lives,
And I, the goddess of all these, command
Aeneas ride as Carthaginian king.   (IV, iv, 65-78)

This extraordinary statement, for which Marlowe's source contains not the remotest suggestion, raises issues as to the powers of the sovereign which were of living importance in the sixteenth century. Moreover, it probably represents the poet's views, as the sequel will show. For both reasons it demands careful study.

Dido says that she not only owns all the lands and movables of her subjects but also disposes of their lives absolutely. She has the right to execute anyone who even questions her command. Her will is supreme law. Clearly this is the ultimate in despotic theory. And, just as clearly, it is directly opposed to the main traditions of western thought from the classical period to the Renaissance.[1] Plato, Aristotle, and their followers taught that the law-making power resided in the social body as a whole and that, no matter what the political system, the agents of government were under the law, not above it. The same general mood carried on through such thinkers as Cicero and Seneca in the Roman period, Augustine in the patristic, John of Salisbury and Aquinas in the medieval. Its inheritors in Renaissance England were Fortescue, Sir Thomas Smith, and Hooker. This, then, was the prevalent political ideal. It

1. See R. W. and A. J. Carlyle, *A History of Mediaeval Political Theory in the West* (Edinburgh & London: Wm. Blackwood & Sons Ltd., 1936), Vol. VI; J. W. Allen, *A History of Political Thought in the Sixteenth Century* (London: Methuen & Co. Ltd., 1928); and the Introduction to Lester Born's translation of Erasmus' *The Education of a Christian Prince* (Columbia University Press, 1936).

remained prevalent in England even while Tudor practice encroached on those parliamentary liberties in which the ideal had gradually been embodied during the Middle Ages. From Henry VIII to Elizabeth no substantial body of writing can be found which exalts the royal prerogative above the law.

But a contrary ideal was growing up in France during the latter half of the sixteenth century under the influence of renewed study of the Roman civil law. The great figure there is Bodin, whose conception was that the sovereign is limited only by the laws of God and nature. These prevent him from violating the lives and property of his subjects, but in all other respects he has the right to make any edicts he pleases without their consent.[2] Bodin goes far enough, but apparently there were others in France who went farther. The famous Protestant manifesto, *Vindiciae contra Tyrannos*, published in 1579, violently attacks the opinion that the king is master of all life and property:

The Minnions of the Court hold it for an undeniable Maxime, That Princes have the same power of life and death over their Subjects, as anciently, Masters had over their slaves, and with these false imaginations have so bewitched Princes, that many, although they put not in ure with much rigour this imaginary right yet they imagine, that they may lawfully do it. . . . But we affirme on the contrary, that the Prince is but as the Minister and Executor of the Law. . . .[3]

And again under the section heading, "Whether the goods of the people belong to the King," the author complains:

2. Jean Bodin, *The Six Bookes Of A Commonweale* (trans. R. Knolles; London, 1603), Bk. I, pp. 88, 92, 95, 104, 108, 130; Bk. II, pp. 200ff. Bodin's thought was highly influential. It can be traced not only in many French treatises but also in the British works cited below.

3. I quote from the English translation printed in London, 1648, p. 66. The quotation below is from p. 80.

In these dayes there is no language more common in the
Courts of Princes, then of those who say all is the Kings ...
and this opinion hath gained so much power in the minds of
some Princes, that they are not ashamed to say that the paines,
sweat and industrie of their Subjects is their proper rev-
enue. . . .

Absolutist theory went on to achieve dominance in
France during the seventeenth century and to cast a shadow
in England dissipated only by the victory of Parliament
in the civil war. As early as 1556 in England Bishop Ponet's
A Short Treatise of politike power gave a negative answer
to the question, "Whether All the Subiects goodes be the
Kaysers and kinges owne, and that they maie lawfully take
them as their owne?" [4] Unfortunately, the answer was not
always negative. After long study of the civil law in France,
the Scottish writer, Adam Blackwood, published in his
Adversus Georgii Buchanani Dialogum (1581) an extreme
version of the doctrine that all citizens and their possessions
belonged to the king.[5] Shortly after Marlowe's death appeared King James's *The True Lawe of Free Monarchies*
(1598) with the same thesis:

And as ye see it manifest that the King is ouer-lord of the
whole land: so is he Maister ouer euery person that inhabiteth
the same, hauing power ouer the life, and death of euery one
of thē. For although a iust Prince will not take the life of any
of his subiects without a cleare law: Yet the same lawes,

4. Fol. E8ʳ. The question is similarly answered in Christopher Good-
man's *How Superior Powers Oght To Be Obeyd* (Geneva, 1558),
chap. XI, p. 149, and Charles Merbury's *A Brief Discourse Of Royall
Monarchie* (London, 1581), p. 45.
5. Apud F. Pagaeum, 1581. See p. 68, quoted in Carlyle, p. 437:
"Neque enim ita rerum ignarus es, ut nescias non modo personas
omnium regibus obnoxias ac veluti mancipio nexuque teneri, verum
etiam res omnes popularium, atque fortunas ita regum esse proprias, ut
usu dumtaxat, ac fructu, singulorum esse videntur."

whereby he taketh them, are made by himselfe, or his pred-ecessors.[6]

The power to make laws, he says, is in the king alone. This high royalist doctrine was shared by a small group of other Britons, among whom it is interesting to find John Cowell, doctor of civil law at Cambridge in 1584 and later professor of civil law there.[7] Cowell's prominence at the university during Marlowe's student days tells us some-thing of the political atmosphere breathed by the growing dramatist. In this connection, Kyd's remark to Puckering at the time of Marlowe's death also haunts the mind:

He wold perswade with men of quallitie to goe unto the k of Scotts whether I heare Royden is gon and where if he had liud he told me when I sawe him last he meant to be.

Probably this means only that by 1593 Marlowe foresaw that James would be the next king of England and knew the advantage of coming early into his favor. But the re-semblance between the *Dido* speech and the views of James remains a tantalizing coincidence.

What we have, therefore, in the *Dido* passage is a dra-matically violent expression of a political idea which, while repugnant to the main stream of western European thought, was in the ascendant in France and was gaining some cur-rency with a minority group in Britain, especially Scotland. The puzzling question is why it should have appeared at all in Marlowe's first play. Quite unsolicited by the source or by anything in the surrounding context, it springs sud-

6. Printed at London by T. C., 1603, fol. D1ʳ. Also fols. C6ᵛ and C7ʳ.
7. Cowell's book, *The Interpreter*, printed at Cambridge in 1607, went so far in placing the king above the law that Parliament forced its prohibition in 1609. See its definitions of "Prerogative," "King," "Parlia-ment." Another work in the same tradition is Sir Thomas Craig's *The Right of Succession* written and dedicated to King James in 1603 but not published until 1703. See especially pp. 154 and 161 of the edition of 1703.

denly out of a scene of amorous reconciliation between
Dido and Aeneas. No particular purpose of characterization
seems to be served, since it makes no difference to the plot
whether Dido is an absolute or a limited ruler and her status
as queen is not elsewhere drawn in question. The explanation best agreeing with the political complexion of the
sequence of Marlowe's dramas is that he himself held these
ideas at this time and brought them in simply because he
held them. What was the "pestilent Machiuilian pollicie"
which Robert Greene reproached him for studying? "For
if *Sic volo, sic jubeo* hold in those that are able to command: and if it be lawfull *Fas et nefas* to doe anything
that is beneficiall, onely Tyrants should possesse the
earth...." Dido's speech is merely an expansion of the
maxim, *Sic volo, sic jubeo*, which Greene says Marlowe
himself subscribes to. And the same maxim underlies the
program of virtually every one of the great domineering
figures who possess or climb to power in every one of the
dramas. It is the logical expression in the area of politics
of the high-pitched egoism which they share with their
creator.

In applying this dictum to the two parts of *Tamburlaine*,
we should first consider the nature of Marlowe's sources
and their ideological contributions to the play. As a historical personage Tamburlaine had, on the whole, a highly
favorable reputation in Renaissance literature. Particularly,
the two English accounts in Thomas Fortescue's *The Forest*
and George Whetstone's *The English Myrror*,[8] most likely

8. Fortescue's main version appears in Pt. II, chap. xiv of the 1576
edition of *The Forest*, Whetstone's in Bk. I, chap. xii of the 1586
edition of *The English Myrror*. Both are derivatives of the story written
in *Silva de Varia Lection* (1542) by Pedro Mexia. A recent article by
Thomas Izard, "The Principal Source of Marlowe's *Tamburlaine*,"
MLN, LVIII (June, 1943), 411-17, makes a good argument in favor of
Whetstone as the chief source.

to have served Marlowe as principal sources, show admiration for his prowess and virtues, seasoned at times with blame for his cruelty. So Whetstone begins on a eulogistic note:

Amonge the illustrous Captaines Romaines, and Grecians, none of all their martiall acts, deserue to be proclaimed with more renown, then the conquest and millitarie disciplines of Tamberlaine. . . .[9]

He goes on to describe in the same vein his hero's early exploits:

. . . notwithstanding the pouertye of his parents: euen from his infancy he had a reaching & an imaginatiue minde, the strength and comelinesse of his body, aunswered the hautines of his hart . . . he parted the spoyle continually among his companions, & intertayned them with such faithfulnes and loue, as the rumour thereof dayly increased his strength . . . Tamberlaine ioyned with y⁰ kings brother: and so valiantly behaued him self, yᵗ he ouerthrew the king & seated his brother in the kingdom: the new king created Tamberlaine, chiefe captaine of his army: who under colour to inlarge his kingdom, raised many people, & found the means to make them reuolt from their obedience, & so deposed y⁰ new king . . . & then made him selfe king of Persia: redeeming (by this industry and dexterity in armes) his country from the seruitude of the Sarizens and kinges of Persia. . . .

In all this sounds no word of disapproval for the rebellion. Where it is not neutral, it is laudatory. Then follows a commendation of the excellent discipline among his soldiers and the love they bore him. His treatment of Bajazeth is narrated simply as making the latter an example of the uncertainty of worldly fortune. The slaying of the Damascus citizens is condemned marginally, "A great cruelty." The

9. Bk. I, p. 79. The other passages quoted are taken in sequence from the next three pages.

protest of the merchant of Genoa, found in most of the accounts, is duly related, together with Tamburlaine's wrathful reply that he is the Scourge of God. Whetstone concludes with the comment:

And in truth Tamburlain although he was endued with many excellencies & vertues: yet it seemed by his cruelty, y^t God raysed him to chasten the kings & proud people of the earth. In the ende this great personage, without disgrace of fortune, after sūdry great victories, by the course of nature died, & left behind him two sons, euery way far unlike their father....

Here, then, is an Elizabethan account, written the year before Marlowe's play, in which the Scourge of God is a predominantly admirable and virtuous figure, dying not by the vengeance of God but "by the course of nature."

Except that it is longer, the treatment in Fortescue's *The Forest* is substantially the same. If anything, Tamburlaine's virtues are amplified despite his mission as Scourge:

By meane of which his vertues, & others that we shall heere-after remember, he in short time acquired such honour, and reputation: as it is to be supposed man neuer shall doo again....
He was very courteous, liberall, dooing honor to all men, according to their demerits, that would accompany or follow him, feared therefore equally and looued of the people....[10]

In two passing references to Tamburlaine elsewhere in his book, Fortescue follows an uneven course, once classing him with a list of cruel monsters who have carried God's anger over the earth, and once urging men of base parentage to follow his example "to aspire to the seate of Vertue and honoure."[11] Nevertheless, his prevailing attitude is that

10. Chap. xiv, fols. 67^v and 68^r.
11. The latter is in Pt. II, chap. xviii, fol. 82^v, the former in Pt. I, chap. xv, fol. 35^r.

given in the main part of his narrative, as indicated above. Other Renaissance accounts vary in tone a good deal.[12] The great majority of Tamburlaine's biographers, however, were so won by his brilliance that they dropped only a few perfunctory crumbs of indignation for those episodes of his career which were offensive to morality, and expatiated instead on the sheer magnificence of the man. Renaissance opinion in the large thus united with the English accounts chiefly available to Marlowe in depicting a hero whose savagery as an executor of God's vengeance could not outweigh his wonderful force of character and his many milder virtues. It is clear from a reading of the plays that Marlowe intends the same estimate.

He so presents the rebellions of Tamburlaine, first against Mycetes and then against Cosroe, as to win the favor of the audience for both. This difficult feat he performs by making Mycetes a brainless idiot incapable of the throne and a butt of scornful laughter. The welfare of Persia requires his overthrow. Justification of Tamburlaine's rising against Cosroe is achieved mainly by giving him a magnificent first word in his plans to "ride in triumph through Persepolis" and an even more magnificent last word in his

12. Long encomiums were written by Cambinus in *Two very notable commentaries of the originall of the Turcks* (trans. J. Shute; London, 1562), Bk. I, fol. 3[r]ff., and Le Roy, *Of the Interchangeable Course, or Variety of Things* (London, 1594), fols. 107[v]ff. Fairly frequently in other works Tamburlaine is held up as a model for those aspiring to high honor; e.g., John Ferne, *The Blazon of Gentrie* (London, 1586), p. 21; Whetstone, *The Honourable Reputation of a Souldier* (London, 1585), fol. B2[r]; Fregoso, *Baptiste Fulgosi de dictis factisque memorabilis* (1518), fol. xc[v]. On the other side, La Primaudaye's *French Academie* (Pt. I, chap. xxiii, p. 253) and Sebastian Muenster's *La Cosmographie Universelle* (1552, pp. 1185ff.) apply a stricter ethical standard which admits his dynamic vigor but finds him guilty of excessive pride and cruelty. The somewhat later narratives by Du Bec-Crespin (*The Historie of the Great Emperor Tamerlan*, London, 1597) and Richard Knolles (*The General Historie of the Turkes*, London, 1603, p. 210ff.) are extremely eulogistic.

vindication against the dying curse of his antagonist: "Nature that fram'd us of four elements...." The strategic placement and irresistible eloquence of these speeches justify him as nothing in the sources ever could. By such arts does the dramatist make palatable even the cardinal crime of rebellion.

To enlist sympathy for Tamburlaine's attack on Bajazeth, Marlowe had only to show him as a rescuer of Christian slaves tortured in the galleys of the bragging Turkish despot. Incidentally, Marlowe's transfer of the Scourge of God role to this episode from the scene of slaughter at Damascus, where it is given in all the sources, is another indication that he means it to enhance Tamburlaine's good name. A more delicate question is posed by the later scenes of the torture and death of Bajazeth and his wife. Even if the comic prose bits be disregarded as probably not Marlowe's, and even if full allowance be made for the strong stomachs of the Elizabethans and their hatred of the Turk, much remains in the text to point up the brutality of Tamburlaine and draw sympathetic attention to his captives' sufferings. Marlowe develops from the sources the conception of Bajazeth as a grand victim of fortune in the medieval manner. Especially effective to this end is the pity so plangently voiced by Zenocrate. We recall also that most historians considered Tamburlaine very cruel in this instance; Zenocrate herself shares this opinion. It is significant, notwithstanding, that she does not relinquish her loyalty to him. Nor should we. Tamburlaine is at his worst here, but he is still the hero, though a dire one, still executing the purposes of God. Abhorrence, pity, and moral revulsion are intended to be felt by the audience, but only as undercurrents which, in a sense, really accentuate by contrast the dominant reactions of devotion and awe. A like method helps to save the admitted cruelty of Tamburlaine in the butchery of Damascus. He feels some pity for his victims and yields partially to the entreaties of Zenocrate. Thus he is ruthless indeed, but not ruthless enough to pass beyond the pale of all ethical toleration, dramatically sustained above serious blame, as he always is, by the sweep and oceanic roar of his blank verse.

The contours of the whole portrait are softened also by the success of his more intimate human relationships. He has three loyal friends in whom he more rejoices than does the King of Persia in his crown. His soldiers adore him: not all the gold in India's wealthy arms will buy the meanest one of them. Best of all, loving Zenocrate, he respects her chastity until the time comes for marriage. Her beauty calls forth bursts of lyric passion which reveal at once his love of the human and his aspiration to the divine. In still other passages he has a zeal for high intellectual endeavor. Qualities like these would help to reconcile to him even the most severe Elizabethan moralist.

The ethical situation is about the same in Part II, except perhaps that the episodes of cruelty are less relieved by the tenderness of which we have just spoken. And of course Tamburlaine is made to suffer here, as he never does in Part I, through the death of Zenocrate and finally his own mortal illness. In this way, the motif of the fall of the mighty, subordinated in Part I and pertinent only to Bajazeth, rises uppermost. What should be insisted on, however, is that Tamburlaine in his own person is ethically the same as in the first play, possessed of the same virtues and vices and subject to the same chiefly sympathetic judgment. As shown in the chapter on religion, neither his death nor that of Zenocrate is a divine punishment for sin. They are strictly human disasters. Very dubious also is the interpretation that grief for the death of his wife drives Tamburlaine to a new fury of cruelty amounting to madness. If the massacres of innocents seem somewhat more plentiful in Part II, it is probably because Marlowe, running out of historical material, was working hard to keep the interest of his audience. Any greater bloodiness in the hero tends to be counterbalanced sympathetically by his greater pitiableness.

Scrutinized in the cold light of Renaissance ethical theory, no doubt Marlowe's hero in both parts can be found gravely wanting. He is a rebel and a usurper. He suffers from the vices of ambition, pride, and cruelty. He delights in frankly offensive wars of conquest, where theory permits only defensive war,[13] and murders his captives where theory universally recommends mercy.[14] Reason does not rule his passions properly. His anger is intemperate, as is his taste for magnificent robes and sumptuous feasting. His conception of his relations with God are irregular, sometimes blasphemous, and his function as Scourge cannot excuse his barbarism if he performs it with egoistic, rather than devout, motives.[15] Only it may be said on his behalf that he is just to his soldiers, loyal to his friends, chaste in his love for Zenocrate, and capable of glimpses of a higher life through beauty and knowledge.

So far the ethical theorist. And, in greater or lesser degree, there was something of him in every Elizabethan who went to see Marlowe's play. But there was also, and perhaps rather deeper, the primordial brute exulting in naked energy and power. A few purists might still de-

13. Erasmus, *op. cit.*, chap. XI; Justus Lipsius, *Sixe Bookes of Politickes* (London, 1594), p. 129; Barnabe Barnes, *Foure Bookes of Offices* (London, 1606), Bk. 2, p. 110; Sutcliffe, *Practice, Proceedings, and Lawes of armes*, p. 9; and many others. Wars motivated by ambition were almost uniformly condemned.

14. Sutcliffe, *op. cit.*, pp. 11-12; John Norden, *The Mirror of Honor* (London, 1597), Address to the Reader; J. Hurault, *Politicke, Moral, and Martial Discourses* (trans. A. Golding; London, 1595), pp. 199ff.

15. See Institor and Sprenger, *Malleus Maleficarum*, Pt. I, Ques. 15.

nounce "that atheist Tamburlaine." And quite possibly the drama helped to spread in some quarters Marlowe's reputation as a man of dangerous opinions, for it is poised precariously at the outer limits of moral acceptability. But the audiences as groups were certainly swept away. So much so that the prologue of the contemporary drama, *The Troublesome Raigne of King Iohn,* pleads for an equally favorable reception:

> You that with friendly grace of smoothed brow
> Have entertained the Scythian Tamburlaine,
> And given applause unto an Infidel:
> Vouchsafe to welcome (with like curtesie)
> A warlike Christian and your Countreyman.

Inevitably in the foregoing survey of ethical questions a number of the political issues have already been discussed. It remains to look more closely at some aspects of Tamburlaine's theory of kingship. The man of low birth has as much right to the throne as anyone else. Though born of shepherd parents, Tamburlaine calls himself a lord, "For so my deeds shall prove." In Part II he applies the same doctrine to his three sons, assuring his youngest boy that he will succeed to the royal title

> If thou exceed thine elder brothers' worth,
> And shine in complete virtue more than they.
>
> (I, iv, 50-51)

And when he apportions crowns to his three friends his exhortation is:

> Deserve these titles I endow you with,
> By valor and by magnanimity.
> Your births shall be no blemish to your fame;
> For virtue is the fount whence honour springs,
> And they are worthy she investeth kings.
>
> (Pt. I, IV, iv, 128-32)

The sceptre, then, should go to the most deserving, regardless of birth or legal title. Now this is an extension and reapplication of the standard Renaissance definition of nobility, as stated, for instance, in Elyot's *Governour:*

Thus I conclude, that Nobilitie is not after the vulgare opinion of men, but is onely the praise and surname of Vertue, which the longer it continueth in a name or linage, the more is nobilitie extolled and meruayled at.[16]

True nobility, true honor are the reward for a man's virtuous deeds, not for the accident of his birth. But what a strange new twist Marlowe gives to the doctrine! By it he justifies unlawful seizure of sovereignty, as Renaissance theory never would, and gives an entirely unconventional meaning to the word "virtue." I do not think it necessary to say that Marlowe fetched this meaning from the Italian "virtu," signifying native energy. He is only following his old habit of bringing over an orthodox Elizabethan idea into a situation where its application was never dreamed of by his contemporaries.

The theory of a king's powers held by Tamburlaine and his associates is no less absolute than was Dido's. Typically, Theridamas' expectation is

To wear a crown enchas'd with pearl and gold,
Whose virtues carry with it life and death;
To ask and have, command and be obeyed;
When looks breed love, with looks to gain the prize,
Such power attractive shines in princes' eyes.
(Pt. I, II, v, 60-64)

16. London, 1580, Bk. II, cap. IV, fol. 95ʳ. To the same effect are La Perriere, *The Mirrour of Policie* (London, 1598), fol. 131ᵛ; Ferne, *op. cit.*, p. 14; Palingenius, *Zodiake of life*, Bk. VI, p. 91, and many others. Cf. Lyly's *Campaspe*, II, i, 73-74: "Well Ladies, for so your vertues show you, whatsoeuer your birthes be, you shalbe honourably entreated."

These arbitrary powers over life and death, this certainty
of obtaining whatever one asks, are evidently not attributes
of any constitutional monarch. Of course Tamburlaine
never doubts that he can do what he pleases. Kings make
the law, he tells his friends when he sends them off to
their several kingdoms (Pt. I, V, ii, 463-65). And his dying
warning to his son is that he can retain the throne only
by being stronger than any challenger (Pt. II, V, iii,
234-40).

However, the statement that really goes full depth is that
in the "Nature that fram'd us of four elements" speech
(Pt. I, II, vii, 12-29) to which detailed attention was given
in the chapter on religion. Tamburlaine retains there a religious basis of a kind for his political and ethical conclusions
but places in heaven a god who is himself a rebel, and
substitutes a law of force for a law of justice in nature
and the world of human affairs. Jove is a divine "precedent"
for usurpation (note the legal term). Nature "wills us"
—all of us, that is, not Tamburlaine alone—to seek power.
Let the strongest rule. Thus in effect the Renaissance divine
right of kingship becomes the divine duty of rebellion.
Whatever measures are necessary to achieve the throne,
and to maintain it after it has been achieved, become
morally right. So all ideas of moral goodness as generally
understood are reversed. It is evident that this theory goes
well beyond Tamburlaine's actual practice, which respects
many elements of the moral code.

How utterly alien this whole view of the law of nature
and the qualities of kingship is to the normal doctrine will
appear immediately from a few typical Renaissance formu-
lations. Thomas Wilson's *Art of Rhetoric* speaks of the
law of nature in very different terms:

God powred first this law of nature, into mans hart ... that
man should doe as he would be doen unto, the which is

nothing els, but to liue uprightly without any will to hurte his neighbour.[17]

Tamburlaine meets in some respects Sir Thomas Smith's definition of a tyrant:

Where one person beareth the rule they define that to be the estate of a king, who by succession or election commeth with the good will of the people to that gouernement and doth administer the common wealth by the lawes of the same and by equitie, and doth seeke the profit of the people as much as his owne. A tyraunt they name him, who by force commeth to the Monarchy against the will of the people, breaketh lawes alreadie made at his pleasure, maketh other without the aduise and consent of the people, and regardeth not the wealth of his communes but the aduancement of him selfe, his faction, & kindred.[18]

And Erasmus does not think much of the doctrine of *sic volo, sic jubeo*:

Those expressions of a tyrant, 'Such is my will', 'This is my bidding', 'Let will replace reason' should be far removed from the mind of the prince. . . . It is the mark of a tyrant—and womanish, too—to follow the unbridled will of your mind. . . .[19]

In the play there are indeed some few instances of practical limitation on the power of the king, such as Cosroe's investiture in the name of the commons as well as the nobility (Pt. I, I, i, 136-39), and Tamburlaine's asking the

17. London, 1560, fol. 13ʳ. Also J. Hurault, *op. cit.*, p. 79: "...there is not any thing more against nature, and against the lawe of man, than to take from another man, wherewith to profit a mans selfe." Hooker wrote a great exposition of the law of nature in Book I of his *Of the Laws of Ecclesiastical Polity*. But the concept is well developed in medieval thinkers.

18. Thomas Smith, *De republica anglorum* (London, 1583), Lib. I, chap. VII. Selfishness and destruction of law as the distinguishing tests of tyranny were set forth by the Greeks and thereafter accepted by western thought as a whole.

19. *Op. cit.*, chap. I, p. 189.

assent of his followers when he assumes the crown (Pt. I, II, vii, 61-66). But these are echoes of English practice at the investiture of a new monarch, too fleeting to affect the general autocratic theme. No doubt to some extent this theme is called for by the nature of the story, which is essentially military and oriental. But we have to ask the further questions why this type of story appealed to Marlowe, not only here but in his other dramatizations of the struggle for power, and why his justifications of the theory of absolutism are extreme, beyond the needs of the actual plot, not only here but elsewhere.

We shall never, I am convinced, get any satisfactory answers to these questions except from some hypothesis of the dramatist's own personal psychology at this stage of its development. The indications point to a temperament unusually remote from the world of men and their affairs. Studies of his imagery have shown [20] that it is drawn much less frequently from the common details of life than is that of his contemporaries in the drama. Lyly and Greene, for example, wrote about the long ago and far away just as Marlowe did, for this was the preference of the Elizabethan drama, but they did it with a homely touch of present times and English places and people. Marlowe is anything but homely. And judging from the characterizations in his plays, the range of his sympathies for people is quite narrow. Within certain strict limits, which seem to be those of his own personality, he is brilliantly successful. Outside them, the people have no actuality. Visions of the future tend to blot out the present, visions of himself, aspiring, achieving magnificently, falling catastrophically. When such a man came to think of ethics, the natural consequence of his remoteness was to make unreal to him the

20. Caroline Spurgeon, *Shakespeare's Imagery* (New York: Macmillan, 1935), chap. II.

force of the accepted moral code. Its religious basis fell with the Christianity he rejected, and he could not see its purely human cogency as an outlet for the instinct of fellowship and a method for regulating conflict between men who must live together. Similarly, oblivious to the needs of the whole body social and immersed in egocentric dreams of power, he arrived inevitably at an absolutist political theory. Thus his ideas in the several fields of thought were the harmonious products of a psychological attitude. By such a hypothesis we can most fruitfully and coherently reconcile all the phenomena in his biography and his plays. It leaves room, moreover, for developments which we shall watch unfolding in his subsequent work.

The *English Faust Book* offered Marlowe for his next play the same type of hero as before, fired with prodigious desires, but in this case achieving them by methods which threw him into direct conflict with Christianity. Such a theme was sure to have an irresistible appeal for the dramatist. But in accepting it he had to accept also the damnation of Faustus at the end, and therewith the whole scheme of theological and ethical values by which he was condemned. Marlowe kept his bargain with the source materials. His statement of principles throughout the drama is impeccably orthodox. The "self-conceit" of which the Prologue authoritatively accuses Faustus is the cardinal sin of pride, which, according to the preachers, is always the chief agent in man's rebellion against God. It makes him prefer magic before his "chiefest bliss," the *summum bonum* of salvation, and turn to the worship of his own appetite for pleasure. When he explores with Mephistophilis questions not intended for man's knowledge, he manifests the sin of curiosity. Voluptuousness is in his enjoyment of Helen of Troy and other fairest courtesans. If he thinks of repentance, the devils divert him with entertainments or tempt him to suicide, which being in itself a sin, would ensure his damnation. However, the theological vice of despair keeps him from repenting. An epilogue warns the audience to profit by his example and avoid a like "hellish fall" by not exceeding the appointed limits of speculation. All Elizabethan ethics hinged upon obedience to God, but it could be given a theological or humanistic bias depending on the point of view of the commentator. In keeping with the religious theme, Marlowe makes the ethics here highly theological.

Faustus also has royal ambitions. If he were king, he would be as dictatorial as Tamburlaine. He would "reign sole king of all the provinces." Disposal of life and death would be his:

> The Emperor shall not live but by my leave
> Nor any potentate of Germany.

Characteristically, too, the Prologue describes courts of kings as places "where state is overturn'd." No mention, of course, that the court of a king might possibly be a seat of administration. Faustus' ambitions in this kind are part of his vice of "self-conceit" and therefore presumably share in the denunciation which that receives. Herein, then, lies the vast difference between this play and *Tamburlaine*. The longings common to both prosper in the latter, whereas in the former they are branded as evil and are punished by everlasting death. Marlowe's willingness thus to brand qualities so intimately his own betokens growth of a more objective attitude towards them and an increased recognition that they were commonly stigmatized. It is a step closer to acceptance of the world's values.

Much more is this true of the treatment accorded the same qualities in his next play. They are given, for one thing, far less prominence in Barabas than in the two earlier heroes. And especially they are associated, for the first time, with overshadowing traits of knavery. Thus corrupted, they lose almost all vestige of sympathetic appeal. Barabas, unlike Tamburlaine, passes far beyond the pale of ethical toleration, passes indeed into caricature. He is villain and clown, frankly proffered to the hatred and jeers of the groundlings. Here is further concession to conventional standards of moral judgment. We have noticed indeed in a previous chapter that Marlowe frequently validates Barabas as a spokesman for heterodox religious and ethical criticism. Even then, however, Marlowe is showing new interest in the contemporary scene. He is beginning to descend from the clouds and look at the social landscape.

Walking on the stage as Prologue, Machiavelli claims Barabas as one of his. He thus presents us with the whole question of the nature of Machiavelism in England and the extent of its influence on Marlowe.

It is already a truism that the popular Machiavelism of the Elizabethan stage was very different from the Machiavelism of Machiavelli himself. The Florentine statesman in his *Discourses on Livy* and *The Prince* recommended observance of the moral code except where deviations were regrettably necessary for the safety of king and kingdom. He kept in view as the end of all statecraft the stability and peace of the realm rather than the selfish advantage of its prince. These books may have circulated among educated Englishmen in Italian and French versions, but not sufficiently to correct the popular misconception, which became current in England as early as the 1580's, of Machiavelli as an advocate of everything evil in statecraft. Causes of the misconception were manifold. Not only Gentillet's vilifying *Contre-Machiavel* but scores of continental books brought in the defamation. The Huguenot pamphlets pouring in from France habitually denounced Catherine de

Medici and her party as Machiavels, partly because of her Italian origin. In England, the established reputation of Italy as a sinister land of vengeance, murder, and poison, where the people had no morals, contributed further elements. So did the voluminous literature against atheism. When the dramatists began to put this material on the stage they amalgamated with it old traditions of villainy, including that of the Senecan tyrant and the Vice of the morality plays. Additionally, political treatises from Aristotle on down were filled with detailed accounts of the methods of tyrants, actual and prospective. Or the dramatist could and did go to the chronicles of England for practical examples of intrigue. The conclusion to be stressed, then, is that almost from its inception in England Machiavelism had so wide a latitude of meaning as almost to cease to mean anything at all. Any underhanded, "atheistic" machination in politics was dubbed Machiavellian. A dramatist, therefore, had at first a virtually free hand in making his own private concoction of evil ingredients under that label.

Marlowe wrote *The Jew of Malta* about 1589, before the characteristics of the Machiavellian villain as a stage type had become crystallized by tradition, and was himself, in fact, along with Kyd, one of the chief founders of the type. The statement is often made that he knew the books of the Florentine at first hand. It may be true, but, if so, the effect does not appear demonstrably in his plays. Not one passage in them, so far as I can see, expresses an idea which might not just as well have come from some form of the popular misconception, or from Seneca, or from the literature of politics in general, or from just mere knowledge of the operations of depraved cunning in political affairs. On the contrary, many passages express ideas which are the direct opposite of what Machiavelli actually says. Similarly, I find it difficult to see any specific influence by Gentillet's work.

Now one would think that if Marlowe dramatized any-where the principles of Machiavelli, or Gentillet's inter-pretations of them, he would do so in the Prologue spoken by Machiavelli. Let us see:

> Admir'd I am of those that hate me most: 9
> Though some speak openly against my books,
> Yet will they read me, and thereby attain
> To Peter's chair; and when they cast me off,
> Are poison'd by my climbing followers.
> I count religion but a childish toy,
> And hold there is no sin but ignorance.   15
> Birds of the air will tell of murders past:
> I am asham'd to hear such fooleries.
> Many will talk of title to a crown:
> What right had Caesar to the empery?
> Might first made kings, and laws were then most sure   20
> When, like the Draco's, they were writ in blood.
> Hence comes it that a strong built citadel
> Commands much more than letters can import:
> Which maxim had [but] Phalaris observ'd,
> H'ad never bellow'd, in a brazen bull,   25
> Of great ones' envy: o' the poor petty wights
> Let me be envied and not pitied.

It is known [21] that the model for this is a Latin poem writ-ten by Gabriel Harvey in 1578, *Epigramma in effigiem*

---

21. The debt was first pointed out in Edward Meyer's famous thesis, *Machiavelli and the Elizabethan Drama* (Weimar, 1897), p. 22. Meyer, however, was much too certain of the influence of Gentillet's work on Marlowe, not taking account of the many similar political ideas already afloat in Elizabethan literature, dramatic and non-dramatic. The defect was partly rectified by M. Praz in his British Academy lecture for 1928, *Machiavelli and the Elizabethans* (*Proceedings of the British Academy*, Vol. XIII). It appears to me that Praz still did not go nearly far enough to show how indefinable was the thing called Machiavelism in England, and how practically impossible is the task of isolating its effects from those of ideas already prevalent.

Machiavelli, picturing Machiavelli as declaiming his resolution to be "Aut nihil, aut Caesar" by means of fraud or force, his scorn of the unambitious herd, his delight in blood and crime. The poem itself is a melodramatic misreading of a few of Machiavelli's more spectacular ideas. In other words, Marlowe's prologue is already at one remove from the Florentine in its inspiration.

The specific ideas are even more distant. Reference to those who attain Peter's chair by studying Machiavelli is one of those frequent Elizabethan pleasantries about the crimes of the popes.[22] Gentillet is silent on the point, and obviously, the real Machiavelli also. The latter, moreover, does not advocate poisoning. Gentillet mentions it a few times in passing but without particular stress. The next lines contemning religion do not represent Machiavelli's attitude, which is one of respect for religion while recognizing the utility of a show of religion where none genuinely exists.[23] They are somewhat closer to Gentillet's perversion of the doctrine into a general contempt for religion.[24] However, what they most resemble is Marlowe's own scorn of the "bugbeares and hobgoblins" of Christianity which peculiarly deserve the epithet "childish," especially since the line "Hold there is no sin but ignorance" has no counterpart in any kind of Machiavelism, whereas it is highly characteristic of the poet himself. Equally, the mocking of the Christian doctrine that murder will out, if necessary by a miracle, is of a piece with his

22. *The Restorer of the French Estate* (London, 1589), p. 71: "As for the Popes, most of them haue clymbed up to the holy See by lyes, hypocrisie, guiles and deceipt, by money, armes, massacres, poysonings and Magicall arts."

23. *Discourses on the First Ten Books of Titus Livius,* Bk. I, chaps, XI and XII in Vol. II of *Writings of Niccolo Machiavelli* (trans. C. E. Detmold; Boston: Houghton Mifflin & Co., 1891).

24. Innocent Gentillet, *A Discourse Upon The Meanes of Wel Governing* ... (trans. Simon Patericke; London, 1602), pp. 92-94.

known derision of miracles. After that come lines (18-21) approving the taking of thrones by force. In a general way these might have been inspired by the Florentine, but we notice that Machiavelli lengthily denounces the usurpations of that very Caesar whom the Prologue uses as a favored example.[25] Or they might have come from Gentillet, but they do not strictly resemble any given maxim. We are principally reminded, however, of the views formulated in *Tamburlaine*. "What right had Caesar to the empery?" is clearly a descendant of "What better precedent than mighty Jove?" And the following statement that "Might first made kings" is the earthly equivalent of the divine precedent of the latter. Machiavelli's theory of the origins of kingship was quite the opposite, holding that the first men chose their king by agreement because they saw the need of a social order to prevent violence.[26] Gentillet is silent. A monograph might be written about the different Renaissance theories on this topic. Marlowe, however, has the backing of much authority. La Primaudaye writes:

The first soveraigne government was established either by the violence of the mightiest, as Thucidides, Caesar, Plutark, and others write: and the holie historie testifieth the same unto us. ... Or if any will beleeve Demosthenes, Aristotle, and Cicero, the first soveraigntie was instituted upon their will & good liking, who for their owne commoditie, rest and securitie, submitted themselves to such as excelled most in vertue in those times, which they called heroicall.[27]

25. *Discourses*, Bk. I, chap. x. In *The Prince*, chap. vii and *Discourses*, Bk. I, chap. ix, Machiavelli analyzes favorably the careers of Caesar Borgia and Romulus as founders of states without title, but he conceives of both as men "whose object is to promote the public good." In *The Prince*, chap. viii, he condemns the crimes of Agathocles and Oliverotto da Fermo in attaining sovereignty.
26. *Discourses*, Bk. I, chap. i, p. 95, and chap. ii, p. 100.
27. *The French Academie* (London, 1594), Pt. I, chap. liv, p. 552. The same view is held by Bodin, *Six Bookes of a Commonweale*, Bk. IV,

On the question of severity of the laws, Machiavelli believed the prince should be just by preference, cruel or
lenient sometimes as occasion required.[28] He denounced
the tyranny of Phalaris.[29] In the *Discourses* he pronounced
absolutely against the maintenance of fortresses, but in *The
Prince* said that they might be needed by a prince who
fears his own people more than he does foreigners. However, his repeated advice is that it is much better for him
to be loved than hated; his best fortress is the affection of
his people.[30] Nothing could well be more contrary to these
doctrines, whether in letter or spirit, than lines 20 to 27 of
the Prologue. With regard to fortresses, Gentillet repeats
Machiavelli rather fairly,[31] but lays a misleading stress in
attributing to him the maxim that "It is better for a Prince
to be feared than loved." We remark that it is not exactly
love vs. fear that the Prologue discusses but envy vs. pity,
a somewhat different matter.[32] However, if the two be
considered approximately the same, the comment should be
made emphatically that Gentillet is very far indeed from
being the only writer to enter either the fortress or the
love vs. hatred-envy-fear debate. These questions had been,
since ancient times, the standard subject matter of treatises

---

p. 412, by many of Seneca's plays, e.g. *Hippolytus*, ll. 525ff., and by
British writers sharing King James's doctrines; e.g. Blackwood, *op. cit.*,
p. 57. But contrast Plato, *Laws*, Bk. III; Aristotle, *Politics*, V. viii. 5;
Cicero, *Republic*, I. xxv; Sir Thomas Smith, chap. xii; Hooker, *Ecclesiastical Policy* (ed. Keble; Oxford, 1888), Bk. I, chap. x, secs. 3, 4.

28. E.g. *Discourses*, Bk. III, chap. xix; *The Prince*, chap. xvii.

29. *Discourses*, Bk. I, chap. x.

30. On the fortress question see *Discourses*, Bk. II, chap. xxiv; *The
Prince*, chap. xx. On the question of love or hatred by the people see
The Prince, chaps. xvii and xix; *Discourses*, Bk. III, chap. vi.

31. "Of Policie," Maxime 33, p. 347. His discussion of fear vs. love
comes under Maxime 9, "Of Policie," p. 216. This should be compared
with its original in *The Prince*, chap. xvii.

32. Cf. Seneca's *Hercules Furens*, ll. 339ff., wherein the usurper
Lycus meditates: "Shall envy and the common people's talk restrain my
hand? 'Tis the first art of kings, the power to suffer envy (*invidiam*)."

on politics;[33] they were favorites in Seneca's essays and dramas.[34] Influence of Gentillet on Marlowe cannot be proved by citation of such commonplaces.

Simply to illustrate the almost unlimited incidence of the ideas underlying the Prologue, and to demonstrate the dangers of ascribing every case of political wickedness on the Elizabethan stage to Machiavelli or Gentillet, the advice of Pothinus to the king of Egypt in Book VIII of Lucan's *Pharsalia* may be cited:

Expediency is as far from the right as the stars from earth or fire from water. The power of kings is utterly destroyed, once they begin to weigh considerations of justice; and regard for virtue levels the strongholds of tyrants. It is boundless wickedness and unlimited slaughter that protect the unpopularity of a sovereign. If all your deeds are cruel, you will suffer for it the moment you cease from cruelty. If a man would be righteous, let him depart from a court. Virtue is incompatible with absolute power.[35]

In sum, Marlowe's Prologue seems to be composed partly of subjective elements, partly of commonplace ideas which might possibly have been suggested by Gentillet and quite as possibly by a hundred other originals. The contradictions to the principles of the real Machiavelli are numerous and sharp; the agreements well nigh nonexistent. On the

---

33. E.g. Isocrates, *To Nicocles* (Loeb), secs. 15 (p. 49) and 21 (p. 53); Plato, *Republic*, Bk. IX; Aristotle, *Politics*, V. viii. 6ff.; Cicero, *De Officiis*, II, vii. 23 and 25; Erasmus, *op. cit.*, chap. 1, p. 180; Lipsius, *op. cit.*, Bk. IV, chap. vii; Charron, *Of Wisdome* (London, 1612), Bk. III, chap. iii, pp. 400ff.

34. E.g. *Oedipus*, ll. 703ff.; *Phoenissae*, ll. 654ff.; *Thyestes*, ll. 204ff. Also the *De Clementia*, I, xii, 4. In early Elizabethan drama the topic was very widely introduced, e.g. *Misfortunes of Arthur*, II, ii, 1-45; *Damon and Pithias* (Dodsley, Vol. XL), p. 50.

35. Lines 487ff., quoted from the Loeb edition. Marlowe, of course, knew this poem well, having translated Book I of it himself. Compare also the advice of the evil counsellor, Hermon, in *Gorboduc*: "Know ye that lust of kingdomes hath no law...." (II, i, 143ff.)

basis of this showing, one could better argue Marlowe's complete ignorance of the Florentine's works than his intimate acquaintance with them. As for popular Machiavelism, nothing so vague and general could have more than a vague and general influence, which by its very nature is practically incapable of demonstration.

If space permitted, every other instance of putative Machiavellian influence in *The Jew of Malta* might be subjected to the same analysis, with, I think, the same results. However, we must content ourselves with two major observations. First, Barabas as a Jew automatically inherits a reputation as a poisoner,[36] hypocrite, miser, traitor, and general unmitigated devil. Disclosing his treachery in the final act, Ferneze explains, "Now, Selim, note the unhallow'd deeds of Jews" (V, v, 92)—not of Machiavellians, we notice. His crimes, accordingly, should not all be attributed to Machiavellian influence, as Meyer would propose. Second, we do not yet know what was the source of the play, or whether there was a source. If it should be discovered one day that most of the deviltry of the action is taken from some story, Machiavelism would be even further discredited as a formative influence. This mistake is often made in interpreting the character of Guise in *The Massacre at Paris*, where virtually every incident has a firm historical basis and is given a ready-made interpretation in the sources. In such cases the sources determine the character. Then Machiavelism is not much more than a label pinned on *ex post facto*, warning the audience "This is a

36. In the anti-Leicester pamphlet, *A Copie of a Leter, Wryten By a Master of Arte of Cambridge* (London, 1584, p. 80), the Earl is accused of keeping "Iulio the Italian and Lopas the Iewe, for Poysoning...." John Stow's *Annales* (London, 1592), records that in the year 1319 "aboue 12000 Iewes" were killed in Germany for poisoning wells. The poisoner in *Selimus*, sc. xviii, is a Jew. See Kittredge, *Witchcraft in Old and New England*, chap. vi, p. 137, citing many authorities on the point.

bad fellow; look out for him." I do not wish to disintegrate entirely the prevalent conceptions about Machiavelism in Marlowe, but the closer we come to it the more it resembles a mirage vanishing into the indefinable and undemonstrable.

For practical purposes it may be disregarded in a study of *Edward II.* Neither Gaveston nor Mortimer formulates any distinctive maxims; neither is "atheistic" or diabolical beyond what is suggested in the chronicles. Both, indeed, are typical Marlovian egoists, but that is another matter. The real interest of the play lies in a different direction—in its notable redistribution of the emphasis in dramatizing the historical materials. Holinshed, the primary source, draws Edward as a misguided and incompetent king but puts most of the onus on Gaveston and the Spensers.[37] The barons are at first presented in a good light as seeking to free the king of evil counsellors. When they actually rebel, however, the chronicler blames them and shifts rapidly to pity for Edward:

All these mischeefes and manie more happened not onlie to him, but also to the whole state of the realme, in that he wanted iudgement and prudent discretion to make choise of sage and discreet councellors, receiuing those into his fauour, that abused the same to their priuate gaine and aduantage, not respecting the aduancement of the common-wealth ... in so-much that by their couetous rapine, spoile, and immoderate ambition, the hearts of the common people & nobilitie were quite estranged from the dutifull loue and obedience which

37. *Chronicles* (London, 1587), III, 342. Other expressions of opinion occur on pp. 318, 319, 320. Holinshed even approves (p. 321) the manner of Gaveston's execution, which in Marlowe is said to be "against the law of arms," as indeed it was. On page 325 he laments the misfortunes of England under Edward's weak rule, and presents the early actions of the nobles favorably. Some sympathy for the Queen is voiced on page 336. Stow's *Annales* (pp. 320-45) gives an almost exactly parallel treatment.

they ought to haue shewed to their souereigne, going about by force to wrest him to follow their wils and to seeke the destruction of them whome he commonlie fauoured, wherein suerlie they were worthie of blame, and to tast (as manie of them did) the deserued punishment for their disobedient and disloiall demeanors. For it was not the waie which they tooke to helpe the disfigured state of the common-wealth, but rather the readie meane to ouerthrow all. . . .[38]

These judgments undergo some modification in the play. The defeat of Edward on the battlefield is a dividing line, before which the sympathy of the audience swings evenly between him and the opposing barons, and after which it swings sharply to Edward. The change, therefore, comes mostly in the early acts of the play. Marlowe begins, for example, with a more kindly portrait of Gaveston. Holinshed treats him merely as a selfish flatterer and parasite.[39] In the drama he is still the overbearing minion, ruffling it with treasure of the realm and drawing the pliant king which way he pleases, but mixed confusedly, and humanly, with his selfishness is a real devotion to Edward. Marlowe has dignified the whole relationship between the two men with many traits taken from classical friendship theory.[40]

38. See *Chronicles*, p. 327.

39. By strict Renaissance political ethics this is the proper attitude towards Gaveston. The flatterer of a king was regarded as highly mischievous to the state. Flattery is condemned in all treatises, including Castiglione, *The Courtier*, Bk. IV; Elyot, *op. cit.*, Bk. II, cap. xiv, fols. 139ᵛ and 140ʳ; Patricius, *A Moral Methode of ciuile Policie* (London, 1576), fol. 53ʳ. Du Bartas' comment in *Divine Weeks*, 4th Day of 1st Week, p. 136, reflects this attitude:

> I'll boldly sing (bright Soueraigne) thou art none
> Of those weake Princes Flatt'rie works upon,
> (No Second Edward, nor no Richard Second,
> Un-kinged both, as Rule-unworthie reccon'd)
> Who to enrich their Minions past proportion
> Pill all their Subiects with extreme extortion. . . .

40. See L. J. Mills, "The Meaning of *Edward II*," *MP*, XXXII (1934), 11-31. As recommended by Aristotle in the *Ethics* and Cicero in *De*

Then, too, when Gaveston, the low born, retorts to the contempt of the lordly peers who sit at home and eat their tenants' beef, Marlowe the low born cannot help breathing a favoring warmth into his words (II, ii, 74ff.). Again, Holinshed applies a severe moralism to the "iesters, ruffians, flattering parasites, musicians, and other vile and naughtie ribalds" with whom Gaveston entertained the king.[41] But does not Marlowe describe them with the eloquence of favor (I, i, 50-71)? However, lest the estimate should grow too partial, we hear the nobles set forth in indignant detail the taxation under which the whole realm groans, the defeats in Scotland, the loss of provinces in France. But as good Elizabethans we cannot side entirely with the nobles either, because then we should be siding with their allies, the hated Catholic prelates who threaten to excommunicate Edward and give his subjects liberty of rebellion if he does not consent to banish Gaveston. The parallel to the Pope's current bulls against Queen Elizabeth is so perfect as to make every loyal Englishman cheer Edward's speech, "Why should a king be subject to a priest?" (I, iv, 96ff.).[42] Moreover, the barons are put in the wrong frequently by their insolence and threats of revolt. Yet we are antagonized also by Edward and Gaveston when they are cruel to Queen Isabella. So the issue of sympathy is indeterminate until the Queen herself takes Mortimer for her

---

Officiis, Edward considers Gaveston an alter ego with whom he shares all that he has. But he errs in not choosing for his friend a good man equal to himself in station.

41. P. 318.

42. The depth of English feeling against these bulls and fear of their potential political consequences can be seen, for example, in Lord Burghley's *The Execution of Iustice in England* (London, 1583), fol. A3ʳ. References to them in contemporary literature are endless. On the stage two dramatizations of the reign of King John prominently treated the subject: Bishop Bale's *Kynge Johan* and the anonymous *Troublesome Raigne of King Iohn.*

lover and with him raises successful rebellion. Then their treason is roundly condemned by the Earl of Kent, whose judgment throughout the play represents a kind of ethical norm. Marlowe invites attention to the tragic sufferings of the king, as well as to the hypocrisy of the lovers and Mortimer's ambitions. Commons and nobles join finally with Edward's son to punish the malefactors.

Marlowe demonstrates at every stage of the action his ability to call upon the political and ethical judgments normal to an Elizabethan audience for the purpose of directing their sympathies as he wishes. Thus he obtains in the first division of the play a dramatic clash between two parties, both of whom are half wrong and half right, and in the second division a dramatic concentration on pity for the defeated. Whether this is a good method for tragedy may perhaps be open to question. But the point we intend to urge is that the whole performance is, for Marlowe, signally objective. More than in any of his previous dramas, he is writing consciously for the theatre a type of history play already well established on the boards, creating balanced groups of characters instead of a single paramount individual, appealing to familiar standards of thought and behavior. The old individualism is still, indeed, not a little recalcitrant. It lives, I think, in his more luminous poetic realizations of the schemes of Mortimer and Gaveston; it colors the friendships of Edward with a forbidden passion of homosexuality; [43] and, above all, it determines the theme of the play according to the old formula of ruthless strength

43. He and Gaveston use images of sexual love, like the Hero-Leander image in I, i, 6-8, and the Danae image in II, ii, 52-58 to describe their affection, and the Queen compares them to Jove and Ganymede (I, iv, 180), a notorious instance of the passion which Marlowe himself had already utilized in the opening scene of *Dido*. The physical endearments go far beyond those customary between Elizabethan friends exemplified in such plays as *Damon and Pithias*, Lyly's *Campaspe*, *The Taming of a Shrew*, and *Mucedorus*.

triumphant over weakness. In the main, nevertheless, *Edward II* marks the further retreat of defiant individualism, and the advance of a more normal social consciousness. Marlowe still expresses himself, but it is a different, more placable self.

One significant phase of this development can be seen beautifully in what happens to Edward's theory of kingship. His offer of power to Gaveston is absolute:

> Fearst thou thy person? thou shalt have a guard:
> Wantest thou gold? go to my treasury:
> Wouldst thou be lov'd and fear'd? receive my seal;
> Save or condemn, and in our name command
> Whatso thy mind affects, or fancy likes.   (I, i, 166-70)

This is the usual despotic theory of Dido, Tamburlaine, Faustus, or Barabas. The gold in the treasury is the property not of the people but of the king. His word determines life or death. *Sic volo, sic jubeo*, as before. Mortimer as lord protector likewise exults:

> I seal, I cancel, I do what I will.
> Fear'd am I more than lov'd—let me be fear'd.
>
> (V, iv, 51-52)

And when fallen Edward surveys the past, he concludes that his one great mistake was failure to rule sternly enough:

> Yet how have I transgress'd,
> Unless it be with too much clemency?
>
> (V, i, 122-23)

He has learned too late the dying lesson of Tamburlaine to his son to "bridle the steeled stomachs of these jades." This is only putting into other words also Mortimer's warning to Isabella to

take heed of childish fear
For now we hold an old wolf by the ears
That, if he slip, will seize upon us both....

(V, ii, 6-8)

Power is dangerous; only power can retain power.

But the play as a whole gives the lie now to these doctrines that went unchallenged in the earlier work. Edward may think that his one fault was too much clemency, but obviously he is mistaken. His fault was in not ruling wisely and justly. The barons rebelled because he gave himself up to wantonness with corrupt favorites while the kingdom sank to ruin. And he was deposed finally by an act of Parliament representing the will of all classes in the state. Marlowe somewhat tones down this latter point in order to keep high the sympathy for Edward, but it is sufficiently indicated.[44] Two new factors have thus emerged. One is the fundamental principle of Renaissance political science that the sovereign must observe justice. The second is the elementary awareness that the nobles and the commons are political forces of prime importance. That is, the shallow perspective of the first plays, which shows us the king's throne in the foreground and nothing much behind it, broadens and deepens to display an entire scene of realistic political activity. We see it, for example, in Mortimer's maneuvering for popular support:

Then may we with some colour rise in arms;
For howsoever we have borne it out,
'Tis treason to be up against the king;
So shall we have the people of our side,
Which for his father's sake lean to the king,
But cannot brook a night-grown mushrump,
Such a one as my lord of Cornwall is,
Should bear us down of the nobility.

44. II, ii, 155ff.; V, i, 38-39, and 84-85; V, iv, 1-2.

And when the commons and the nobles join,
'Tis not the king can buckler Gaveston;
We'll pull him from the strongest hold he hath.

(I, iv, 279-89)

The open-eyed quality of this speech would have been quite beyond the younger Marlowe. To a degree we may, if we wish, explain these new developments as due partially to the nature of the chronicles, which are realistic above any of the sources he previously used. But Holinshed attributes no absolutist doctrine to Edward or Mortimer, for instance. We must ask, as always, why Marlowe chose these particular sources and treated them in this particular way. By this route we return to the familiar biographical hypothesis.

On the burning political and religious issues raised in *The Massacre at Paris*, Marlowe could do nothing else but take the attitudes made mandatory by English sympathies. This meant glorifying the Huguenots, headed by Navarre, and vilifying the Catholic League, led by Guise. It meant painting Henry III black in the early years when he participated in the massacre of St. Bartholomew, and white later on when he assassinated Guise and allied himself with Navarre. It meant raising a cry of horror when he was subsequently murdered by a Catholic monk, and the drawing of obvious parallels to the Pope's efforts to murder Queen Elizabeth. All this is obvious concession to prejudice on the lowest popular levels. Marlowe's heart is not in it. He writes badly. Navarre, the supposed hero of the piece and historically a figure of grand proportions, is the veriest blank. Only Guise, villain, hypocrite, harboring giant dreams of rebellion, has vitality.

For this, hath heaven engender'd me of earth;
For this, this earth sustains my body's weight,

(II, 56-57)

he cries, formulating a divine duty of rebellion like that claimed by Tamburlaine. Cloyed by the orthodox tenets of this drama which he himself officially promulgates, Marlowe seems homesick for evil. We should be warned by this not to overestimate his progress towards normalcy.

The same caution is suggested by *Hero and Leander*, which he left unfinished at his death. It is a paean to sex, and to all the pleasures of sense, unabashed and uncondemned. Other Elizabethan poems were erotic enough, but Marlowe's work has also a homosexuality which sets it apart. The existence of this trait in the scene of Neptune's toying with Leander (Sestiad II, ll. 155ff.) is, I think, undeniable. If it occurred here only, one might prefer to make little of it. But when it enters also the friendship between Edward and Gaveston, and the Jupiter-Ganymede scene in *Dido*, and when Baines attributes to Marlowe the statement "That all they that love not Tobacco & Boies were fooles," we are forced to take the matter seriously. The theme was just as taboo with the Elizabethans as with us,[45] though they were accustomed to reading of it in the classics. At the very least, its treatment in three of Marlowe's works shows his willingness to tamper with a dangerous topic, and more probably it betokens some degree of personal passion.

The full scope of Marlowe's nonconformity stands out clearly only against the background of early, as distinguished from late, Elizabethan drama. Its derivation from both Seneca and the morality plays made this drama a highly moralistic body of work, fond of spectacular forms of

45. In England "buggery" was a capital offense punishable by death. The "sinne of Sodom" was, of course, condemned in the Bible. Protestants often accused Catholic prelates of committing it. See John Nichols, *A declaration of the recantation of Iohn Nichols*, fols. H3ᵛ and H4ᵛ.

horror and evil, but quick to denounce them and also to
theorize about them in terms made conventional by the
dominant ethical and political thought of the day. In Marlowe there is far less denunciation. His early plays, *Dido*
and especially *Tamburlaine*, do not denounce. The conception of evil grows into the mature plays, but even there
the application of moral judgment tends to have either a
perfunctory or a bizarre note, whereas the depicting of
what is ostensibly blameworthy is prolonged, enthusiastic,
and poetically brilliant. Theorizing about principle either
does not occur at all or is strikingly unorthodox. Almost
any play by Lodge, Greene, or Peele refers often to the
Aristotelian doctrine of the mean, or to the rule of reason
which is basic in all ancient as well as Renaissance philosophy, or, let us say, to the law of nature which controls
human conduct. I do not recall a single reference by Marlowe to any of these principles, except, symptomatically,
his entirely strange views of the precepts of nature in the
famous Tamburlaine speech. It would seem that he was
willing to pass the conventional judgments on specific
conduct in his plays, but not to accept conventional theory.
This observation, of course, has its limits. Marlowe does
refer often to particular vices and virtues in their usual
significations, such as magnanimity, covetousness, lechery,
and pride. But even here the omissions are noteworthy.
The anaylsis of virtue into four cardinal aspects, Temperance, Fortitude, Justice, and Prudence, popularized by Plato,
had been almost universally adopted ever since. Fortitude
is a favorite with Marlowe, but he never once mentions
Temperance or Prudence, or gives to Justice its full
theoretical meaning.

The Aristotelian virtue of friendship, on the other hand,
was one of his few real enthusiasms within the limits of

orthodox principle. He developed the various friendships of Tamburlaine, Faustus, and Edward far beyond anything required by his sources, and gave them a warmth greater than he gave to love or to any other relationship. I am speaking now not of the well-worn Renaissance dictum that friendship is superior to sexual love, but of the emotional verity of Marlowe's treatment. This emotion constituted, apparently, the one egress from egoism that was thoroughly natural to his temperament. To a man like him it would be the clearest revelation of human worth, and an intimation, perhaps not of immortality, but of the presence of a spirit of love abroad in a fierce and lonely universe. It would always be a bond drawing him towards further participation in gentler ideals.

The story of the plays, as we have seen, is the story of the fate of the doctrine of *Sic volo, sic jubeo*, stately and proud in the morning, and in the evening fallen so low beneath a rising conception of personal and social justice. Even in Marlowe's latest work, however, there are abundant signs that in his heart he was more at home with the old ideal. And the closing events of his life likewise show how far he was from complete realization of the new. At the time of his death he had such loyal friends as Thomas Walsingham, Royden, and Blount, but he showed another face to his enemies. Gabriel Harvey hated him for his arrogance. "He was intemperate & of a cruel hart," said Kyd, adding that he feared Marlowe's "rashness in attempting soden pryvie iniuries to men." In the previous year Chettle had heard such evil report of the dramatist that he cared not if they never made each other's acquaintance. To the end, the man whose plays we have watched struggling towards a conception of justice was capable of so irrational an outburst of individualism as to say that "he had as good a right to coin as the Queen of England." The poet who wrote with all tenderness the agonies of Faustus and Edward was killed while attacking Frizer in a quarrel over the price of a meal. All men fail. But, more than most, Marlowe never found the way to translate into deeds the mind's inner glory.

9. ASTRONOMY AND METEOROLOGY

THE STUDY OF MARLOWE'S ASTRONOMY IS IN many ways crucial to an understanding of his mind and art. It furnishes a measure of his proficiency in the natural sciences—his grasp of first principles, his accuracy and scope in details, his recourse to ancient or modern authorities. In particular, it is a test of his acquaintance with the scientific research being carried on by Harriot. If he had such an acquaintance, then some special quality of expertness, some degree of advanced information about new theories and instruments should be perceptible somewhere in his thinking. Perhaps most significant of all, study of astronomy touches the deepest springs of Marlowe's thought and feeling. For him, this was one of the fields of human knowledge that mattered. Especially during the early years, contemplation of the ordered beauty of the stars fed his intellect and enlarged his vision. Not only for glorious passages of aspiration in *Tamburlaine* and *Faustus* but also for more workaday images scattered all through his pages he turned freely to the science. More than any other region of the mind, save only divinity, it was his home.

One would like to be able to say that Marlowe's plays, so keenly in the forefront of religious controversy, were equally eloquent of the current issues in astronomy between the rival systems of Ptolemy and Copernicus. The fact, however, is otherwise. Except in one very doubtful single passage which I shall discuss later, the dramatist adheres to the old Aristotelian-Ptolemaic cosmology and never shows the slightest acquaintance with the Copernican theory although, as Francis Johnson has demonstrated,[1] it was already fairly well known in England in Marlowe's day. We should not hastily conclude that Marlowe himself was ignorant of it. Like Milton, he may have chosen to write of the old system because it better responded to the needs of poetry or because his audience expected to hear of it. But these excuses seem insufficient. Marlowe was not the man patiently to keep on doling out old ideas to his audience if he himself believed in new. And poetry may be made out of any cosmology to which a poet gives real imaginative acceptance. It must follow, I think, that either Marlowe did not know Copernican thought or, if he did, he had already irrevocably given his allegiance to the system of Aristotle and Ptolemy. In this situation, one might add, he had the company of the great majority of the literary men of his time.

Marlowe's most concentrated exposition of cosmology occurs in the dialogue between Mephistophilis and Faustus (II, ii, 33-80).[2] That the earth is the center of the whole system is stated in Faustus' question:

> Are all celestial bodies but one globe,
> As is the substance of this centric earth? (ll. 36-37)

1. Francis Johnson, *Astronomical Thought In Renaissance England* (Baltimore: The Johns Hopkins Press, 1937), chaps. iv-viii.
2. In line 34 Faustus requests that they converse "of divine astrology," and his questions show that he means what we would call astronomy. The word is used in this older sense also in the *Kalender of Shepardes* (*ca.* 1570), cap. xxxi, sig. I 5ᵛ.

Faustus is asking whether the entire cosmos is spherical as is the earth which lies at its center. Mephistophilis replies affirmatively:

> As are the elements, such are the heavens,
> Even from the moon unto the imperial orb,
> Mutually folded in each others' spheres,
> And jointly move upon one axletree,
> Whose terminine is termed the world's wide pole;
> Nor are the names of Saturn, Mars, or Jupiter
> Feign'd, but are erring stars. (ll. 38-44)

That is, just as the uppermost element of fire encloses the element of air, which in turn encloses the other two elements of water and earth, so the various spheres, the outermost of which is the imperial sphere and the innermost the moon's sphere, enclose one another. Of these spheres, as Gemma Frisius puts it, "tousiours le superieur embrasse & comprend par sa circonference les inferieurs."[3] And, explains Robert Recorde:

> ...all partes of the globe moue, excepte the two endes of that Axe tree, wheron it mooueth, and they mooue not out of their place.... Those twoo pointes are named the poles in a sphere...bicause it [the world] is rounde, it muste haue a centre (whiche I dyd affirme before to bee the earthe) and by this centre, we may imagine a right line to run from the one pole to the other, whiche righte lyne muste be called the Axe tre of the world.[4]

3. *Les Principes D'Astronomie & Cosmographie* (Paris, 1556), chap. 1, fol. 4ᵛ. A more lengthy commentary on the same point is made by Robert Recorde, *The Castle of Knowledge* (1556), Bk. I, p. 9.

4. Bk. I, p. 19. Recorde explains that of course this axletree is only a mathematical creation and has no physical reality. For the purposes of poetry, however, Marlowe sometimes chooses to give it concrete existence; e.g., "...Clymene's brainsick son / That almost brent the axle-tree of heaven" (1 *Tam.* IV, ii, 49-50).

We see that when Faustus in his first soliloquy exults,

> All things that move between the quiet poles
> Shall be at my command,   (I, i, 57-58)

he intends dominion over all the operations of the orbs and
of the elements of the universe.

The designation of Saturn, Mars, and Jupiter as "erring"
or wandering is a conventional reference to the quick
variations in the positions of the seven planets as contrasted
with the relative immobility of the stars. Thus Peurbach:
"Atque hae septem stellae quae tam diuersis afficiuntur
motibus, vocantur ... errones, quia habent varios, sed
tamen non incertos aut vagos motus." [5] One can only guess,
however, why Mephistophilis feels it necessary to add that
the names of the three planets are not "feign'd." Possibly
the allusion is to the common Renaissance notion that the
fables about the gods, whose names the planets bore, were
"feign'd" (i.e. invented) by the poets, and there may also
be a pun on the word "erring" in the light of certain
Olympian escapades.

Mephistophilis remarks that there are nine spheres or
heavens: "the seven planets, the firmament, and the imperial
heaven" (ll. 60-61). This is the Aristotelian view in all save
the addition of the imperial heaven, or empyrean.[6] The
empyrean, first suggested by ancient neo-Platonic thinkers,
had been imported into the Christian universe by the early
Church Fathers [7] and had become, so to speak, a standard
piece of cosmological equipment. Shining with a clear,
stainless light it lay outside the other spheres. Unlike them,
it did not rotate. It was the habitation of God; and Marlowe

---

5. *Theoricae Novae Planetarum* (Parisiis, 1558), Praefatio, fol. 1ʳ.
Also Recorde, Bk. I, p. 8.
  6. Aristotle, *De Caelo* (Loeb), II, ivff.
  7. Johnson, chap. II, p. 56.

so treated it whenever he mentioned it in *Tamburlaine* or elsewhere.[8]

The firmament, the sphere of the fixed stars, was for Marlowe, as for Aristotle, the *primum mobile* or activating sphere which gave east-west motion to all the other spheres enfolded within it. Tamburlaine declares:

> The chiefest God, first mover of that sphere,
> Enchas'd with thousands ever shining lamps,
> Will sooner burn the glorious frame of heaven
> Than it should so conspire my overthrow.[9]
>
> (1 *Tam.* IV, ii, 8-11)

And we notice that Mephistophilis does not specify any *primum mobile* apart from the firmament of fixed stars.

Mephistophilis denies the existence of two other spheres, "*coelum igneum, et cristallinum.*" The crystalline heaven was supposed to lie just outside the sphere of fixed stars. M. Cortes' *The Arte of Nauigation* thus describes it:

> The Christaline heauen compasseth about, or conteyneth within it the heauen of Starres. This Christaline heauen, is transparent, and perspicuous, as cleare water or glasse that may be seene through.... It is by another name called, the heauen of water, whereof holy Scripture speaketh saying, *Aquae quae supra caelos sunt, laudent nomen Domini....*[10]

8. See, for example, Orcanes' famous invocation of God, beginning, "Open, thou shining veil of Cynthia, / And make a passage from th' imperial heaven" (2 *Tam.* II, ii, 47-48). Jupiter also is said to have placed himself "in the imperial heaven" (1 *Tam.* II, vii, 15). Accounts of the empyrean are given in *Batman uppon Bartholome*, Lib. viii, cap. iv, fol. 122ʳ, and in John Blagrave's *The Mathematical Iewel* (London, 1584), Bk. I, chap. ii, among other treatises.

9. The conception of God as the *Primus Motor* of the outermost sphere is likewise Aristotelian, as Miss Ellis-Fermor notes on page 141 of her edition of *Tamburlaine* (1930). Cf. 2 *Tam.* IV, i, 118, and *Jew of Malta*, I, ii, 165.

10. M. Cortes, *The Art of Nauigation* (London, 1584), Pt. I, chap. v, fol. 7ʳ. See also T. Hill, *The Schoole of Skil* (London, 1599), p. 13; W. Cunningham, *The Cosmographical Glasse* (London, 1559), Bk. I, fol. 10.

This ninth or crystalline sphere had not been mentioned by Aristotle [11] but had been postulated by Ptolemy to account for the precession of the equinoxes, a phenomenon unknown to the great Greek Philosopher.[12] As the foregoing quotation shows, Scriptural authority led to its being frequently considered as composed of water. In view of the almost universal acceptance of this ninth sphere into the Ptolemaic system, its rejection by Marlowe raises a question of some moment. Is Marlowe thereby denying wholesale the validity of the Ptolemaic scheme and reverting to Aristotle as being closer to the truth of things? I think not. Numerous other passages in the dramas, notably the discussion of the periods of the planets, stand upon the Ptolemaic view. And there seems to be no conceivable reason why Marlowe should prefer Aristotle to the scientific developments of later centuries. The best explanation, I should guess, comes not from Marlowe's science but from his religion. Just as "hell's a fable," so the crystalline heaven is a fable because its very Scriptural authority damns it in his eyes.

Mephistophilis' rejection of *coelum igneum* is less important. Some thinkers of antiquity, Philolaus and Anaxa-

11. The authority of the Arabian interpreters of Aristotle was likewise against it; e.g., Alfraganus, *Liber de aggregationibus scientiae stellarum* (ed. R. Campani in *Collezione Di Opuscoli Danteschi*, Vols. LXXXVII-XC, 1910) cap. xii, p. 109. So also was that of Copernicus, who believed that the sphere of the fixed stars extended outwards infinitely into space. His English followers accordingly rejected any possible ninth or tenth sphere, as Thomas Digges did in his Addition of Leonard Digges' *A Prognostication euerlastinge* (London, 1576), sig. N3ʳ. But the geocentric views in the remainder of the *Faustus* dialogue remove the possibility that Marlowe could be adopting Copernicanism at this point.

12. Johnson, chap. ii, p. 51. An excellent statement of the relations between the contributions made by Aristotle and Ptolemy to the Aristotelian-Ptolemaic world scheme is given in chapter ii of Dr. Johnson's book. In general, Aristotle provided the physics, Ptolemy the mathematics, of the system.

goras among them, had described the world as completely surrounded by a circle of fire, but this phenomenon had found no place in the usual medieval and Renaissance world scheme.[13] It is to be distinguished, of course, from the element of fire just beneath the moon's sphere, of which Marlowe, like almost every other contemporary, frequently speaks. That element, being below the spheres, would not be termed a *coelum*. And it is evident that the whole course of the dialogue between Mephistophilis and Faustus is about the spheres of heaven, not the elements.

The assertion of Mephistophilis that every sphere has "a dominion or intelligentia" probably takes its ultimate provenance from the Platonic doctrine that the heavenly bodies are living beings endowed with divine intelligence, and from the similar Aristotelian dictum that "we ought to think of them as partaking of life and initiative." [14] The very widely read "Dream of Scipio" in Book VI of Cicero's *Republic* afforded it popular statement:

...man...has been given a soul out of those eternal fires which you call stars and planets, which, being round and globular bodies animated by divine intelligences, circle about in their fixed orbits with marvellous speed.

This seems to have been transformed by the Middle Ages into the more anthropomorphic view that an angel intelligence guided every orb. Boyle, *Enquiry, Notion Natural*, (1685), declared, "The School Philosophers teach the Coelestial Orbs to be moved or guided by Intelligences, or

13. Aristotle, *Meteorologica* (trans. E. Webster; Oxford: Clarendon Press, 1923), I, 339; Johnson, chap. II, p. 30. John Chambers' *A Treatise Against Iudiciall Astrologie* (London, 1601, chap. III, p. 19), has this fabulous version: "Some were of opinion, that heauen without was compassed round about with fire, and that the eighth Sphere was full of holes, through which the fire made shew of starres."

14. *De Caelo*, II, xii, 207; Plato, *Timaeus* (Loeb, 1929), pp. 79, 81, 85.

Angels." [15] And in *Purchas his Pilgrimage* Samuel Purchas alluded to the possibility of considering "the Starres animated, or else moued by Intelligentiae." [16] But this bit of medievalism, although familiar to the Elizabethan age, was not then commonly accepted, especially by the scientists. Further remarks by Mephistophilis ard Faustus have to do with "the double motion of the planets": [17]

Meph. All move from east to west in four and twenty hours upon the poles of the world; but differ in their motions upon the poles of the zodiac. . . .
Faustus. . . . the first is finish'd in a natural day; the second thus: Saturn in 30 years; Jupiter in 12; Mars in 4; the Sun, Venus, and Mercury in a year; the Moon in 28 days.

(II, ii, 46-55)

In other words, although all of the seven planets are carried completely around the earth from east to west by the force of the *primum mobile* once every twenty-four hours, each of the seven also has its own opposite motion from west to east which achieves a complete circuit of the sky in the period indicated. Caxton has an illustration which helps to clarify the matter:

15. Quoted in Boas' edition of *Faustus*, p. 92. See also A. W. Ward's edition (Oxford, 1892), p. 171, citing Albertus Magnus and Cornelius Agrippa.
16. Samuel Purchas, *Purchas his Pilgrimage* (London, 1614), Bk. I, chap. II, p. 10.
17. This phrase of Marlowe's comes directly from the vocabulary of astronomy, as has been shown by A. Marquardsen ("Christopher Marlowes Kosmologie," *Shakespeare Jahrbuch*, XLI, 1905, 54-80), quoting the heading of Lib. VIII, cap. XXII of *Batman uppon Bartholome*: "Of double mouing of the Planets." But Marquardsen's argument that Marlowe used Batman, Albertus Magnus, Roger Bacon, and Cardan as specific sources must be rejected, since the parallels he cites are common to any number of contemporary treatises.
The description of Hero's undecided mind "like a planet moving several ways / At one self instant" (*Hero & Leander*, I, 361-62) is a beautiful adaptation of the same idea.

...and so eueryone of them [planets] hathe ii mouynges lyke wyse as a whele which tournyth one wey / & upon that whele there crepyth a flye which goth the contrary way. This flye must haue ii. mouynges.[18]

The backward path of the planets is not exactly from west to east, however, because the zodiac, the great band through which they move, intersects the equator of the cosmos at an angle of about 23° 28'. Thus "the poles of the zodiac" mentioned by Marlowe are also about 23° 28' distant from "the poles of the world"; [19] in fact, the former in their daily rotation describe the celestial arctic and antarctic polar circles.

Claude Dariot's *Astrologicall Iudgement of the Starres* provides a highly typical statement of the planetary periods, which shows how conventional Marlowe is in this respect:

...Saturne whiche is the highest of thē all, & hath gretest circle, finisheth not his course or revolutiō but in 30 yeres: Iupiter in 12 yeares: Mars in 2 yeares: the Sonne in 365 dayes, and about 6 houres: Venus and Mercury keepe their course like the Sunne: the Moone maketh her reuolution in 27 dayes, and about eyght houres.[20]

Dozens of exactly similar lists might be adduced.[21] Upon scrutiny, we see that Marlowe names the planets from

18. *The Myrrour & dyscrypcyon of the worlde* (London, [1527]), I, xiii, a translation by Wm. Caxton of a work attributed to Bellovacensis Vincentius.

19. The difference between the poles of the zodiac and the poles of the world is fully clarified by Hill, Pt. I, pp. 7, 17. See also Johannes de Sacrobosco, *Sphaera* (Venice, 1562), cap. II, p. 36; Recorde, Bk. II, pp. 41-42.

20. London, 1598, chap. II, sig. C4ʳ.

21. E.g. Leonard Digges, *Prognostication euerlasting*, fol. 15ᵛ; Macrobius, *In Somnium Scipionis Libr II* (Parisiis, 1585), Lib. I, XIX, 74; L. Le Roy, *Of the Interchangeable Course...of Things* (London, 1594), Bk. I, fol. 1ʳ&ᵛ; Pliny, *Historie*, (trans. Holland; London, 1601), II, viii.

farthest to nearest in the same order as does Dariot. By both men, the sun is thought of as circling the earth, and the periods assigned to the several planets are the same, with the significant exception of Mars. Dariot, like all the other astronomical writers I have encountered,[22] gives Mars a period of two years. Marlowe has four years, which is an obvious error. Unless the printer of the play was at fault (and this is unlikely, since the error appears not only in Q1 in 1604, as well as all its derivatives, but also in the radically different quarto of 1616), it looks very much as if Marlowe forgot the correct figure. There is an outside possibility that he was reading from some erroneous old treatise, but even then we could scarcely hold him totally excused.

To Faustus' question why the stars and planets are not in the same relative positions to one another at the same time each year so that the same eclipses, conjunctions, etc., occur, Mephistophilis answers succinctly, "Per inequalem motum respectu totius." That is, all have not the same speed and direction. Only at the end of "Plato's wondrous year," [23] an epoch of thousands of solar years according to

---

Fault has sometimes been found with Marlowe for lumping the Sun, Venus, and Mercury all together as having a period of one year. But this is an objection based on modern science, and therefore inapplicable. Using the earth as a center of reference instead of the sun, the Ptolemaic astronomy calculated that the circuits of Venus and Mercury were completed within a few days of that of the Sun. Accordingly, when the periods of the planets were being listed in round numbers, as here, these three were customarily spoken of as being one year. This statement can be found in Leonard Digges, Le Roy, Macrobius, and many other writers.

22. See on this point, in addition to the authorities cited in the preceding footnote, Alfraganus, XVII, 131; Sacrobosco, cap. I, p. 12; Caxton, I, xiii; Batman, VIII, cap. xxii, fol. 128^r; Hill, p. 26; Recorde, Bk. IV, p. 276.

23. Mentioned in 1 Tam. IV, ii, 96. The reference is to Timaeus, p. 83. See note ad loc. in Miss Ellis-Fermor's edition of the play.

some Renaissance belief, would all the stars and planets return to their original positions and the full cycle of celestial phenomena begin anew.

This, then, in broadest outline, is Marlowe's universe. It is a single, finite world. Marlowe's thought did not reach out, as did that of Democritus and others of the earliest Greek philosophers, to the possibility of a plurality of worlds. It is a world, moreover, which was created by God and will be destroyed again by fire when God so wills. Faustus and Mephistophilis both say so; and there are references to the final conflagration in *Tamburlaine* and *Edward II*.[24] Herein the poet departs from the Aristotelian tradition, which taught that the world was uncreated and everlasting, and follows the Platonic and Christian.[25] Some deference to a contrary idea, however, is paid in an occasional passage, like that praising the beauty of Olympia:

> In frame of which, Nature hath shewed more skill,
> Than when she gave eternal Chaos form,
> Drawing from it the shining Lamps of heaven.
>
> (2 *Tam.* III, iv, 75-77)

Before going on to discuss in detail the further particulars of Marlowe's astronomy and meteorology, I should like to consider the one doubtful passage, previously mentioned, which might seem to show knowledge of the Copernican hypothesis. In 2 *Tamburlaine* I, ii, 9-13 Orcanes says:

> Stay, Sigismund; forgetst thou I am he
> That with the cannon shook Vienna walls,
> And made it dance upon the continent,
> As when the massy substance of the earth
> Quiver about the axle-tree of heaven?

24. *Faustus* II, ii, 68-76; II, i, 125-27; 2 *Tam.* III, v, 82, and ii, 7; *Edward II*, IV, vi, 101-2.

25. *De Caelo*, I, iii; *Timaeus*, p. 51. A passage in Ovid's *Metamorphoses* (Loeb, I, 253ff.) envisages the end of the world by fire.

The concluding line might seem to mean that (1) the earth is not at the center of the celestial sphere but circles about the "axle-tree" in the manner of other planets, or (2) the earth is at the center of the sphere but rotates on its own axis, which is a section of the axis of the celestial sphere. But the much more plausible interpretation is that Marlowe intends merely to describe a violent earthquake which causes the stationary, central earth to shake about the axis of the celestial sphere which runs through it. Orcanes is comparing it with the tottering of walls under his cannonade.

Here and there in his dramas Marlowe makes numerous references to the fixed stars, so called not because they were stationary but because they seemed to maintain the same formations relative to one another. The stars, he says, receive their light from the sun, or from Zenocrate, who is the sun:

> Now, bright Zenocrate, the world's fair eye,
> Whose beams illuminate the lamps of heaven....
>
> (2 *Tam.* I, iv, 1-2)

For the Renaissance, the illumination of the stars by the sun was not poetic whimsy but scientific fact:

The Sunne the fountaine of light, doth not onely giue light and make shine cleare the inferiour bodies, but the superiour also, by the brightnesse and light of his beames.[26]

Stars and planets were thought to be solid globes of the same fifth element, the quintessence, which constituted their orbs and indeed everything else from the moon upward. The sizes of the several planets were computed with varying degrees of accuracy, and the distances between

26. Hill, p. 11. To the same effect, Palingenius, *Zodiake of life,* "Aquarius," p. 219; Peter De Medina, *The Arte of Nauigation* (London, 1581), Bk. I, chap. vii; Recorde, Bk. IV, p. 148.

them were badly underestimated. Stars were known to be far larger than the earth. Their real magnitude and remoteness, however, was not suspected. Ancient astronomers had fixed their number at 1022, but Renaissance observers were well aware that many others existed, too fine for sight. The Milky Way, for example, was considered by some thinkers to be "nothing else but innumerable little starres, which with their confuse light, caused that whitenesse," as Fulke reports.[27] He continues:

The Poets haue foure fables of it.... The second, that it is the high street in heauen, that goeth streight to Iupiters palace, and both sides of it the common sort of gods doe dwell.

The same idea inheres in Tamburlaine's visionary ambition:

> Then in my coach, like Saturn's royal son
> Mounted his shining chariot gilt with fire,
> And drawn with princely eagles through the path
> Pav'd with bright crystal and enchas'd with stars,
> When all the gods stand gazing at his pomp,
> So will I ride through Samarcanda streets,
> Until my soul, dissevered from this flesh,
> Shall mount the milk-white way, and meet him there.[28]
> (2 *Tam.* IV, iii, 125-32)

Of the particular constellations Marlowe describes three: the Hyades, Orion, and Boötes. The storm-raising qualities of the Hyades, a group of stars in the forehead of Taurus, which the poet relates in the lines

> As when the Seaman sees the Hyades
> Gather an army of Cimmerian clouds
> (1 *Tam.* III, ii, 76-77)

27. W. Fulke, *A most pleasant Prospect into the Garden of naturall Contemplation* (London, 1602), Bk. III, fol. 38ᵛ.

28. Likewise in *Hero and Leander* (I, 298-99) Hero's tears are said to make on her face "milk-white paths, whereon the gods might trace / To Jove's high court."

were, of course, traditional. Pliny speaks of "the seuen starres called Suculae, which the Grecians of raine name Hyades, because they ever bring foule weather." [29] Similarly, Orion's "drizzling look" (*Faustus* I, iii, 2) was matter of ancient knowledge. According to Aristotle, *Meteorologica:* "Both the setting and the rising of Orion are considered to be treacherous and stormy." [30] Boötes Marlowe names in connection with Boreas in such a way as to show his knowledge that it is one of the farthest northern constellations (1 *Tam.* I, ii, 206). Further, he displays a very nice bit of fancy about it in these lines:

> The sun, unable to sustain the sight,
> Shall hide his head in Thetis' watery lap,
> And leave his steeds in fair Boötes charge;
> For half the world shall perish in this fight.

> (2 *Tam.* I, vi, 41-44)

The conceit revolves about the fact that Boötes was customarily pictured as a driver of oxen, as explained in Hill's *Schoole of Skil:*

> [Among the northern constellations is] the image named Arctipholax, or Bootes, which in English may bee named the Heardman, or rather the keeper of the wagon, in that he seemeth to follow the wagon: that is the Northerly stars.[31]

Boötes, then, would be a proper person to look after the horses of the Sun's chariot when the Sun fled from the sight of the slaughter dealt out by Tamburlaine.

The dramas contain only one reference to an individual star, and that is to Aldeboran, one of the Hyades, in the speech of Tamburlaine:

29. *Historie*, II, xxxix, 19; Batman, Lib. VIII, cap. xxxvi, fol. 137^r.
30. II, 361; Digges, fol. 7^v; Recorde, Bk. IV, p. 267.
31. Pt. II, p. 84. Ovid (*Metamorphoses* II, 176-77) speaks of the clumsy ox-cart of Boötes.

> If Jove, esteeming me too good for earth,
> Raise me to match the fair Aldeboran,
> Above the threefold astracism of heaven,[32]
> Before I conquer all the triple world.
>
> (2 *Tam.* IV, iii, 60-63)

Tamburlaine is of course thinking that at his death Jove may turn him into a star in the manner of the heroes of classical mythology. The comparison to Aldeboran is well taken, because that star is one of the brightest in all the heavens. Enumerating the Hyades, Robert Recorde writes:

... amongst whiche, one is more notable then all the reste, and is called Oculus Tauri, the Bulles eye: but the Greekes call it Lampadias and ... the Arabitians Aldebaran.[33]

Scattered passages in the plays reveal a considerable body of information about the moon. Like the stars, it borrows all its light from the sun. Consequently it is eclipsed when the earth passes between it and the sun. Such an eclipse is described in Tamburlaine's apostrophe to Zenocrate as one

> Whose heavenly presence, beautified with health,
> Gives light to Phoebus and the fixed stars,
> Whose absence makes the sun and moon as dark
> As when, oppos'd in one diameter,

32. I can make nothing definite of the phrase "Above the threefold astracism of heaven." An astracism is supposed by *NED* to be a corruption of "asterism," meaning constellation. The phrase is obviously balanced by "all the triple world" of the following line, which refers to the three geographical regions comprising the then known world: Europe, Asia, and Africa. It would seem, therefore, that Tamburlaine is thinking of three regions which comprise heaven. He may mean the constellations south of the zodiac, those within the zodiac, and those north of it. This is the partition of the constellations made, for example, by M. Maestlin, *Epitome Astronomiae* (Tubingae, 1624), Lib. I, pp. 36-38. Or possibly he makes a different division: the stratum of elements, the stratum of planets and fixed stars, the stratum of the empyrean. This latter division is made by Purchas, Bk. I, chap. II, p. 6, and by G. Scribonius, *Naturall Philosophy* (London, 1631), chap. I, p. 1.

33. Bk. IV, p. 265.

Their spheres are mounted on the serpent's head,
Or else descended to his winding train.

(2 *Tam.* II, iv, 49-54)

It is not an eclipse of the sun that is here being dealt with,
because that can occur only when sun and moon are on
the same side of the earth, not "oppos'd in one diameter."
The terms "serpent's head" and "train" were standard
astronomical terms designating the two points at which the
moon's orbit passed over the sun's orbit. Blagrave's *Mathematical Iewel* gives a clear summary:

The Sun neuer digresseth from the Eclipticke, but the way
of the moone lyeth by, as 5. degrees from the Eclipticke,
crossing him alwaies in 2. opposite points, of which the point
Northwards is called Caput draconis, the other Southwards
Cauda draconis. In these points only is the moone in the
Ecliptick, and in or very neere them, the moone is at all
Eclipses. . . .[34]

Hence Marlowe is accurate in using the word "mounted
on" for the northward point, the serpent's head, and "descended" for the southward, its train. When he calls the
sun dark during an eclipse of the moon he may be taken
to mean that it is invisible, though still radiant, since it is
on the other side of the earth from the observer of the
eclipse.

Marlowe's frequent references to the moon's pull upon
the tides need no comment save in one instance which has
sometimes been misjudged. Bajazeth boasts:

34. Bk. III, chap. LX. Other expositions of the eclipse of the moon,
couched in the same terminology, are given in Sacrobosco, cap. IV, pp.
74-76; Alfraganus, cap. XII, p. 114; Cortes, Pt. II, chap. VIII, fol. 33ᵛ-34ʳ;
Thomas Blundeuile, *The Theoriques of the seuen Planets* (London,
1602), pp. 61-62, 174-76. The conceptions are as old as Pliny (II, x, 7).

As many circumcised Turks we have,
And warlike bands of Christians renied,
As hath the ocean or the Terrene sea
Small drops of water when the moon begins
To join in one her semicircled horns.

(1 Tam. III, i, 8-12)

The implication is that there is more water in the sea at the full moon than at other times. This idea is set forth in Galen's *De Diebus Decretoriis*, as expounded in William Cunningham's *The Cosmographical Glasse*:

...in the spring, and ebbe tides, the seas do encrease, & decrese maruelously: whiche happen but twise euery mōth, & this is that, which Galen ment. And as for daily ebbing, & flowinge, the seas do not increase, or decrease therwith. And therfore properlye called fluxus, et refluxus, but th'other Augmentum et Decrementum maris.[35]

One cannot turn over many pages of the plays without encountering a good deal of that miscellaneous information which was to be found in Proclus or Sacrobosco or almost any other standard textbook of astronomy. Gaveston in *Edward II* (I, i, 16-17), for example, knows that during summer in the arctic circle the sun never sets. Tamburlaine (2 *Tam.* III, ii, 29-31) refers to the fact that the stars of the south polar circle are not visible from the northern hemisphere. One idea that seems to fascinate Marlowe particularly is that when night shadows any part of the earth, day lights its antipodes.[36] Very vivid is Faustus' image of the black cone of night leaping into the sky and revealing the stars (I, iii, 1-4). But when he declares that the shadow

35. Bk. IV, fol. 146.
36. It is applied fancifully in *Hero and Leander*, I, 50: "Since Hero's time hath half the world been black." Cf. also I, 189-91. L. C. Martin seems to me in error when he interprets the line as referring to the Ethiopians (p. 30 of his edition of Marlowe's poems, 1931).

of the night is projected "from the antarctic world" he is
less accurate than if he had said from the antipodal world.
Marlowe indulges in the same looseness a number of times.
The tropic zones, the parallels of latitude, the meridian,
zenith, and horizon, and "the quarters of the sky" formed
by the intersection of the celestial horizon and meridian
also come in for occasional mention, as in the Prologue to
Act III of *Faustus*.

The subject of Renaissance meteorology was allied to
astronomy not only by the fact that the phenomena of both
took place mainly above the earth's surface but also by the
consideration that meteors of all kinds were caused by the
stars and planets, notably the sun. Some notion of the content of the subject can be gained from Aristotle's definition
in the *Meteorologica*:

It is concerned with events that . . . take place in the region
nearest to the motion of the stars. Such are the . . . comets, and
the movements of meteors. It studies also . . . the causes of
winds and earthquakes and all the consequences the motions
of these kinds and parts involve. . . . Further, the inquiry is
concerned with the falling of thunder-bolts and with whirlwinds and fire-winds, and further, the recurrent affections
produced in these same bodies by concretion.[37]

What Aristotle wrote in this field remained largely up to
date in the Renaissance and for many years afterwards.
Even Copernicus did not attempt to replace the old meteorology with a new. Whether the earth stood motionless
at the center of the universe or swung about the sun, it was
thought to be enveloped by a layer of air, and outside that
by a layer of fire, within which operated the anciently
stated Aristotelian laws. It is true that Copernican astronomers argued that the laws of growth and decay which

37. I, 338.

operated within the circle of the elements operated also outside them in the ethereal regions which Aristotle had declared to be forever changeless,[38] but this heresy, although a major shock to the Aristotelian astronomy, seemed to disturb the meteorology not at all.

Certainly no comet of innovation swept across the horizon of Marlowe's plays. In orthodox fashion he wrote of the stratum of fire encircled by the orb of the moon and encircling in turn "the triple region of the air." [39] Concerning the latter element Fulke says:

...the aire is deuided into three regions, the highest, the middle and the lowest. The highest because it is next to the region of the fire, is exceeding hoate: the lowest being next the earth and the waters, is temperate, & by repercussion or striking backe of the Sunne beames waxeth hoat, & by absence of them is made colde, being subiect to winter and summer. The middle region of the ayre, is alwaies exceeding cold....[40]

Beneath the air, of course, is the earth, and the water washing the earth. Now the earth is without motion, but the air and the fire have a circular motion imparted to them by the whirling spheres above. Further, the moon draws the sea. The sun sucks vapors and exhalations from earth and water into the air. The other planets and the stars, in lesser measure, do likewise. All these forces produce the varied phenomena of meteorology.

Comets ("blazing stars"), shooting stars, and similar fiery apparitions provide Marlowe with some of Tamburlaine's most spectacular outbursts:

38. Johnson (pp. 154-60) shows how strong was the effect of the appearance of a super-nova in the constellation of Cassiopeia during 1572 in securing acceptance of this Copernican point of view.
39. 1 *Tam.* IV, ii, 30.
40. Bk. I, fol. 5ᵛ. Also Cunningham, Bk. I, fol. 45.

So, burn the turrets of this cursed town,
Flame to the highest region of the air,
And kindle heaps of exhalations,
That being fiery meteors, may presage
Death and destruction to th'inhabitants!
Over my zenith hang a blazing star,
That may endure till heaven be dissolv'd,
Fed with the fresh supply of earthly dregs,
Threatening a death and famine to this land!
Flying dragons, lightning, fearful thunder-claps,
Singe these fair plains, and make them seem as black,
As is the island where the Furies mask.

(2 *Tam.* III, ii, 1-12)

A Renaissance scientist would find here much that was familiar. He would recognize the exhalations as one of the two kinds of fume drawn out of the earth by the sun and other heavenly bodies, the other being vapor. Vapor, composed chiefly of water, rose to the lowest and middle regions of the air, where it formed clouds, rain, hail, and snow. Exhalations, however, were of a different nature.

Exhalations are as smokes that be hoat and dry, which because they be thinne, and lighter then Vapours, passe the lowest and middle region of the ayre, and are carried up euen to the highest region, where for the excessiue heat, by neerenesse of the fire, they are kindled, & cause many kind of impressions. They are also sometimes viscose, that is to say, clammie, by reason whereof, they cleauing together and not being dispersed, are after diuers sorts set on fire, and appeare sometimes like Dragons, sometime like Goats, sometime like candels, sometime like speares.[41]

In the light of this exposition, Tamburlaine's fancy that the flames of the burning town will ignite the exhalations is

41. Fulke, Bk. I, fol. 2ᵛ-3ʳ. The analysis is based on Aristotle, *Meteorologica* I, 341.

seen to be unscientific (though none the less poetic),[42] for exhalations in the upper air are kindled by the heat of the neighboring element of fire. But his flying dragons turn out to be the accepted data of science.[43] So also the concluding words of the quotation last given, "sometime like speares," show the scientific origin of the imagery in another Tamburlaine passage:

> I will persist a terror to the world,
> Making the meteors, that, like armed men,
> Are seen to march upon the towers of heaven,
> Run tilting round about the firmament,
> And break their burning lances in the air.[44]
>
> (2 *Tam.* IV, i, 201-5)

The details of Tamburlaine's "blazing star" or comet in the first passage quoted likewise have unimpeachable authority. Fleming, *Of Blazing Starres*, observes:

> ... Aristotle ... supposed that a Blazing starre did consist of a drye vapour, which beeing drawn upward into the highest ayre, is there set on fire: and that this blazing starre taketh substance of earthly exhalations, very hote, dry, fat and clammy: which beeing carried into the upper region of the ayre, is there kindled and burneth: to whom all Philosophers (in a manner) of this our age haue subscribed, and some Astronomers also ... the drie vapour in it is kindled, burneth, and lasteth with the light of the flame, which is moued to and

42. Even wilder, of course, is Tamburlaine's similar conceit that such flames could "Incense the heavens and make the stars to melt" (2 *Tam.* IV, i, 195-96). In Renaissance view, fire always blazed immediately under the moon's sphere without damaging it.

43. Similarly, Batman (Lib. XI, cap. 1, fol. 157ᵛ) describes a fiery impression which "is called, a Dragon spowting fire." See also Scribonius, chap. IV, p. 16.

44. The same phenomenon is utilized in *Dido* (IV, iv, 117-20): "Not bloody spears, appearing in the air, / Presage the downfall of my empery...." It is discussed by Abraham Fleming, *A Treatise of Blazing Starres* (London, 1618), chap. II, sig. B2ʳ, and Pliny, II. xxv, 15.

fro, by the under ayre: where vapours of like nature, quality and substance arising, giue continuance and length thereunto: . . . [45]

And Scribonius adds the familiar idea: "It foreshewth war, Pestilence, drought, and barrennes of the earth." [46]

Also with regard to exhalations, there is an interesting speech by Guise in *The Massacre at Paris*, triumphant at the death of Mugeroun, the king's favorite, whom he has just assassinated:

> Thus falls imperfett exhalation,
> Which our great sonn of France cold not effecte:
> A fyery meteor in the fermament.
> Lye there, the kinge's delyght and Guise's scorne! [47]

The task of interpretation is made easier by Fulke's definition:

The Meteors are deuided after three maner of wayes: first, into bodies perfectly and imperfectly mixed. . . . They are called imperfectly mixed, because they are very soone chaunged into another thing, and resolued into their proper elements of which they ·doe most consist, as doe all impressions, fyrie, ayrie, watrie: . . . The last sort, namely earthlie Meteors, are called perfectly mixed, because they will not easily be chaunged and resolued from that forme which they are in, as be stones, metalles and other mineralles. [48]

In short, then, Mugeroun was a fiery exhalation and hence

---

45. Chap. VI, sig. B4ᵛ. Other discussions occur in Blagrave, Bk. III, chap. LXXII, p. 62; Palingenius, Bk. XI, p. 222.

46. Chap. III, p. 14. Some difficulty exists as to the meaning of those other lines of Tamburlaine: "So shall our swords, our lances, and our shot / Fill all the air with fiery meteors" (1 *Tam.* IV, ii, 51-52). Perhaps a reference is intended to the belief held in antiquity that missiles flying through the air caught fire and melted. It is expressed by Aristotle in *De Caelo*, II, vii, 179, and by Ovid, Lucretius, Virgil, and others.

47. Appendix A, ed. Bennett, p. 255.

48. Bk. I, fol. 1ᵛ-2ʳ.

unstable. The "great sonn of France," the king who lifted him from the earth and formed him, could not "effect" him, make him perfect, or for long keep him from resolving back into his elements.

Renaissance meteorology also studied the phenomena of the middle and lower regions of the air. These included those "freezing meteors and congealed cold," namely snow, hail, and ice, which Marlowe knew to besiege the arctic wastes. But cold was essential to the formation of clouds even in the temperate zones:

A cloude is a vapour joyned together by the extreme cold of the middle region [of the air]. Cloudes hang in the Ayre by the Sunnes heat, which draweth them up, and by the moving of the windes are tossed up and downe.[49]

Wind was currently defined as "a hot & dry exhalatiō, ingendred in the bowels of th'Earth, which once breaking forth, is driuen rounde aboute the face of the same."[50] With this, Marlowe's description of wind as made up of "reeking water and dull earthly fumes" (*Hero & Leander* II, 115-16) only partly tallies. Showing his usual favor for the tempestuous, he several times alludes to the properties of whirlwinds, notably their power of raising objects high above the earth.[51]

Thunder and lightning may be caused by the collision of clouds driven by winds, according to one body of Renaissance opinion. "Also meeting & comming together of Clowdes, setteth oft the ayre on fire and flame, and ingendereth lightening and thundering," we read in *Batman*

49. Scribonius, chap. IV, p. 17; Fulke, Bk. IV, fol. 46ᵛ.
50. Cunningham, Bk. IV, fol. 153; Aristotle, *Meteorologica* II, 360-61.
51. See Tamburlaine's blasphemous challenge to Mahomet, "Why send'st thou not a furious whirlwind down, / To blow thy Alcaron up to thy throne...?" (2 *Tam.* V, i, 191-92). Whirlwinds which snatch up objects to great heights are mentioned by Fulke, Bk. III, fol. 33ᵛ, and Aristotle, *Meteorologica*, III, 371.

uppon Bartholome.[52] This idea is turned into poetry in 1 *Tamburlaine* III, ii, 76-81:

> As when the seaman sees the Hyades
> Gather an army of Cimmerian clouds,
> (Auster and Aquilon with winged steeds,
> All sweating, tilt about the watery heavens,
> With shivering spears enforcing thunderclaps,
> And from their shields strike flames of lightning)....

An alternative explanation of the cause of lightning and thunder is thus stated in Leonard Digges' *Prognostication Euerlasting:*

> ...thunder is an exhalation, hot and dry, mixt with moisture caryed up to the middle Region, there thicked and wrapped into a cloud, of this hotte matter coupled w^t moystnes, closed in the cloud, groweth a strife, the heate beatinge, and breaking out the sides of ye cloude wyth a thundringe noyse: the fyre then dispersed, is the lightninge.[53]

This likewise has its poetic counterpart in Marlowe:

> My sword struck fire from his coat of steel,
> Even in Bithynia, when I took this Turk;
> As when a fiery exhalation,
> Wrapt in the bowels of a freezing cloud,
> Fighting for passage, makes the welkin crack,
> And casts a flash of lightning to the earth.
>
> (1 *Tam.* IV, ii, 41-46)

However bizarre these principles of science may seem to us, Marlowe was well in accord with the most conservative opinion of his time in making them into poetry. But certain others of his images were near the outer verge of legitimate science, if not altogether beyond it. A good example is

52. Bk. XI, cap. IV, fol. 160^v. Cf. Ovid, *Metamorphoses*, VI, 687ff.
53. Fol. 13^v. To like effect are Fulke, Bk. III, fol. 27^r & ^{v}, Pliny II, xliii, 20, and Aristotle, *Meteorologica*, II, 369.

Tamburlaine's vaunt of the massacres he has made in Africa:

> And here in Afric, where it seldom rains,
> Since I arriv'd with my triumphant host,
> Have swelling clouds, drawn from wide gasping wounds,
> Been oft resolv'd in bloody purple showers,
> A meteor that might terrify the earth,
> And make it quake at every drop it drinks; . . .
>
> (1 *Tam.* V, ii, 395-400)

One might quickly dismiss this as outrageous fustian were it not for Fulke's statement, "After the same maner, the Sunne also from places where blood hath beene spilt, draweth up great quantity of blood, and so it rayneth blood."[54] On the other hand, most authors content themselves with saying that under some conditions the color of the sky is like that of blood.[55] Many cite the authority of Pliny, who said:

> There appeareth in the Skie also a resemblance of bloud, and . . . a fierie impression, falling from out of heaven to earth: like as it happened in the third yeere of the hundred and seven Olympias, at what time as king Philip made all Greece to shake with fire and sword.[56]

Another apparently peculiar thought is in Bajazeth's prayer:

> Make heaven to frown and every fixed star
> To suck up poison from the moorish fens,
> And pour it in this glorious tyrant's throat!
>
> (1 *Tam.* IV, ii, 5-7)

But compare Fleming's words, ". . . it is likewise knowne, that by force of Starres, many enuenomed and infectious

54. Bk. IV, fol. 52ʳ.
55. Batman, Bk. XI, cap. vii, fol. 162ʳ; Digges, fol. 13ʳ.
56. II, xxvii, 17.

vapours ascend. ..." [57] The extent to which the poetry of
Tamburlaine is rooted in the scientific information of Marlowe's time must be, I think, matter for recurring surprise.

The inner workings of such everyday matters as rain,
dew, and snow did not particularly concern Marlowe and
need not concern us. But earthquakes were gigantic enough
to fit well into *Tamburlaine:*

> And these, that seem but silly country swains,
> May have the leading of so great a host
> As with their weight shall make the mountains quake,
> Even as when windy exhalations,
> Fighting for passage, tilt within the earth.
>
> (1 *Tam.* I, ii, 47-51)

This passage suggests why the study of earthquakes was
embraced within the field of meteorology. Earthquakes
were believed, at least since the age of Aristotle, to be produced by the pressure of winds within the earth. The earth,
says Abraham Fleming in his *Bright Burning Beacon,*

is made to quake by the violence of winds shut up & kept
close in the hollowe places of the same. ... Now these winds
thus shut up, seeking a vent here & there to breake out, and
trieng by all meanes they can make to haue passage, that
breaking out of prison (as it were) they might be set at
libertie, and blow at large, whiles this is intended, the earth
trembleth, rocketh, & reeleth as though it wold fall. ...[58]

In another place Marlowe describes fountains of water as
being cast up by an earthquake (1 *Tam.* V, ii, 285), a hap-

---

57. Chap. XIV, sig. E1ᵛ. The power of the stars to draw up ordinary
exhalations and vapors from the earth was widely accepted. See Le Roy,
Bk. I, fol. 4ʳ. This idea is embodied in Faustus' last soliloquy:
> You stars that reign'd at my nativity,
> Whose influence hath allotted death and hell,
> Now draw up Faustus, like a foggy mist,
> Into the entrails of yon lab'ring cloud. ...   (V, ii, 161-64)

58. London, [1580], chap. II, pp. 13-14. See Aristotle, *Meteorologica,* II,
365-66; Pliny, II, lxxix, 37.

pening which Gabriel Harvey, for instance, likewise describes in *Three Letters*, citing Aristotle and Pliny as authority: "... the earth to quake, to stirre ... to cast out ... great ouer flowing waters, and fountaynes." [59]

A general consideration of the cosmology of Marlowe's plays leaves one struck by the very large number of allusions to the subject, many more than I have been able to discuss here, and by the ease and naturalness of their introduction. During the period of the composition of *Tamburlaine* and *Faustus* the poet's mind must have been so thoroughly impregnated with these ideas that upon every occasion they germinated into new forms and images by the pressure of an inevitable fecundity. Any question as to his real originality in thus using the accepted data of contemporary science need scarcely be argued. One has only to read the excerpts of pedestrian prose from the scientific textbooks, quoted in this chapter, and then read the verse of Marlowe. By all canons of Renaissance criticism, much more than by our own, the poet lay under obligation to reflect the learning of his age. The high degree in which Marlowe's plays answered this expectation has not been adequately realized.

On the other hand, it would be idle to pretend that Marlowe displayed anything resembling real scientific attainments. Naturally, the popular drama was not quite the place for exhibiting such gifts. Nevertheless, the failure even to mention Copernicanism must tell somewhat against Marlowe as a thinker. Nor can it well be overlooked that even his Ptolemaic details are distinctly on the elementary side. His works give the impression that the universe was a relatively simple affair of homocentric spheres. Quite absent

59. Ed. Grosart, I, 58-59. Aristotle's statement as to such fountains is made in *Meteorologica*, II, 368, and Pliny's in the passage cited in the preceding footnote.

are all references to deferents, equants, epicycles, and other troublesome complexities of Ptolemaism. It is hard to believe that this absence was due solely to Marlowe's wish not to overtax the intelligence of his public.

If these things are so, then we must of course forego all use of his dramas as proof of his intimacy with Harriot. It is also to be remembered that our only evidence of contact between the two men comes in the year 1593, whereas the large majority of Marlowe's astronomical references appear in dramas dating 1587 and 1588, as discussed below. Some possibility still exists that late in his career Marlowe talked over facts and theories with the great mathematician, but his dramas and poems do not show it.

The biographer of the dramatist will note with interest that the material we have been examining is almost wholly confined to *Tamburlaine* and *Faustus*, which are early plays. Incredibly, such later plays as *The Jew of Malta* and *The Massacre at Paris* contain only one or two astronomical references each; *Edward II* has half a dozen; *Hero and Leander* perhaps a dozen; *Dido*, another early play about the same number. Now this relative abandonment of astronomy after *Faustus* coincided with an important change in the spirit and meaning of the plays, as indicated in previous chapters. *Tamburlaine* and *Faustus* were plays of universal aspiration and essentially solitary temper; the subsequent plays dealt with limited ambition in an increasingly well-realized human environment. Marlowe's absorption in astronomy, then, was associated with and symbolic of his youthful stage of lonely aspiration. His reading and thought about the heavens brought him spaciousness and power and the exaltation of high intercourse. These qualities, at least, are apparent in much of what he wrote during those first years, before that species of splendor passed away.

10. ART OF WAR

IN THE FOREGOING CHAPTERS MUCH HAS BEEN SAID about Marlowe's erudition. But any image of him sitting forever pallid among his books like a statue of his grandsire cut in alabaster must be dispelled at once. Marlowe was young. Marlowe was a swordsman who used rapier and dagger against William Bradley in the Hog Lane affray of 1589. Kyd, and others, feared him for his rashness in "attempting soden pryvie iniuries to men." Marlowe died with a dagger in his hand. In short, his nature had a tempestuously active side. Now a lover of action who is also a lover of thought takes special delight in any practical science which affords outlet for both kinds of energies. That is why, one supposes, Marlowe was attracted to the science of geography, measuring coasts and kingdoms and planning global voyages. It accounts likewise for his enthusiasm for military tactics. His mind could be busy with the techniques of attack and defense, while in imagination he marched with the troops, smelled gunpowder, and stormed cities.

Marlowe was content with no mere superficiality in the science. His approach shows his customary blend of methodical reading with zestful interpretation. So much of technical information enters into *Tamburlaine*, especially, that all of the action and much of the characterization of the play leap into full significance only against a background of sixteenth-century warfare and military usage. The same thing is true, but in much lesser degree, of others of Marlowe's early dramas. We must go with him to the military treatises of the age to recover the codes of conduct, the weapons, the maneuvers, all the clangor of battle which enter so integrally into the work.

It goes almost without saying that the armies and tactics described in *Tamburlaine* are, except in a few superficial details,[1] neither oriental nor early fifteenth century as historical realism would require. Witness the host of Tamburlaine:

> Three hundred thousand men in armour clad,
> Upon their prancing steeds disdainfully
> With wanton paces trampling on the ground;
> Five hundred thousand footmen threatening shot,
> Shaking their swords, their spears and iron bills,
> Environing their standard round, that stood
> As bristle-pointed as a thorny wood;
> Their warlike engines and munition
> Exceed the forces of their martial men.
>
> (1 *Tam.* IV, i, 22-30)

Save for the inordinate numbers it mentions, Marlowe's passage is a fairly apt review of any contemporary European force, as a short survey of some typical western troops and formations will disclose.

1. E.g., the reference to the Turkish janissaries. But Marlowe is mistaken in speaking of them as "Mounted on lusty Mauritanian steeds" (1 *Tam.* III, iii, 16). The janissaries were footmen. See Paulus Jovius, *A short treatise upon the Turkes Chronicles* (trans. P. Ashton; London, 1546), fol. cxxii[v]. On the other hand, Marlowe's description of the battle array of the Turks in "The figure of the semicircled moon" (2 *Tam.* III, i, 66) is authentic. Jovius (fol. xi[v]) declares: "...Frosert...writeth that y[e] winges of Bayazets hoste, beyng set very thinne...bent after y[e] fashion of the newe moone, couered more thā vii miles of groūd...."

Most European armies had as their core and inner substance the massed battalion of pikemen, protected by
cuirasses and armed both with eighteen-foot pikes and with
short swords.[2] These are the "spears" and "swords" that
Marlowe speaks of. The pikes, developed by the Swiss and
recognized as highly formidable weapons, were used on the
offensive to break the enemy infantry ranks by sheer
weight of pushing and so make them vulnerable to a cavalry
charge. On the defensive, pikes braced on the ground could
repel any assault by even the most heavily armed cavalry.[3]
The swords came into play both offensively and defen-
sively against enemy footmen after the pikes had been
broken or swept aside and the two armies pressed against
each other at close quarters. In a melee of that sort each side
would seek to penetrate to the midst of the opposing formation "environing the standard round" and seize the enemy's
ensign. For its defense the ensign was always surrounded by
a small group of guards wielding halberds,[4] or "iron bills"
as Marlowe calls them, shafts five to eight feet long sur-
mounted by a large axe head and a keen spike.

Pikemen and halberdiers alike were, of course, helpless
against firearms. Hence every large body of infantry was
flanked on both sides by troops of "shot," footmen carry-
ing calivers, arquebuses, or muskets ("threatening shot," as

2. Sir John Smythe, *Certain Discourses...Concerning the formes and
effects of diuers sorts of weapons* (London, 1590), fol. 4ᵛ; Machiavelli,
Arte of Warre (London, 1588), Bk. II, fol. 22ʳ. Spanish pikes were fifteen
feet long. When these weapons were held upright by troops standing
in serried ranks they would suggest Marlowe's simile, "As bristle-pointed
as a thorny wood."

3. T. Styward, *The Pathwaie to Martiall Discipline* (London, 1582),
Bk. II, p. 157; Sutcliffe, *Practice, Proceedings, and Lawes of armes,* chap.
xII, p. 185. See Sir Charles Oman's account of the victories of the Swiss
pikemen over the mailed feudal chivalry during the fourteenth and
fifteenth centuries, *A History of the Art of War in the Middle Ages*
(London, Methuen, 1924), Vol. II, Bk. xi.

4. G. Clayton, *The Approved order of Martiall discipline* (London,
1591), fol. 18.

Marlowe says.)[5] As firearms became more and more deadly during the sixteenth century, the ratio of "shot" to pikemen increased, but few commanders cared as yet to have much more than half their infantry strength in "shot," since these alone could not hold their ground against either pikemen or cavalry in open country. It was the duty of the "shot" to skirmish with the foe, and so soften both his offensive and his defensive power. The issue of most battles, however, was decided by the shock of pikemen or heavy cavalry, and once a determined charge was launched in the open field the "shot," after firing their pieces, usually retired to the rear or sought safety behind the pikes of their comrades.[6] This interdependence of the various infantry arms had been recognized since the French campaigns in Italy at the opening of the century.

Marlowe's greater interest, however, is in the heavy cavalry arm, to which Tamburlaine and his sons, as leaders of the army, properly belong:[7]

> Well done, my boy! thou shalt have shield and lance,
> Armour of proof, horse, helm, and curtle-axe,[8]
> And I will teach thee how to charge thy foe,
> And harmless run among the deadly pikes.
>
> (2 *Tam.* I, iv, 43-46)

5. The musket, heavier and more powerful than either the arquebus or the caliver, seems to have been used extensively for the first time by Alva's army in the Netherlands in 1566. It could pierce armor at much greater distances (about 200 paces) than could other portable firearms, and rapidly superseded them.–R. Williams, *A Briefe Discourse of Warre* (London, 1590), p. 40; O. Spaulding, H. Nickerson, and J. Wright, *Warfare* (New York: Harcourt Brace & Co., 1925), p. 451. Marlowe seldom makes specific mention of any sort of small firearm.

6. L. Digges, *Stratioticos* (London, 1590), Bk. III, pp. 109, 121, etc.

7. In feudal times the kings, nobles, and lesser gentry always fought, of course, as mailed horsemen. The practice continued through the sixteenth century and beyond.

8. "Curtle-axe" (cf. cutlass) is not an axe at all but a short heavy sword. See Williams, p. 18, who says, "These Launtiers...al carrie a curtilace, I meane a good broad sword."

This was the ponderous steel equipment and these were the shock tactics of the western armored horseman even so late as Marlowe's day. They were, however, swiftly becoming obsolete, and extremely heavy armor, already inadequate against musket bullets, was being shed in order that the cavalryman might move more freely. Military treatises published during Marlowe's lifetime discuss three main sorts of horsemen. A few of the most heavily armored were retained for shock tactics. Less thickly covered, especially in the lower limbs, were the demi-lances; these might be called the cavalry norm. Then there were light horsemen, some of them completely unarmored, who were used for scouting, for convoying, and for disrupting the enemy's communications.[9] To these functions Marlowe several times refers:

> Two thousand horse shall forage up and down,
> That no relief or succour come by land.[10]
>
> (1 *Tam.* III, i, 61-62)

He has nothing to say, however, about that growing branch of the cavalry, the argoletiers, mounted men whose chief weapon was an arquebus, or about the mounted pistoleers. In fact, he makes the error of thinking that the German reiters were lancers, "Almaine rutters with their horsemen's staves," whereas they were preeminently pistoleers.[11] It seems, generally, that his imagination was less attracted by the smaller firearms than by "the slicing edge," by the massive onslaughts of the mailed knights, and by the detonations of great artillery. Archers he scarcely mentions at all, and one gathers that he would have had little sympathy

9. Styward, Bk. II, p. 158.
10. For other passages see 1 *Tam.* II, ii, 39-42; 2 *Tam.* III, iii, 47-48, where scouting is mentioned.
11. *Faustus*, I, i, 126. Reiters are defined by Smythe, fol. 45ᵛ, and Sutcliffe, chap. XII, p. 174.

with Sir John Smythe's efforts to revive the use of the long-bow. He has several particularly vivid pictures of the wild cavalry charge:

> Hast thou not seen my horsemen charge the foe,
> Shot through the arms, cut overthwart the hands,
> Dyeing their lances with their streaming blood.
>
> (2 *Tam.* III, ii, 103-5)

In Renaissance military theory, the cavalry should be stationed on either flank of the shot, who, in turn, flanked the pikemen. Nearest the shot were placed the "men at arms," the heavy cavalry. Outside them rode the lighter horse. The field artillery, guarded by squads of pike and shot, was ordinarily set up somewhere in front, either in the center or on the farthest flanks of the array. It was relatively ineffective, since it often had not chance to fire more than once or twice and accuracy of aim was rare. Marlowe, however, gives one account of the solid shot ploughing through an enemy formation:

> Hast thou beheld a peal of ordnance strike
> A ring of pikes, mingled with shot and horse,
> Whose shattered limbs, being tossed as high as heaven,
> Hang in the air as thick as sunny motes,
> And canst thou, coward, stand in fear of death?
>
> (2 *Tam.* III, ii, 98-102)

The line, "A ring of pikes, mingled with shot and horse," has seemed to most editors either to be corrupt or to indicate Marlowe's ignorance of military tactics. Their argument is that a mingling of pikes, artillery, and cavalry is not a feasible military combination.[12] But "shot" here does not mean artillery; according to universal Renaissance usage it means infantry with small firearms. All sorts of combinations of pikes with shot were discussed and prac-

12. U. M. Ellis-Fermor's edition (1930), p. 226, note.

tised during the sixteenth century. A difficulty remains
with respect to the horsemen. The ring or circle was a well
known close defensive formation for pikemen;[13] but to
introduce cavalry in the midst of it would be both highly
unorthodox and quite ruinous to its steadiness. The problem
may be solved with credit to Marlowe, however, if we may
suppose that "mingled with" means "closely flanked by."
The disposition of troops would then be completely orthodox, as has already been shown.[14]

Naturally enough, full accounts of battle maneuvers are
lacking in Marlowe's dramas, but suggestive details keep
continually flashing in. Usumcasane, for example, wants to
take the advantage of higher ground to "Drive all their
horses headlong down the hill" (1 *Tam.* I, ii, 135). Tamburlaine, knowing that the approach of his army is not
expected by the Soldan of Egypt, advances with all expedi-
tion. Earlier, he has been cunning enough not to fight
against Theridamas when the odds are too heavy. Meander
resorts to an ancient stratagem, flinging gold over the
battlefield to tempt the enemy to break their array (1 *Tam.*
II, ii, 59ff.). Frontinus' *Stratagems*, a Roman treatise very
popular in the Renaissance, recommended this device:

When the Gaules shuld fyght with Attalus, they delyuered all
theyr golde and syluer, to be kepte of certayne men, that
myghte scatter it abroode, if it happened them to be putte to

13. Styward, Bk. I, p. 68; Clayton, fol. 55: "But say it happeneth, that
their enemies come suddainly uppon them, so that they cannot set their
men in order of battaile as they woulde: then it shall be good for those
Captaines to cast their men in a Ring ... with the greatest part of their
shotte in the midst of their Pikes, your Holbards or Billes next the
Ensigne, being placed in the middest of all...." Marlowe also refers to
"a ring of pikes" in *Dido*, II, i, 196.

14. Pikes and shot were sometimes distributed among horsemen to
strengthen them against superior enemy horse: Sutcliffe, chap. vi, pt. 2,
p. 119; Du Bellay, *Instructions for the Warres* (trans. P. Ive; London,
1589), Bk. II, chap. i, p. 121. But they would not then be in the ring
formation.

flyghte, to the entent they myght the more easily escape theyr ennemyes, beinge let with gatherynge up the praye.

Tryphon kynge of Siria, being vanquyshed, scattered money all the way that he fledde, and so he hyndered Antiochus horsemen, that pursued hym....[15]

Since at least three widely read military text books of Marlowe's day repeated this material,[16] the probability is that the dramatist picked it up somewhere during his reading. Richness and veracity of effect are given to the play by many other small details of strategy and maneuver.

Apparently, the branches of military science which Marlowe finds most absorbing are fortification and siegecraft, for he brings long treatments of them into scenes ii and iii of Act III of 2 *Tamburlaine*, and makes frequent slighter mention of them elsewhere. These sciences had achieved high technical development in the wars in Italy during the early sixteenth century. At first the unprecedentedly powerful French artillery train had given the advantage to besiegers, but equilibrium between offense and defense had been restored by subsequent improvements in fortification. As all large cities and many small ones were powerfully fortified and an invading army could not afford to leave strong enemy positions in its rear, campaigns frequently settled down into a long series of sieges.

The main passage in Marlowe having to do with fortification comes in Tamburlaine's promise to instruct his sons in the science:

> But now, my boys, leave off, and list to me,
> That mean to teach you rudiments of war.

.   .   .   .

15. Trans. R. Morysine; London, 1539, Lib. III, cap. viii, sig. Hiv^v.
16. Digges, Bk. III, chap. xxiii, p. 335; Du Bellay, Bk. II, chap. ii, p. 132; Barnabe Rich, *A Path-Way to Military practice* (London, 1587), sig. H4^v.

Then next, the way to fortify your men;
In champion grounds what figure serves you best,
For which the quinque-angle form is meet,
Because the corners there may fall more flat
Whereas the fort may fittest be assailed,
And sharpest where th' assault is desperate;
The ditches must be deep, the counterscarps
Narrow and steep, the walls made high and broad,
The bulwarks and the rampiers large and strong,
With cavalieros and thick counterforts,
And room within to lodge six thousand men.
It must have privy ditches, countermines,
And secret issuings to defend the ditch;
It must have high argins and covered ways
To keep the bulwark fronts from battery,
And parapets to hide the musketeers,
Casemates to place the great artillery,
And store of ordnance, that from every flank
May scour the outward curtains of the fort,
Dismount the cannon of the adverse part,
Murder the foe and save the walls from breach.

(2 *Tam.* III, ii, 53-82)

As Danchin first pointed out,[17] many of the details of this speech were drawn by Marlowe from Paul Ive's *Practise of Fortification*, published in London in 1589. But because Marlowe picks these details from many different parts of Ive's book and throws them together without definition and without orderly connection, they do not give us any clear picture of a fortified place. A brief sketch of a typical Renaissance fortress will help to formulate the scene.[18]

17. "En marge de la seconde partie de Tamburlaine," *Revue Germanique* (Jan.-Fév. 1912).

18. Consult, besides Ive, the long and excellent treatments of the theory of fortification written by Sutcliffe, chap. xvii; R. Barret, *The Theorike and Practike of Moderne Warres* (London, 1598), Bk. V, pp. 123-32; G. Maggi, *Della Fortficatione Delle Citta* (Venetia, 1564); Williams, pp. 48-54.

Main fortifications of inland cities consisted of a complete circuit of wall surrounded by a deep ditch; in addition, there were usually some minor defenses on the outer bank of the ditch. A primary consideration was the shape or "figure" to be given to the whole defense system. Triangular and quadrangular figures were regarded as very weak because some of their angles were too sharp, and hence too easily pulverized by enemy cannonade.[19] The larger the angle, the thicker the earthworks inside it and around it could be made, and the more space there would be in which to throw up new ones if the enemy succeeded in making a breach at that point. Hence multi-angled figures were favored. A great projecting work called a bulwark, roughly heart-shaped with the point outward, was erected at each angle, as a station for heavy artillery which could sweep the whole length of the wall (called the "curtain") between it and the next bulwark, thus taking the enemy in the flank as he advanced to the assault on the wall. These guns, also, of course, sought to silence the opposing cannon. Their two functions are thus stated by Marlowe:

> And store of ordnance, that from every flank
> May scour the outward curtains of the fort,
> Dismount the cannon of the adverse part,
> Murder the foe and save the walls from breach.
>
> (2 *Tam.* III, ii, 79-82)

In order that this flanking fire be effective, the stretch of wall between bulwarks had to be straight, and could not be concave. Moreover, it should not be longer than about 200 paces,[20] the maximum range of real effectiveness of most guns in Marlowe's time. So devastating was the shot

19. Ive, *Practise of Fortification*, chap. III, p. 7; P. Whitehorne, *Plattes of fortification*, fol. 16ᵛ, included in his translation of Machiavelli's *Arte of Warre;* Barret, Bk. V, p. 124.

20. Sutcliffe, chap. XVII, p. 259; Machiavelli, Bk. VII, fol. 94ᵛ; Williams, p. 50.

of these flankers if the bulwarks were properly constructed, that the besiegers always had to put them out of commission before delivering an infantry assault upon any section of wall which they commanded. The defensive fire of the bulwarks was usually supplemented by that of artillery set on the walls themselves, either on outer protuberances called "platforms" or inner elevations called "cavalieros."[21]

Marlowe speaks of "walls made high and broad." Typically, they might rise about 45 feet from the bottom of the ditch,[22] difficult to scale with ladders and yet not so heavy as to collapse easily under the impact of the solid cannon balls. Stone, bricks and mortar were preferred for their composition, but earth and faggots might be used if nothing better were available. The thickness, greater at the bottom than at the top, might average 12 or 15 feet, and the whole structure was strengthened internally by braces (Marlowe's "thick counterforts")[23] running from outer to inner edges. Supporting the wall from behind stood the rampart ("rampiers large and strong"), an immense heap of earth which had a level breadth of at least 30 feet at its summit about 5 feet below the top of the wall, and which sloped downwards to the town below so gradually that the defenders could easily run up and down it. The five-foot difference in height between wall and rampart served as the "parapets to hide the musketeers" who harried the attacking forces. "Casemates to place the great artillery" were chambers in the walls and bulwarks down near the bottom of the ditch which came into play after the enemy had succeeded in entering the ditch.[24]

21. For descriptions see Sutcliffe, chap. xvii, p. 261; Barret, Bk. V, pp. 125-26.

22. Sutcliffe, p. 258; Ive, p. 19.

23. Ive gives specifications and diagrams for these, pp. 19-23.

24. Barret, p. 126; Ive, p. 26; Sutcliffe, p. 250. Marlowe cannot mean the defensive earthworks built within the ditch itself, also called "casemates," for these were not emplacements for heavy guns.

Marlowe's whole description implies a dry ditch. Probably as many Renaissance strongholds had wet ditches as had dry ones, and theorists saw advantages and disadvantages in either. A dry ditch had to be as wide as a wet ditch, and deeper. Depths of 30 or 40 feet and widths of 60 or 70 feet were recommended.[25] Often, running in the center of the main ditch was an extra "privy ditch" going a number of feet deeper as an obstacle to infantry and to mines. The "countermine" was not quite the same. It was an underground tunnel as far as possible beneath the ditch and circling the walls, from which the enemy's mining operations could be detected and intercepting tunnels dug.[26] Behind the shoulder of the bulwarks, at the bottom of the wall were small doorways ("secret issuings to defend the ditch") permitting townsmen to send forces into the ditch to drive out any besiegers who might effect an entry.

Around the outer brink of the ditch ran the "covered way," so called not because it was roofed over but because it was protected from enemy fire by the argin, an earthwork high enough to cover defending infantry.[27] This was the town's first line of defense.

Here its troops could gather to sally out upon the foe and prevent him from bringing his artillery too close to the walls and bulwarks:

25. Sutcliffe, p. 264; Ive, p. 12; Machiavelli, fol. 94ᵛ. Williams, p. 49, wants a dry ditch to be "100. paces broad, and fiftie foote deepe...."

26. Ive (p. 16) directs: "... make the countermine 25. or 30. foot distant from the wall, and so deepe in the ground, as an enemie may go with a mine. Which countermine must be 4. foote broad, and 6. or 7. foote high, and must haue vents made in the top of it, whereby it may receiue light." Italian artificers often placed the countermine within the foundations of the wall.

27. Ive (p. 27): "The couered way round about the Fort must be ten foote broad, and the argin or banke so high that a man be not seene behind it"; B. de Mendoza, *Theorique and Practise of Warre*, trans. E. Hoby (1597), p. 122, desiderates a twenty-foot breadth for the covered way. Sutcliffe, p. 265, says four feet.

> ... high argins and covered ways
> To keep the bulwark fronts from battery.

This whole outermost ring of defense was sometimes given the name "counterscarp." [28] When Marlowe writes that the counterscarps must be "narrow and steep," therefore, he probably means that the sides of the ditch and the argin should be steep, and the covered way narrow. If the latter were broad, enemy fire could more easily sweep it. Both the argin and the covered way were lower than the top of the city walls and would therefore be dominated by the defenders' gunnery in case the counterscarp were taken by the assailants.

From the foregoing discussion it appears, I believe, that although Marlowe may have taken much of his information verbatim from Paul Ive's *Practise of Fortification* there are no such serious errors in his use of the terms, nor any such slavish copying of single passages, as would suggest that he did not understand what he was saying. Even the often questioned lines on the shape of the fort need not be condemned as lacking military sense.

> But now, my boys, leave off, and list to me,
> That mean to teach you rudiments of war.
>
> . . . .
>
> Then next, the way to fortify your men;
> In champion grounds what figure serves you best,
> For which the quinque-angle form is meet,
> Because the corners there may fall more flat
> Whereas the fort may fittest be assailed,
> And sharpest where th' assault is desperate.
>
> (2 *Tam.* III, ii, 53-67)

---

28. Sutcliffe, p. 250. It is a pity that Marlowe puts all his nouns in the plural in Tamburlaine's speech. Properly, there was only one counterscarp and one covered way. But Ive has the same loose usage.

If Marlowe means that the five-angled form is meet for flat country because the sharp angles (those least defensible, as stated above) may be placed where the avenue of assault is hardest ("desperate") and the obtuse angles (best defensible) where the assault is easiest, his words do indeed betray confusion. In flat country, free from natural obstacles, every side of the fort must be equally assailable. But the text bears a different interpretation: "I'll teach you what figure is best for flat country, and also for which kinds of country (other than flat) the quinque-angle is suited because its strong and weak points may be placed so as to take advantage of the inequalities of the terrain, which render some sections more assailable than others." This makes good military logic and does not seem to torture the grammar of Marlowe's sentence. In the back of his mind may also be the idea that the quinque-angle fort is less expensive to build than one with more numerous angles [29] and is, at the same time, adequately defensible, as a fort with fewer angles is not.

The concluding lines of his fortification passage describe

> a fortress in the raging waves,
> Fenc'd with the concave of a monstrous rock,
> Invincible by nature of the place. (2 *Tam.* III, ii, 88-90)

---

29. This possibility is suggested by Ellis-Fermor, p. 225, note. But the remainder of her interpretation seems to me vitiated by her misconceptions of the quinque-angle as having "the shape of a five-pointed star." Such a star would have ten angles, not five. I must disagree also with Danchin's view that Marlowe has probably misunderstood Paul Ive's description of the quinque-angle. As I see it, Marlowe was not trying to follow Paul Ive's outline for any one particular fort, but was combining details from several different discussions by Ive so as to form a new composite of his own. Thus part of the material for the passage comes from chapter II of Ive, part from chapter III, and the facts about counter-forts, counterscarps, and casemates from still later sections of the book. The only question for us, therefore, should be whether or not Marlowe's lines have military intelligibility.

They attest Marlowe's familiarity with the distinction, often made in contemporary treatises, between places strong by nature and those strong by art. As Machiavelli declares:

> You ought to know y^t towns and fortresses, may be strong either by nature or by industrie: by nature those be strong, which be compassed about with rivers, or with Fennes, as Mantua is and Ferrara, or which be builded upon a rocke....[30]

Matched against the complicated technique of Renaissance fortification was the equally intricate technique of siege. The latter is treated by Marlowe with great detail in 2 *Tamburlaine* III, iii, almost as if he were balancing it against his treatment of fortification in the scene immediately preceding. The material here and elsewhere in the play will be found to follow closely the accepted Renaissance theory of siege.[31]

Excluding the possibility of inducing treachery among the garrison, there were four principal siege methods which might be used singly or in combination. One was to starve out the defenders by drawing lines of trenches around the city or patrolling all paths of ingress. Techelles employs this method against Balsera:

> Captain, these Moors shall cut the leaden pipes
> That bring fresh water to thy men and thee
> And lie in trench before thy castle walls,
> That no supply of victual shall come in.
>
> (2 *Tam.* III, iii, 29-32)

30. Bk. VII, fol. 94^r. Very much the same language is used by the Roman authority Vegetius, *Military Institutions* (trans. Lt. J. Clarke; London, 1767), Bk. IV, p. 169; Clayton, fol. 73; Digges, Bk. III, chap. xxiii, p. 315; Du Bellay, Bk. III, chap. ii, p. 234.

31. Full discussions of siege operations will be found in Williams, p. 20ff.; Mendoza, pp. 87-99; Du Bellay, Bk. III, chap. ii; Sutcliffe, chap. xvi, p. 229 ff. The methods of the Turks in capturing Tripoli in 1551 are carefully described in Nicholas Nicholay's *The Navigations . . . made into Turkie* (trans. T. Washington; London, 1585), Bk. I, chaps. xvii and xviii, which, as Ethel Seaton has shown, Marlowe probably knew.

Bajazeth likewise employs it in his siege of Constantinople.[32]

A second method was "to scale a castle wall" with ladders at all possible points at the same time. This was not likely to succeed unless tried in conjunction with an effort to storm breaches already made in the defenses, or unless the defenders were taken by surprise. Theridamas captures Babylon in this fashion.

Undermining was a third device much practised, especially since the invention of gunpowder rendered it possible "to make whole cities caper in the air." The objective was to dig a winding tunnel under the foundations of the walls, store a dozen kegs of powder there, lay a train, then stop up the mouth of the tunnel and set fire to the train,[33] holding troops in readiness to charge up the breach made by the explosion before the people within had time to throw up secondary defenses. For the besieged, on the other hand, the task was to listen carefully to the subterranean movements of the enemy, discover the path of his mine, and either drive him out of it or dig vents which would make the explosion harmless. Some very weird underground struggles resulted. Wet ditches or rock formations removed the danger of mines.

The siege tactics most relied upon in the sixteenth century, however, were knocking a large hole in the walls by the concentrated fire of heavy guns and storming the breach with infantry. For this purpose an army thought itself well equipped if it had forty or fifty guns of large caliber.

32. 1 *Tam.* III, i, 58-60. Sutcliffe (pp. 216, 217, 238) cites many examples of towns reduced to desperation by the cutting of their water supply, including Rochelle where the French king in 1573 "To depriue the townsmen of fresh water . . . caused the conduit pipes to be cut." Marlowe could have read of conduit pipes at Constantinople in Nicholay, Bk. II, chap. xv, p. 50 or Paulus Jovius, fol. lxii^r, but neither of these works, nor any other that I know of, declares that the pipes were cut during siege of the city by the Turks.

33. The technique is set forth by P. Whitehorne in chapter xxviii, "*Of Mynes,*" bound in with his translation of Machiavelli's *Arte of Warre.*

Guns were then very far from being standardized, but speaking roughly the heaviest included the culverins (a 16- to 20-pound shot), demi-cannons (24 to 30 pounds), cannons (40 to 70 pounds), double cannons and basilisks upward to several hundred pounds. Light artillery consisted chiefly of falcons, falconets, minions and sakers, all discharging a bullet of less than seventeen pounds.[34] Marlowe mentions nearly all of these in one passage or another.[35] All shot, of course, was solid. The guns were usually cast of the best possible iron, but preferably were of bronze. Although the range varied with the particular weapon, few were of much use at a distance of over a half mile, and even at two or three hundred paces the battering of walls could not proceed with any dispatch. The optimum was to get the guns entrenched right in the counterscarps. If this could not be attained, they must be advanced to within sixty or seventy paces at most.[36] It is for this reason that Techelles advises Theridamas:

> Both we, Theridamas, will intrench our men,
> And with the Jacob's staff measure the height
> And distance of the castle from the trench,[37]
> That we may know if our artillery
> Will carry full point blank unto their walls.
>
> (2 Tam. III, iii, 49-53)

34. Barret, Bk. V, pp. 124, 134; N. Tartaglia, *Colloquies concerning the Arte of shooting* (1588), pp. 26-27.

35. Basilisk (1 *Tam.* IV, i, 2, and *J. of M.* V, iii, 3); culverin (*J. of M.* V, iv, 3); cannon, so frequently that no citation is needed; "minions, falc'nets, and sakers" (2 *Tam.* III, iii, 6). Especially interesting is *Faustus* III, i, 42, where "double cannons forg'd of brass" is Marlowe's substitution for the much vaguer "great pieces" of the *EFB*. His preference for brass as a more sturdy metal extends even to bullets: "And with brass bullets batter down your towers" (*J. of M.* III, v, 24).

36. Sutcliffe, p. 230; Lucar's *Appendix* (bound in with Tartaglia), chap. LXX; Mendoza, p. 91.

37. Range-finding by means of the gunner's quadrant and similar instruments was a well developed department of Renaissance gunnery. There are expositions of the science in Lucar and in L. Digges' *Panto-*

At point blank the force of the guns would, of course, be greatest.

The weak points of the defenses having been surveyed and the best site for the siege ordnance having been selected, the problem was to get the guns into position. This work was carried on as much as possible during the hours of night when the defending cannoneers and musketeers could not only fire blindly into the darkness. But the attackers usually found it necessary to set large corps of pioneers to work digging trenches along which the ordnance might safely be drawn to the desired position for battery. There, as a shield to the gunners, gabions were erected, from four to eight feet broad and some seven feet high. These consisted of earth packed into a circle of stakes set in the ground and bound with osier twigs or similar materials. Theridamas gives directions for this work:

> Then see the bringing of our ordinance
> Along the trench into the battery,
> Where we shall have gabions of six foot broad,
> To save our cannoneers from musket shot;
> Betwixt which shall our ordinance thunder forth.
>
> (2 *Tam.* III, iii, 54-58)

Even behind gabions, the siege guns ordinarily had to be set low in trenches also. Lacking any elevated ground on which to plant their battery, the besiegers would adopt one of two procedures. They might capture the counterscarp and cut it away so that their shot could strike the bottom of the wall. Or they might build an artificial mound to dominate the defenses and the city within, as Theridamas threatens to do at Balsera:

---

metria (1571), among others. A book on the use of the Jacob's staff for measuring heights and distances was published in London in 1590: Thomas Hood's *The use of . . . the crosse staffe and the Iacob's staffe.*

These pioneers of Argier in Africa,
Even in the cannon's face shall raise a hill
Of earth and faggots higher than thy fort,
And, over thy argins and covered ways,
Shall play upon the bulwarks of thy hold
Volleys of ordinance till the breach be made
That with his ruin fills up all the trench.[38]

(2 *Tam.* III, iii, 20-26)

Fire would be centered upon some weak point in the wall and upon the two bulwarks flanking it. Once fire had begun, it should continue with unintermitted fury, in order that the besieged might have no time to build new trenches and ramparts behind the growing breach. When the opening was wide enough to admit a broad rank of footmen and the ditch had been bridged by rubble from the wall or thoroughly possessed by advanced units, the final assault was delivered.[39] Marlowe has this vigorous account of these climactic moments:

38. In those of the probable sources of *Tamburlaine* which I have had opportunity to examine, such as Paulus Jovius, Cambinus, Chalcondylas, Newton, Fortescue, Fregoso, and La Primaudaye, this mound-building is the only feature of siege work prominently attributed to Tamburlaine. All of Marlowe's descriptions of digging trench approaches, setting up gabions, measuring the cannon range, cutting off food and water, and so on should probably, therefore, be considered additions out of his own knowledge. So many contemporary books provided information of this sort that it seems impossible to isolate a single source for it.

39. A useful summary of all these various steps in the process of assault is given by Sir John Smythe in the Proeme Dedicatorie to his *Certain Discourses*: "... all Generalls and Chiefetaines of all Nations of anie iudgement, upon the approch of any Citie, Towne, or place fortified, haue used to approch the same with trenches, crosse-trenches, gabions, and diuerse other ordinary and extraordinary inuentions, (according unto the scituation of the ground) for the preseruing, and sauing of the liues of their Souldiours, and that they haue not offered to giue any assault, untill by the battery and effect of great Ordinaunce planted uppon the Caueleeres (by us called Mounts) or by battery from the counterscarfe cut, and opened the flankers of the bulwarkes, platformes, and reuelins haue beene taken way, and the Artillerie of the

> ...our ordinance thunder forth,
> And with the breaches fall, smoke, fire, and dust,
> The crack, the echo and the soldiers' cry,
> Make deaf the air and dim the crystal sky.
>
> (2 *Tam.* III, iii, 58-61)

With a shout the pikemen and the swordsmen would then rush up the debris, led by heavily armoured squads, preceded by a barrage from their own musketeers and cannoneers. They had to press on through mines, traps, and enfilading fire towards the garrison ensconced behind hastily constructed trenches and earthworks. Wildfire, to which Marlowe has several references,[40] might be thrown among them or projected on the points of swords and pikes. Those who survived the last hand to hand clash might take the town.

Before leaving the subject of siegecraft, I should like to indicate that the scheme by which Barabas gives possession of Malta to the Turks is described by writers on military history as having operated at other sieges. Barabas admits the Turks through the "vault" of a sewer which discharges its waters outside the city fortifications (*J. of M.* V, i, 86-94). Du Bellay, *Instructions for the warres*, says:

---

inward Mounts dismounted, and a sufficient breach in the Curtine made assaultable, with the drie or wet ditches filled to take away the effectes of Casamates, as also to make the entrance of the Souldiours into the ditches and breach more easie, and with lesse daunger...."

40. "The sword with a ball of wildfire on it" (1 *Tam.* V, ii, 249); "sulphur balls of fire" (2 *Tam.* III, ii, 41); "balls of wildfire in their murdering paws" (*Dido*, II, i, 217). Digges, *Stratiotocos*, Bk. III, chap. XIX, p. 254, prescribes the making of "Truncks, Balles, Arrowes, and all other sortes of Wild-fire, and for the continuall supply of thē, they ought to haue in readinesse great store of Sulphure, Salt-peter, Rosin...." P. Whitehorne, in the chapters appended to his Machiavelli, has some elaborate recipes; see chap. XXXIV, fol. 42ᵛ, which is headed "How to make balles of wilde fire, to shoote in ordinaunce or to throw with handes." Most of these mixtures apparently were merely incendiary, but some were explosive.

The Generall should also enquire, and cause it to be dili-
gently searched, if there were no vault, or water-course that
issued into the ditches, for they might be very necessarie helps
to get a Towne by. Naples was taken by Bellisarius in the
yeare 538, by means of a conduct of water. It was likewise
taken in the self-same place by King Remus in the yeare 1463.
Monopole was taken by the Marques of Guast, by meanes of
an old caue that lay buried under ground.[41]

Inasmuch as Du Bellay's book was published in English in
1589 bound in the same volume with Paul Ive's *Practise of
Fortification*, which Marlowe is known to have used, the
clear possibility exists that the passage just quoted formed
the basis of the incident in *The Jew of Malta*. No other
satisfactory source has ever been pointed out. If this passage
was not Marlowe's actual source, then at least it describes a
certain kind of siege trick, known to tacticians, which came
to his attention by some other route.[42]

Whether a captured stronghold would be sacked and the
inhabitants cruelly treated depended on the character of
the general commanding the victors, the temper of his
troops, and the circumstances of the particular siege. There
was no firmly established practice, even in western Europe.
Renaissance ethical theory, however, required that mercy
be shown to the conquered. It would definitely condemn
the savagery of Tamburlaine in massacring all populations
who refused to surrender before he displayed coal black
colors on the third day of beleaguerment, and would simi-

41. Bk. III, chap. II, p. 248.
42. Cf. Sutcliffe, p. 226, quoting Guicciardini: "The Venetians tooke
Brescia from the French, entring by a grate through which the riuer
issued. The Protestāts by a grate likewise entred Nismes an. 1569." See
also the narrative of the siege of Jerusalem by Joseph ben Gorion, *Com-
pendious... Historie of the latter times of the Iewes common weale*
(London, 1575), fol. 216, describing the entry of the Romans "through
the vault."

larly denounce his torture of Bajazeth.[43] This trait in his
hero, of course, Marlowe takes over from his sources.[44]

Outside the field of actual combat, also, the dramatist
introduces many a detail having to do with apportionment
of booty, and the disciplining of soldiers. One typical
example is Tamburlaine's equal distribution of the captured
concubines of Bajazeth among his men, with the added
stern injunction against disorders:

> Brawl not, I warn you for your lechery;
> For every man that so offends shall die.
>
> (2 *Tam.* IV, iii, 75-76)

Tamburlaine's foes may taunt him with being the leader of
a disorderly rout, but it is plain in many scenes that his
soldiers have "desires of discipline in arms" and that he
himself never forgets the necessity of strict control. There
are several reasons why Marlowe may wish to stress this
characteristic. The historical Tamburlaine, as he was presented in those western sources likely to have been read by
the poet, was noted for the strong hand he held over his
troops. An often repeated story is thus summarized by
Hurault: "Tamerlane king of Tartarians, made a souldier
of his to be put to death, for taking but a cheese from a
poore woman." [45] An auxiliary reason for emphasizing discipline in the play is that it is constantly emphasized by all
military writers of the sixteenth century as a quality of the
ideal general. The chaotic conditions in most of the armies
of the period made such emphasis highly requisite.

43. These practices of Tamburlaine's are specifically censured by T.
Fortescue, *The Foreste*, Bk. II, chap. xiv; A. Cambinus, *Two very
notable Commentaries* (1562), Bk. I, fol. 5ʳ; La Primaudaye, *French
Academie* (1586), chap. xxiii, p. 253; and by many others.

44. See Ellis-Fermor's edition of the play, p. 139, note.

45. J. Hurault, *Politicke, moral, and martial discourses*, Pt. II, chap.
iii, p. 200. Other emphatic statements occur in Fortescue, Bk. II, chap.
xiv; Cambinus, Bk. I, fol. 4ʳ.

One episode in the play, above all, is often misunderstood because it is not recognized as involving an act of military discipline. This is Tamburlaine's stabbing of his son Calyphas, who has refused to fight in the battle against Callapine (2 *Tam.* IV, i). Many of the worst vices of the soldier are exemplified in Calyphas. He is insubordinate, slothful, a gamester, and a lecher. Granted that for the sardonic pacifism of this remarkable character Marlowe has a strong undercurrent of sympathy, the fact remains that Calyphas deserved death under every code of contemporary military law,[46] and only the exceptional Elizabethan would think otherwise. Before and after he stabs Calyphas, Tamburlaine justifies his act repeatedly by appealing to "martial justice," "war's justice," "the argument of arms." And as commander of the army he has a perfect right to impose, and even personally to execute, the death penalty. Although he is undoubtedly tyrannous and brutal in some of his other deeds, from the Elizabethan point of view Tamburlaine is merely heroic in this one.

None of Marlowe's descriptions of warfare warrants our concluding that he ever saw actual service in the field. It is not that they are amateurish or essentially inaccurate; they are not. But all of them could easily have resulted from the reading he did in Paul Ive and similar authorities, perhaps vitalized by conversation with some of the veterans of the struggles in France and the Low Countries. Further, the whole tone of both parts of Tamburlaine is unrealistic, as everyone admits, in the sense that it shows little realization of the darker elements in the experience of war. Almost absent from it are the long, dreary sieges, the

46. Sutcliffe, chap. XXI, pt. 3, p. 316: "All souldiers that wilfully absent themselues without lawfull cause from their colours, or companie, that goeth to charge, or resist the enemie, deserue death." Similarly Machiavelli, Bk. VI. fol. 84ᵛ: Du Bellay, Bk. III, chap. III, pp. 263-64; Styward, Bk. I, p. 57; Digges, *Stratiotocos*, Bk. III, chap. XXII, pp. 272ff.

epidemics of dysentery and plague, the perpetual internal bickerings and delays, the infected wounds and other circumstances which made Renaissance campaigns something less than glorious. Marlowe is a young man dreaming of battle, not a soldier who has undergone its waking and horrible actuality. In the later plays, his attitude is not radically different. Nevertheless, after all this has been said, one must also say that Marlowe does achieve a certain truthfulness of effect in those parts of the military process which he chooses to portray. Especially in *Tamburlaine*, by repeated hints, touches, and more elaborate references to armies and tactics distributed everywhere through the action he keeps us always cognizant of these things, and offers to our imagination three-dimensional scenes busy with the movements and sounds of war.

IV

CHARACTER

11. HUMOR

INASMUCH AS DIFFERENCES OF TERMINOLOGY ARE largely responsible for differences of opinion about Marlowe's humor, a few definitions are in order. Humor, in my view, is an emotion. It is generated by the perception of unexpected contrasts, likenesses, and incongruities either in concrete images or in abstract ideas. Pointed expression of the latter is wit. Irony is wit faintly tinged with bitterness and stated by indirection. When irony is highly charged with hostility it becomes sarcasm. Satire is wit in the service of destructive criticism: it is broader than irony and sarcasm but embraces them both. Comedy I take to mean any literary instance designed primarily to awaken the emotion of humor.

The most dangerous misconceptions about Marlowe have related not to the serious but to the comic side of his genius. Happily, the opinion is no longer current which denied to this master of irony the possession of any comic sense whatever. But even today a just estimate of the pervasive and protean character of his laughter is still to seek. The fact is that his sense of humor, broadly defined, was one of Marlowe's most remarkable qualities. Distinguished by a surprising resourcefulness of matter and method, it served to complement, to curb, and sometimes to rebuke the grandiose passions of his early dramas. In the one play, *The Jew of Malta*, where it was the controlling temper, it achieved a brilliantly unorthodox comedy scarcely equalled in the contemporary theatre. And in the whole range of his work it was a chosen medium through which spoke that most Marlovian of Marlowe's characteristics, his proudly critical spirit.

His earliest work, *Dido*, although a youthfully serious and wooden performance on the whole, has its interest as a preview of the future of this humor. The playful dalliance of Jupiter with Ganymede in the opening scene will develop into the toying of Neptune with Leander in the much later poem. Both episodes treat homosexuality with the zestful amusement we expect of a Marlowe who said, "That all they that loue not Tobacco & Boies were fooles." Again, Juno's sarcasm in her speech over the sleeping Ascanius,

> Say, Paris, now shall Venus have the ball?
> Say, vengeance, now shall her Ascanius die?
> O, no! God wot, I cannot watch my time,
> Nor quit good turns with double fee down told!
> Tut, I am simple, without mind to hurt,
> And have no gall at all to grieve my foes!
>
> (III, ii, 12-17)

is too blatant to draw admiration as a method of characterization. But the same note, considerably subtilized, will be heard again in the retorts of the barons in *Edward II* and in the hostile cynicisms of all of the "Machiavellians." The attitude is already a natural one for Marlowe.

Wit of a milder sort is in Dido's description of how she rejected her former suitors:

> This was Alcion, a musician;
> But, play'd he ne'er so sweet, I let him go:
> .   .   .   .

This, Meleager's son, a warlike prince;
But weapons gree not with my tender years: ...

(III, i, 158-63)

Here the succinct disposal of each man, with the turning
of his main qualification against him, gives a crisply humorous effect often to be used in such a play as *The Massacre
at Paris*. When, a few lines further on, Dido broadly hints
at her love for Aeneas, and then contradicts herself, we
find, long before Shakespeare, a touch of the comedy which
delights us in a Portia or an Olivia, but here much more
crudely executed. It is even possible that Marlowe's scene
of Dido changing her mind back and forth between Iarbas
and Aeneas (III, i) is meant to show a comic mutability,
but one cannot be sure.

No such doubt attaches to the rather similar episode in
which Cupid inspires the Nurse to take a lover despite her
eighty years. Her alternations between love and common
sense are definitely humorous because of the swift contrasts
they provide, not to speak of the incongruity of her being
in love at all at that age. "A husband, and no teeth!" All
told, this is probably the most successful comic bit in the
play. Taken together with a few lighter strokes in the
portraits of Dido herself, it shows that Marlowe had some
feeling for the humor of women in love. Admittedly, the
expression of it in *Dido* is lacking in ease and fine shading,
but after long abeyance it emerged at last with a new
dexterity in the character of Hero, who dropped her fan
or "used but half her strength," to the accompaniment of
much subdued laughter by the poet.

The bathos of a number of the lines in *Dido* has sometimes been taken as proof that the young Marlowe had no
sense of the ludicrous. But this is a confusion of thought. If
we smile at a line like "Gentle Achates, reach the tinder
box," it is because its commonplaceness presents a sudden,

absurd contrast to the inflated heroics of the surrounding lines. Again, we smile at the speeches of forced passion because they are guilty of a kind of hypocrisy. The cause is the stark contrast between what they are and what they affect to be. Now the reason why Marlowe does not see these contrasts is that his literary judgment is still immature. He cannot yet distinguish the several qualities. This is not to say that his sense of the ludicrous in other quarters may not be well developed. Nor is it to say that in the literary field also he will not learn to see how funny these mistakes are. The truth is, of course, that he does learn. The later Marlowe may still write extravagances but he does so in obedience to the tyranny of the theatre, not without some unquietness of spirit and a laugh of self-mockery.

An immense progress is already visible in *Tamburlaine*, in the greater pungency, intellectuality, and adroitness of the humor, and its closer connection with the plot. Of these qualities the comic character of Mycetes furnishes a signal example.

The main trait around which Marlowe has built the character is his fantastically naive misapprehension of the world of fact. Mycetes has learned, in the manner of an imbecile child learning a game, that a king is a great personage who is obeyed by lesser men. He is very anxious to live up to the rules for his own conduct as sovereign, and very petulant with people like Cosroe and Tamburlaine who do not observe the rules for theirs. Sometimes he is not quite certain what the rules are, and has to ask Meander:

> I might command you to be slain for this,
> Meander, might I not?

Or again, he applies them to the wrong situations, as when he haughtily commands his enemy Tamburlaine in the midst of the battle:

Away! I am the king. Go, touch me not.
Thou breakst the law of arms unless thou kneel
And cry me "Mercy, noble king!"

(II, iv, 20-22)

In other words, all that Mycetes expects the law of arms
(the code of honorable conduct on the battlefield) to do
is to make his foeman surrender to him.

One can see his mind groping for the proper rubric in his
question to Meander:

Would it not grieve a king to be so abused,
And have a thousand horsemen ta'en away?
And, which is worse, to have his diadem
Sought for by such scald knaves as love him not?
I think it would: well then, by heavens I swear. . . .

(II, ii, 5-9)

And so, since it is for kings to be grieved under such circumstances, Mycetes resolves to be grieved. When he
thinks he has succeeded in meeting the requirements of
royalty, he is likely to exclaim proudly, "Is it not a kingly
resolution?" And when he knows it is beyond him to give
the requisite "great and thundering speech" he turns the job
over to Cosroe or Meander. This acknowledgement of
weakness is rare, however. Almost always he puffs himself
huge and ludicrously acts out his conception of a monarch.
It is comic enough for a common man to imitate a king, but
for a king to imitate a king is comedy of an exquisite flavor.

The folly of Mycetes being thus established by all the
emphasis of exposition, we cannot believe that one or two
of his sententious sayings prove him to be wise. His ex-
clamations upon the horror of war might be taken seriously
were they not accompanied by self-congratulation at the
"wisdom's lore" he displays in burying his crown in a hole
on the battlefield, "a goodly stratagem," as he says, "And

far from any man that is a fool." In such a context his pacifism merely shows him up as a comic coward.

More complicated is that other occasion when, having heard Meander refer to warriors sprung from dragon's teeth, he asks meekly:

> Was there such brethren, sweet Meander, say,
> That sprung of teeth of dragons venomous?
> *Mean.* So poets say, my lord.
> *Mycetes.* And 'tis a pretty toy to be a poet.
> Well, well, Meander, thou art deeply read;
> And having thee, I have a jewel sure.

(II, ii, 51-56)

There is no twinkle in the idiot eye of Mycetes as he makes these remarks. He is humbly ignorant, and we are to laugh at him for it. But there is a very mischievous twinkle in Marlowe's eye as he writes, for he is mocking at many things—at mythology, at the poet's profession, and, through the latter, at himself as poet. In short, we have here two levels of comic meaning: one appropriate to the character of Mycetes, the other appropriate to Marlowe, who uses the occasion for his own personal jocularity. The way in which Marlowe's subjective comic intention thus flows in to give a double effect to the situation is both very striking in itself and very revealing as to his habits of writing. We learn that he tends to obtrude his own laughter into the dramatic texture. And he has the redemptive gift of humorous self-criticism.

This gift is at work also in other scenes of the play, even those of serious and exultant poetry. After the famous passage in which Tamburlaine glories in the dream of riding in triumph through Persepolis, and Theridamas declares kings happier than gods, Tamburlaine turns to his friend and asks, "Why, say, Theridamas, wilt thou be a king?" There are few things more astonishing in Marlowe than

Theridamas' wry answer, "Nay, though I praise it, I can live without it." What is this but Marlowe gently ridiculing himself in respect to the soaring ambition which dominates his play and surely expresses one element of his own nature? Into the very sanctuary of vision comes critic reason with its slow, astringent smile. For Marlowe, more than most poets, has a dual temper. His eager imagination works often even unto wildness, and his guardian spirit of good sense constantly pulls it back, chastises, and moderates it. As long as the imagination is genuinely fresh and creative, as it is almost throughout Part I of *Tamburlaine*, the critical sense ratifies it and rests content with a few minor sallies. Or perhaps it would be better to say that the critical sense permeates the serious poetry and keeps it brilliantly sane. But when the imagination so flags that Marlowe has to whip it up to strained performance, then occurs a divorce from common sense, which avenges itself in satirical rebellion.

This is the explanation of certain strange upheavals in the character of Calyphas in Part II. It would appear that Marlowe originally intended to make another Mycetes of him, a fatuous coward whose part in the drama was to accentuate by contrast the bravery of Tamburlaine, and, in the scene where his father stabs him, to occasion exercise of the superhuman will of the hero. Calyphas' first speeches are in that tenor:

> But while my brothers follow arms, my lord,
> Let me accompany my gracious mother.
> They are enough to conquer all the world,
> And you have won enough for me to keep.
>
> (I, iv, 65-68)

This is sloth and cowardice in him, not conscious irony, else he would not here be stamped as "mother's boy " And immediately after he speaks, he is overwhelmed by a torrent of Tamburlaine's scorn, to which he ventures no reply. Some forty lines later when Tamburlaine enjoins his sons to cleave the head of Callapine in battle, Calyphas puts in:

> If any man will hold him, I will strike,
> And cleave him to the channel with my sword.[1]
>
> (I, iv, 102-3)

Again, he is making a serious offer, even being naively boastful. It represents his notion of how to be brave and helpful. One can imagine the guffaws of the Elizabethan spectators. And so, similarly, with those other remarks of his that fortifications are "dangerous to be done" and that wounds are "a pitiful sight." If dramatic emphasis means anything at all, he is guilty of womanish weakness in voicing them, for all the other characters scorn him and swell full chorus to the theme of military glory. He makes no defense of himself, conducts no argument.

Then at the start of Act IV comes the scene of his refusal to go to the battle. By all previous signs, this should be another demonstration of his comic futility, a mere fattening of the victim for the ignoble death he is soon to suffer under the dagger of Tamburlaine. But is it? For the first time he really speaks out to his brothers:

> If half our camp should sit and sleep with me,
> My father were enough to scare the foe;
> You do dishonor to his majesty,
> To think our helps will do him any good.

. . . .

---

1. In Beaumont and Fletcher's *The Maid's Tragedy* (III, ii, 31-39), the same sentiment is attributed to Calianax, a comic coward:

> I would give half my land
> That I durst fight with that proud man a little.
> If I had men to hold him, I would beat him
> Till he ask me mercy.

Take you the honour, I will take my ease;
My wisdom shall excuse my cowardice.

. . . .

They say I am a coward, Perdicas, and I fear as little their taratantaras, their swords or their cannon as I do a naked lady in a net of gold. . . .

. . . .

What a coil they keep! I believe there will be some hurt done anon amongst them.

(IV, i, 18-75)

So during eighty incredible lines he holds the stage, gibing sardonically at his father, his brothers, and the whole cult of war and honor. A new Calyphas seems to have come into being, very different from the contemptible comic butt of the prior scenes. This, however, is no part of Marlowe's dramatic intention. Just as, in the Mycetes episode, the remark about poets was an intrusion of Marlowe's private humor, not meant to credit Mycetes with wit, so here on a larger scale, Calyphas' irony is a personal outburst by the dramatist. Calyphas is intended to remain a laughing stock, and no doubt on the stage the momentum of his previously established reputation assists to that end. He even repeats some of the ideas which made him ridiculous before. But the trouble is that now they are given much too lengthy, vivid, and unanswered expression. To the attentive spectator it must sound like a satire on all the basic themes of the play.

Apparently what happened was that, after writing the whole of the first *Tamburlaine* play and half of the second, during which his imagination had been pitched fever high, Marlowe was thoroughly satiated and weary with excess. In the Calyphas scene his outraged sense of proportion took its revenge through mockery. It simply flooded the speeches of the renegade with an ungovernable vitality.

This cannot have been any part of Marlowe's plan for the drama, because obviously it not only confuses the character of Calyphas but also makes Tamburlaine himself ridiculous.[2] After the quiet derision of Calyphas the "great and thundering speech" with which the hero delivers his death-blow sounds too much like rant. Had the poet's humorous self-criticism been consistently active instead of bursting forth with periodic violence, it would have melted away the more florid excesses of the play, like the bragging contest between Zenocrate and Zabina, and the "Holla, ye pampered jades of Asia" theme. Had it been stronger still, Marlowe might never have written the play at all. But at this stage of his growth it was subordinated to his imagination and his capacity for intense feeling. Nor, indeed, was it ever quite to become dominant over them.

Humor of other kinds, however, abounds in the play. When not soaring or raging, Tamburlaine himself has a biting wit. He can take a dig at the practice of delivering an oration to troops before battle: "Or look you I should play the orator?" He can gibe at feminine susceptibility: "Techelles, women must be flattered." Or upon being begged by the Turkish concubines to spare their honors, retort sarcastically:

> Save your honours! twere but time indeed,
> Lost long before you knew what honour meant.
> (Pt. II, IV, iii, 86-87)

2. The same reason seems to me to render untenable the view that Marlowe intended Calyphas even in the earlier scenes to be a quiet mocker of his father, a lurking critic with whom we ought to sympathize. Marlowe's purpose is to keep Tamburlaine high throughout. Calyphas is merely a comic foil and an obstacle to be swept triumphantly away. It is better to regard the desertion-from-battle scene as a momentary, undramatic departure from this plan than to reduce the figure of Tamburlaine to laughter, thus overturning the whole emphasis of the dramatic exposition and violating the spirit in which the play was written.

Most typically of all, he and his followers can laugh with
absolute delight in jeering at and tormenting their captured
enemies. Even if, as seems probable, the prose scenes in
which most of this kind of thing occurs were written by
someone other than Marlowe, there can be no doubt that
Marlowe himself is responsible for those verse passages in
which fundamentally the same conception of humor prevails. A good deal of it is of a perfectly barbaric crudity,
unrelieved by any ingenuity of idea or statement. One can
forgive Marlowe for the cruelty—that was both Tambur-
lainian and Elizabethan—but not so easily for the obvious
crudity.

Not only the macabre joviality just described but virtually all of the humor in the play consists of laughter by
the strong at the weak. Under this principle come both the
ridicule of the buffoonery of Mycetes and Calyphas, who
are weak because they are cowardly and brainless, and
the ridicule of Bajazeth, Zabina, and the other Turks, who
are weak because they are conquered. It is saturated with
pride of power, pride of intellect. In varying degrees it is
hostile, stinging, or callous, but it always revolves in the
orbit of scorn. It is never gay, never kind. Both in what it
is and what it is not, it is functionally related to the play,
whose subject is merciless conquest. Nor are the interpolations of self-ridicule by the dramatist of a very different
caliber. They, too, are derisory. If the serious passions of
the play reveal the mind of the writer, the comedy does
so no less. Mockery at the world and at himself was already
a powerful force in the Marlowe of 1587.

The same spirit obtains in his next play, *Faustus,* but now
directed against religious ideas, as the subject of the plot
requires. We can clear the ground at the outset by con-
fidently putting aside all the comic prose scenes, for these

are not by Marlowe but by Nashe.[3] The humor that remains is chiefly the sardonic scoffing of Faustus in the day
of his prosperity. It is an essence very difficult of detection,
an ironic undertone, a faint apocalyptic glow that comes
and goes in his meditations. It is there in his first soliloquy
as he closes the jaws of his biblical syllogism and throws the
Vulgate aside with a disdainful smile. And it is present
likewise as he takes up the books of sorcery,

> These metaphysics of magicians,
> And necromantic books are heavenly,
>
> (I, i, 50-51)

stressing the last word to imply that, by contrast with a
harsh religion, magic has better claims to be called heavenly.
He achieves the same effect later, saying after he has succeeded in raising Mephistophilis, "I see there's virtue in
my heavenly words." The word "virtue" here also carries
an ironical double meaning. But the culmination of his
blasphemous wit is his appropriation of Christ's dying
words to the signing of his covenant with Lucifer: "Consummatum est; this bill is ended" (II, i, 74). Here Faustus
draws a ludicrous parallel between the ending of his search
for magical powers and the ending of Christ's mission of
salvation. The parallel is terrible as well as ludicrous, however, because we know that what is truly ended forever is
Faustus' possession of his own soul.

Now the remarkable fact is that this method of turning
a sacred text to shameful uses is the same that Marlowe employed so strikingly in the blasphemies of the Baines note.
Clearly, also, the anti-Christian gibing of the play, wherever
it occurs, is of a piece with the scoffing which marked the
poet's conversation as we have it from both Baines and

3. See Kocher, "Nashe's Authorship of the Prose Scenes in *Faustus*,"
MLQ, III (1942), 17-40.

Kyd. Further, in its generally sardonic and critical tone
the humor of *Faustus* has an underlying identity with that
of the *Tamburlaine* plays, as we have seen, and with that
of his subsequent dramas, as we are about to discover. All
these interrelations furnish the strongest kind of proof that,
as a comic writer no less than as a tragedian, Marlowe is
preponderantly subjective. Often the comedy in his plays
is both subjective and dramatic, that is, appropriate to the
character who speaks it, because that character itself is
essentially Marlowe. This is true, for example, of the protagonist of *Faustus*. We might also remark that subjective
self-criticism is absent from this play because *Faustus* is so
authentic a tragedy, so genuine in its inspiration, that Marlowe here found no cause to turn his laughter back upon
himself. And among its great sequences of rapture and
remorse there was but limited scope for even the ironic
humor described above.

With *The Jew of Malta* Marlowe's humor enters into
its kingdom, but it is not the kingdom of heaven. Actually,
the play is more a malicious comedy than anything else,[4]
although it calls itself a tragedy. This can be said even in
the face of the acknowledged grandeur of the conception
of Barabas' character in the opening scenes, and of the
persistence of a fantastically gruesome chain of events
ending in the death of the protagonist. It can be said
because at almost every point in the action Barabas is either
the dispenser or the butt of mockery, many scenes are given
over entirely or largely to comic effects, and the author
himself frequently drops into a mood of burlesque after
Act II.

From the first, much of what Barabas says is pregnant

---

4. As is well known, T. S. Eliot (*The Sacred Wood*, p. 84) has already
expressed the view that this drama is a burlesque rather than a serious
work.

with a bitter wit founded upon disdain. In this vein he refers to the merchant who will "sweat himself to death" counting paltry silver coins. Complacency is in his understatement, "So, then, there's somewhat come," when he hears of the arrival of his richly freighted argosies. Before long the edge of his reflection turns toward Christians, these Christians whose God knows not how to confer upon his subjects true "blessings," measured in wealth, so well as does the God of the Hebrews upon his. And where are these "fruits" of humility, brotherhood, and ultimate salvation, which the Christians preach?

> For I can see no fruits in all their faith,
> But malice, falsehood, and excessive pride,
> Which methinks fits not their profession.
>
> (I, i, 114-16)

The word "methinks" again adds a fine flavor of understatement. This is, of course, only the first of many attacks upon Christian mores, which form the chief topic for the satire of the play. Knowing what we do about Marlowe's opinions, we can have no whit of doubt that Barabas here and elsewhere is a vehicle for the dramatist's own derision. It is probable, indeed, that one of the attractions which persuaded Marlowe to write this play was the opportunity it gave him to voice his absorbing antagonism under a thin disguise. "Into almost every company he comes," said Baines, "he persuades men to atheism." One of the companies into which Marlowe oftenest came was the theatrical audience.

In Barabas' conference with his fellow Jews begins his habit of using an aside in order to end in some treacherous and guileful way a sentence he has been speaking aloud with ostensible friendship to those present:

If anything shall there concern our state,
Assure yourselves I'll look—unto myself.   [*Aside*
                                          (I, i, 170-71)

Barabas does the same thing scores and scores of times in
subsequent scenes. In quantity and skill this use of the
terminal aside by Marlowe is far beyond anything practised
by his contemporaries, or by himself in other plays. He
seems consciously to have been experimenting with a new
method for comedy. Apparently he was not especially
pleased with the result, for he did not employ it again to
any appreciable extent. It is certainly overworked in *The
Jew*. And indeed the number of effects obtainable with it
is distinctly limited. At its best it produces a sardonic sort
of humor, adding secretly a meaning that is quite the contrary of what is said openly. It depends, then, on the sudden
placing together of opposites, in a situation in which Barabas can hug the secret to himself, and enjoy a feeling of
triumph. It carries with it also a certain grimness because
it is often a forecast of disastrous things to follow.

The scene of the confiscation of Barabas' wealth by the
Governor is masterly, but complicated with many currents
and counter-currents through which analysis must feel its
way carefully. When Fernese makes his first approaches
to the subject of taxing the Jews, Barabas parries by pre-
tending to misunderstand. He affects a naive unawareness
which delights him because it puts his inquisitor off and
because it is such a contrast to what he thinks to be his own
genuine cunning. He has already hidden away the greater
part of his wealth. Then when the Governor makes his
demand for money forthright, the real argument begins.
Overtly what follows is designed as cat-and-mouse play,
Fernese being the cat who is to toy argumentatively with
Barabas and finally devour his Jewish wealth. This purpose

was no doubt executed successfully, to the glee of most of the Elizabethan spectators. For anyone, however, who like Marlowe found the Governor's appeals to Scripture meaningless and hypocritical, the force of the debate would strike in the opposite direction, against the Governor, and although the Christians of Malta might swallow Jewish riches they were themselves devoured judicially, morally, and legally. That this is in fact Marlowe's view of the case has already been argued in the chapter on religion.

In this scene as a whole, therefore, several very different varieties of humor are mingled with a subtlety that is sheer and beautiful. The audience is laughing with Fernese at the loss which has come upon the villainous Jew. Fernese himself may be arguing seriously part of the time, but he darts in some derisive thrusts as Barabas relies on pleas of individual innocence and helplessness. Barabas, on the other hand, is rather enjoying the encounter, for most of his gold is safely stowed, and he has his chance to tell these Christians what he thinks of their affectation of religion and morality. Marlowe manipulates it all with a covert smile. Ostensibly he is with Ferneze and the audience against Barabas; actually he is with none of them completely, but through Barabas he is singeing many a Christian beard with entire safety to himself. He has no particular sympathy for Judaism, but a great antipathy for Christianity.

The later part of this same scene, wherein Abigail pretends to turn nun in order to rescue her father's treasure from the convent, has some further acid observations on religion. Barabas glances time and again at the probity of the motives and faith of dwellers in religious houses: "religion hides many mischiefs from suspicion." As before, he is clearly speaking for Marlowe. And this time he would have the audience on his side also, because the reflection is upon an aspect of Catholicism, wherever anything specific is mentioned. The anti-Catholic vein continues with Abigail's first admission to the sisterhood, during which Barabas continually uses the terminal aside to give her directions about the gold while apparently cursing her. It is a comic scene for Barabas, participated in by the audience as against monks and nuns. In addition, Barabas diverts himself with making fun of some technical Christian terms, as for example "mortified," which Friar Jacomo uses to mean removed from the lusts of the flesh, but which Barabas takes in the literal, lay sense of "dead," a sense sardonically appropriate in his (and Marlowe's) opinion for one who goes into a convent. His riposte with the religious word "blind" employed by the Friar is also delectable, because, again in a lay sense, the Friar and all the religious are very blind indeed to Barabas' schemes, as well as blind in religion:

> *Friar Jac.* Barabas, although thou art in misbelief,
> And wilt not see thine own afflictions,
> Yet let thy daughter be no longer blind.
> *Bara.* Blind friar, I reck not thy persuasions.
> The board is marked thus that covers it.
>
> [*Aside to Abigail*
> (I, ii, 352-56)

We are familiar with this method of translating religious meanings into mundane ones of an unsuspected kind.

For a change, in the next scene Barabas himself becomes the object of derision, as he exclaims when Abigail throws down his gold to him from the window: "O girl! O gold! O beauty! O my bliss." He is the comic figure of the miser who so loves his money bags that raptures about them and about his daughter tumble from his lips in queer confusion. In him feelings usually disparate are equalized. But he resumes the satirical offensive in his battle of concealed cross-purposes with Lodowick, son of the hated Fernese.

Lodowick wants Abigail; Barabas wants revenge. It is the latter who wins, laying down as he does so a barrage of puns, some of them made openly and others in the terminal aside. Most of them, it must be confessed, have no great originality or freshness.

In the same scene with this grim comedy comes that confession of crimes by Barabas to Ithamor₂ which has been the subject of so much dispute among scholars. The question is whether Marlowe wrote words like these for Barabas seriously or with his tongue in his cheek:

> *Bara.* First, be thou void of these affections,
> Compassion, love, vain hope, and heartless fear,
> Be mov'd at nothing, see thou pity none,
> But to thyself smile when the Christians moan.
> *Itha.* O, brave, master. I worship your nose for this.
> *Bara.* As for myself, I walk abroad a nights
> And kill sick people groaning under walls:
> Sometimes I go about and poison wells, ...
>
> (II, iii, 170-77)

It is plain that the audience would take it seriously: the description would tally with their ideas of the fiendishness of Jews. It is almost as plain, I think, that Marlowe wrote it as a parody of those very ideas.

My argument is as follows. The speech is set in the middle of a scene which is alight with manifold irony in the jests of Barabas upon Lodowick, upon Christian intolerance, upon the lust of nuns, and upon the philosopher's stone. Marlowe would have had only to let himself be carried along on this mood in order to write a burlesque; but to do earnest character drawing he would have had to pull himself up short and induce a contrary mood. The crimes in which Barabas revels are incredibly numerous, diverse, and destructive if they are viewed with any critical judgment.

Now Marlowe, as we know, was exactly the man to possess such a judgment on this particular question. His rejection of the divinity of Christ would remove any possibility of his holding the Jews to be a nation accursed and devilish. If anything, his own revolt against Christianity would make him regard them with some favor. And his strong common sense would tell him that there were limits to the demoniac traits of even the most obnoxious Hebrew merchant. On the other hand, he could scarcely fail to be maliciously amused by the wild stories his countrymen swallowed about Jewish vindictiveness. He seems to be thus amused when, later in the play, he has Friar Jacomo ask Friar Barnadine concerning Barabas, "What, has he crucified a child?" That, again, is a scene of satire against the friars for their lewdness and their violation of the confidence of the confessional. An additional blow against their credulity about Jews is in keeping with the mocking tone of the whole surrounding action.

But the most important argument has yet to be made. Is it likely that the Marlowe who laughed at himself for permitting the much milder excesses of a Tamburlaine could look with sober face at this Barabas, this most monstrous of all his creations? To say so would be to say that his powers of ironical criticism had not merely diminished but atrophied altogether. The whole evidence of progression in his dramas is to the contrary. The other scenes of *The Jew of Malta*, as well as the other plays, prove that the critical sense becomes an increasingly powerful force in his mentality and at the same time grows ever more sardonic. It would seem, therefore, that as the melodramatic quality of the plot renders the character of Barabas more and more bizarre, Marlowe's judgment turns against him. Laughing at the grotesque he has begotten, Marlowe makes him yet more grotesque, and by turning him into a conscious caricature escapes from the accusations of his own criticism. It is the plot that is at fault. All interpreters of the drama have sensed the deterioration of the character of Barabas after Act II, but they have erred, I believe, in thinking that he becomes unnecessarily debased. What they should say is that in the first two acts he was unduly ennobled. Marlowe must have had the main outlines of the plot in mind before he started to write,[5] and this plot, with its phenomenal procession of murders and treacheries, is not capable of supporting a genuinely grand characterization of Barabas. The play begins with too lofty a treatment, one that could not be maintained when the plot really began to move. Marlowe recognized that in the second act, and threw the character away.

Not absolutely so, of course. Barabas retains his significance as a stalking-horse for satire and an instigator of much brilliant comedy in later scenes. A small but rather novel instance is his persuading Ithamore to poison Abigail in the nunnery. The terms with which Barabas caresses his servant are drawn from classical and Renaissance doctrines concerning friendship. Ithamore is called "my second self," "my love"; he is to be Barabas' heir; during Barabas' life he is to have free use of half his wealth; he is to be given Barabas' keys, and is to buy the costliest garments. This language and these offers bear a very close resemblance to those afterwards used by Edward to his friend Gaveston in *Edward II*.[6] But here, as employed by Barabas wheedlingly to his ragamuffin of a Turkish slave, they sound sus-

5. In all his other plays Marlowe can be shown to have had sources which provided him in advance with a definite plot. Although no specific source for *The Jew of Malta* has yet been discovered, it seems likely that there was one, and unlikely that here alone he improvised a plot as he wrote, without knowing what turn the action was to take next.

6. Their derivation from classical friendship theory is shown by L. J. Mills, "The Meaning of *Edward II*," *MP*, XXXII (1934), 11-31.

piciously like a parody of all those exalted theories. And
the more so because, as Bennett remarks, every performance of the offers is deftly postponed. It would be like
Marlowe to travesty in one play ideas which he dramatized
with intent passion in another.[7]

But the best of Marlowe's comic scenes is that in which
the two friars accuse Barabas of the poisoning. Before the
friars come on stage, Barabas jokes about the yearly swell-
ing of the nuns not caused by poison. No need to poison
the monks: they will all die of grief now that the nuns are
dead. When the friars enter and begin to make their
charges, the comedy at first consists in the adroit way in
which Barabas saves himself, embroils his two antagonists
with each other, and opens to full view their squabbling
worldliness, "which methinks fits not their profession." He
first tries to shunt them away from the dangerous subject
by innocent misinterpretations of their charges. In each case
Barnadine explodes with some words of accusation, which
are interrupted and repeated by the eager Jacomo, who is
in turn broken in upon by Barabas, finishing the sentence
with a safely naive twist.

> *Friar Barn.* Barabas, thou hast—
> *Friar Jac.* Ay, that thou hast—
> *Bara.* True, I have money; what though I have?
> *Friar Barn.* Thou art a—
> *Friar Jac.* Ay, that thou art a—
> *Bara.* What needs all this? I know I am a Jew.
>
> (IV, i, 29-34)

For four or five rounds this comic cycle whirls until
Barabas can no longer keep them from coming to the point.

7. At IV, iv, 95-105, Ithamore speaks a parody of Marlowe's poem,
The Passionate Shepherd to his Love. This may be another instance of
Marlowe's self-mockery. But the parody may have been written by
Heywood, whose hand is suspected in this portion of the play.

He then takes another tack, bursting into a wail of repentance. His sins, he cries, have made him very wealthy, but what is wealth? The holy men who are listening to him know as well as he that according to all Christian doctrine wealth cannot save a sinner, especially a Jewish sinner. If only whipping could help him, how he would whip himself! Ithamore agrees. He, too, is anxious to whip himself; but, he adds quickly, whipping could do no good. Barabas then dwells succulently on the immense extent of his possessions and, by way of climax, announces impersonally to the listening air that he would give all these to any religious house which would accept him as a convert. That sets the friars bidding against each other, with Barabas seeming to favor first one and then the other. We learn that the denizens of one religious house may consider the usages of another religious house too grievous for the flesh. The affair must end in blows, over which Barabas presides gleefully until, employing the phrase so often found in the exhortations of the godly to those more sinful than they, he quiets the tumult with the grave remark, "This is mere frailty: brethren, be content." And so, after a few more girds at the friars, this little masterpiece of satirical farce comes to an end. It is astounding that the man who wrote it should ever have been thought wanting in humor.

But despite the perfection of some of its individual scenes, *The Jew of Malta* as a whole is far more shapeless in construction and confused in meaning than even the *Tamburlaine* plays, and provides a notable contrast with *Faustus*. Not only is it an unreasoned mass of melodramatic incident but it bulges grotesquely under the pressure of Marlowe's satirical impulses, which dart in at every opportunity or no opportunity to scourge Christians for their devout wealth-getting and slack religion. Paradoxically enough, much of this satire would inevitably go over the heads of the audience. The play would still be for most a story about a bad, bad Jew who came to a bad end. Lost upon them, no doubt, would be the full import of the drama as a commentary on Christianity, and certainly the ironic consent with which Marlowe abandoned the figure of Barabas to caricature in the second act. Thus bounded in vision, they could not have understood the piece for all that it assuredly is, a rich complex of many-faceted humor, a carnival of acrid wit.

Edward II, of course, is composed in an entirely different key. It is almost pure tragedy, containing no specifically comic scenes or personages. Religious satire of a sort is not altogether missing in the horseplay by which the Catholic Bishop of Coventry is "christened anew" in the foul water of the gutters, while his residence is confiscated because "What should a priest do with so fair a house?" And Baldock's affectation of a holy exterior "though inwardly licentious enough" may really be a slur at Puritan hypocrisy, as many scholars believe. These, however, are incidentals. The principal type of humor in the play, what there is of it, is not religious, nor is it even political. It lies in the personal sarcasm developed as the various contending factions snarl and bark at one another through all five acts of the drama. Its components are scorn, hatred, and wit.

A characteristic form of this wit is the catching up of something said by the adversary and quickly capping it. This may be done by using the same word, punning on it, and adding an idea which turns the meaning against the other party. So the Bishop of Coventry, when his enemies order that he be "conveyed" to the Tower, rejoins "True, true," taking the word "convey" in its slang meaning of steal. Frequent also is the sarcastic statement which on its face purports to mean one thing but clearly is seen to mean the opposite because of the circumstances under which it is spoken, as when the earls of Warwick and Lancaster threaten the detested Gaveston:

> *War.* All Warwickshire will love him for my sake.
> *Lan.* And northward Gaveston hath many friends.
>
> (I, i, 128-29)

Since the first half of the drama is almost one long quarrel, and this sneering, jeering tone is heard whenever the words begin to fly, the amount of it is vast. Often it shades so imperceptibly into outright anger that one is hard put to say whether or not it is there in any given line of the dialogue. It lurks everywhere in the atmosphere of the scenes of belligerent retort. On occasion it has an artistic subtlety. Far too often, however, it is merely heavy and contrarious, without those spreading overtones which make this species of satire excellent. The differences are due not to delineation of character, inasmuch as they crop out impartially in almost everybody in the dramatis personae, but rather to the varying felicity of Marlowe's sarcastic vein.

At its most ferocious this humor develops into a macabre death's-head jesting. The death of an enemy is made an occasion of witticism. Edward, upon conquering and capturing the rebellious barons, jokes, "methinks you hang the heads, / But we'll advance them, traitors," giving the word "advance" the double meaning of "promote" and "nail high" after execution. And Baldock at the same time remarks,

> These barons lay their heads on blocks together;
> What they intend the hangman frustrates clean.
>
> (III, iii, 89-90)

with a like pun on "lay heads together," meaning both "plot" and "suffer simultaneous beheading." Other examples are frequent. Particularly, the spirit of this humor, and in fact of the humor of the play as a whole, is summed up and made incarnate in Lightborn, the murderer of Edward. He expresses in purest kind its egoistic, mordant, and malignant quality. Thus in his first interview with Mortimer he laughs when Mortimer fears he may relent. "Relent! ha, ha! I use much to relent." The moral element in the possibility does not reach him at all, and he is amused at the wildness of the idea as he looks back over his life's experience. He smiles complacently at Mortimer's failure to understand how expert he is in his profession, that delightful game of whose "tricks" he is such a master. Even about his name hovers a suggestion of irony, that he should be called Lightborn, this creature of the nether darkness.

Not much range is added to the humor of the play by the "Machiavellian" amusement which Gaveston and Mortimer introduce into their soliloquies. It also is acidly contemptuous. For example, Mortimer as lord protector is elated by the consciousness of his power and scornful of those who are deceived by his cloak of humility:

> They thrust upon me the protectorship,
> And sue to me for that that I desire.
> While at the council-table, grave enough,
> And not unlike a bashful puritan,
> First I complain of imbecility,
> Saying it is *onus quam gravissimum;*
> Till, being interrupted by my friends,
> *Suscepi* that *provinciam* as they term it; . . .
>
> (V, iv, 56-63)

The idea that he should achieve his ends by assuming the countenance of a Puritan and pleading incompetence is delicious to him: both these methods are such complete misrepresentations of what he knows himself to be. He can laugh at the gullible peers, at his own ingenuity, and at the figure he must have made while he worked out his designs.

The solemnity of the legal terms involved in the farce is another delightful aspect.

And so it is clear that such humor as we find in this drama is not of the kind to soften or relieve the impact of the tragedy. Rather, it serves to strengthen our impression that we have here to do with a hard world and, for the most part, hard people. Sarcasm is the prevailing note. On almost every face is the slow corrosive smile, the long stare, in every mouth the chosen and taunting speech. Pitiless delight in seeing the adversary go down is combined with pleasure in playing with verbal parallels and antitheses. This latter pleasure may be denominated chiefly intellectual, the former emotionally egoistic. In this play the two are seldom found apart. And both, because of their universal dissemination among the characters and their resemblance to the comic effects in others of Marlowe's plays, seem referable back in some degree to the nature of the playwright.

Death's-head jesting is, again, the most notable feature of the humor of *The Massacre at Paris*. And, as one would expect, Guise is its most skillful practitioner. All three of the murders which he personally commits on the night of St. Bartholomew are dispatched with a joke appropriate to the profession of his victim. He says as he stabs the two schoolmasters, "I'll whip you to death with my poniard's point." Comparing his dagger to the birch rods which they have used to whip their pupils, he turns their own methods against them. He will play at being schoolmaster, but from that birching they will not recover. In like vein, he employs a show of logic in killing the logician Ramus:

> *Argumentum testimonii est inartificiale.*
> To contradict which, I say, Ramus shall die:
> How answer you that? your *nego argumentum*
> Cannot serve, sirrah.—Kill him.

The Latin quotation is from Ramus' textbook on logic.
Guise refutes the principle with the statement "Ramus shall
die," which is a mere personal assertion (*argumentum
testimonii*) and yet will not be *inartificiale* (incapable in
itself of proving the case) but *artificiale*, absolutely conclusive of the truth of what it asserts. Let Ramus deny it if
he can.

A number of other instances of this dire humor turn
upon religious meanings in the Catholic-Protestant struggle
which is a central topic of the play. Guise, killing the
Protestant preacher Loreine, exclaims:

> *Guise.* 'Dearly beloved brother'—thus 'tis written.
>   [*Stabs Loreine, who dies.*
> *Anjou.* Stay, my lord, let me begin the psalm.
>   (sc. v, ll. 69-70)

If I understand this correctly, Guise parodies the ritual of
the Church of England for morning and evening prayer,
in which the preacher, preliminary to the general confession, begins his address to the congregation with the words
"Dearly beloved brethren." With his dagger Guise writes
the affectionate remainder in the unprotected flesh of
Loreine. Anjou's offer to begin the psalm is both an added
parody of the Anglican service, since the general confession
and absolution are followed by the singing of a psalm, and
a claim to share in the assassination.

The play is full of other examples, but only one is of
unusual interest. Just before the slaughter commences,
Guise makes his associates swear by the crosses in their
burgonets that they will kill all whom they suspect of
heresy. Dumaine accedes, "I swear by this, to be unmerciful" (V, 4). It is upon the cross, the symbol of mercy, that
he swears to do unmerciful deeds! This is a very neat bit
of Marlovian irony. The immediate reflection is upon the

Catholic perpetrators of the massacre. But the larger reflection, as usual, is upon all Christians who hide their crimes in the shadow of the cross.

Guise's ridicule of religion, "a word of such a simple sound," rounds out the anti-Christian humor of the drama with its familiar strain. And, all told, it can be said of *The Massacre*, as of *The Jew of Malta* and *Faustus*, that most of the humor deals in some way with religion. It contains also a number of secular elements, however. The cutpurse episode may perhaps not have been written by Marlowe, but it could easily be his. The joke of cutting off the thief's ear and then offering it back to him in exchange for the gold buttons he has stolen is brutal but clever. We know very well that Marlowe can be both more brutal and less clever than this. As for the Soldier's bawdy remarks about Guise's wife, they are certainly worthy, with their string of metaphors drawn from commerce and law, of Marlowe's ingenuity at its best. Their good male lewdness, relatively rare in his dramas, helps to maintain normalcy against the insinuations of the homosexual passages.

It is a relief to pass from the murkiness of this play to the clear, bright air of *Hero and Leander*. In the poem Marlowe leaves behind him the harsh, conquerable world of the dramas and enters a new and lovely region through which he can move lightly. Here in the country of myths, he is far from hated institutions, far from enemies, and there are no rancors in the vessel of his peace. His imagination is delightedly busy in holiday mood, yet with real effort to create something as beautiful as may be. He half believes what he writes. The half of him that does not believe keeps the poem in the spirit of play, and sometimes smiles good-humoredly at the unreal material of the story. But at the same time his imagination affirms the validity of what it creates.

And so arises a form of humor which is largely whimsy, indulging in escapades of playful exaggeration. Its closest kin, strangely, is the wild burlesque of the final acts of *The Jew of Malta*, but here all is airiness and good temper. Even so, Marlovian humor without irony is unthinkable, and there is a trace of it in the situation with which the poem opens. Hero is a priestess of Venus, sworn to preserve herself chaste in the service of the goddess of unchastity. The phrase "Venus' nun" points the contradiction. But it also introduces a further element of humor, since it is Elizabethan slang for prostitute.[8] Chaste Hero has classed herself with the lewdest of her sex. Against this inconsistency in her position, Leander directs a long series of arguments in which Marlowe's logical faculty amuses itself with devising pretty sophistries. There never was a better picture of logic at play.

Then through sheer pleasure in movement and freedom his fancy spins out several long digressions in no wise germane to the plot. It invents a whole new myth to account for the enmity between Mercury and the Fates, and hence for the sad luck scholars have in the world. Marlowe was not forgetting that he himself was one of them. The episode is really too long, but he was carried along on an intent imagination which rejoiced at its own elaborate fabric. It is in the same temper of high-spirited make-believe that the Neptune episode is volunteered. But perhaps the homosexual tone there is not altogether impersonal.

The many fantastic conceits of the poem are likewise the work of a playful fancy:

8. Gosson, *Schoole of Abuse* (London, 1587), sig. E7^r: "Other [prostitutes] there are which...either couch themselues in Allyes, or blind Lanes, or take sanctuary in fryeries, or liue a mile from the Cittie like Venus Nunnes in a Cloyster at Newington...or some such place, where like penitents, they deny the worlde, and spende their dayes in double devotion."

> And as she wept, her tears to pearl he turn'd,
> And wound them on his arm, and for her mourn'd.
>
> (I, 375-76)

Cupid's winding of the tear-turned pearls on his arm is the touch which shows that Marlowe is only toying with the image, heightening it to excess, not attempting any serious poetic effect. And the same mood and method produce some mad excursions into the pathetic fallacy. When Leander swims, the waves

> mounted up, intending to have kiss'd him,
> And fell in drops like tears because they miss'd him.
>
> (II, 173-74)

These are true expressions of the spirit of mischief.

Another important element in the humor is laughter at the maneuverings of the lovers, which leads Marlowe to some wryly sententious comments on human nature, particularly feminine human nature: "Women are won when they begin to jar" (I, 332). In other words, the imaginative, recognizably unreal element in the story is not the only one. At many points the unreality passes over into reality through temporary or partial perceptions of Hero and Leander as actual persons. So an adult telling a fairy tale to his child sometimes becomes grave or faintly ironical as he sees within his tale the inevitable parallels to the world of actual experience.

The smudges of satirical realism, however, are neither very dark nor very numerous. The importance of the poem to our discussion is that here is celebrated at last the marriage of poetical beauty with humor. These have remained antagonistic, or separate, or, at most, only latently coexistent in the plays. There we see a more or less autonomous strand of grand and serious aspiration or suffering, which is Marlowe soaring; beside it is another fairly autonomous strand of irony, which is Marlowe earth-bound and critical. The union of the two in *Hero and Leander* is a product which moves with lovely grace in the middle air. The descriptive beauties of the poem are of the true springs of Helicon. And while he works Marlowe smiles to see the perfect lines drop from his fingers, smiles at the never-changing ways of lovers, their subterfuges and their happiness, touches with whimsy the episodes and images, and plays gently with the mythology of old Greece, so untrue and so true.

The growth of Marlowe's humor is now visible in panorama. *Hero and Leander*, for the very reason that it is so nearly fantasy, stands somewhat apart from the main line of development. In the plays, where the temper is much more realistic, the trend is toward a laughter more and more acid and malicious. And the attendant great advance in skill of execution is measured by the difference between the clumsy foolery of *Dido* and the wild burlesque of *The Jew* or the devil's wit of *The Massacre*. As the plays mature, the frequency of humor also increases. On the whole, however, it is still subordinated to serious tragic purposes: except in *The Jew*, it seldom gets complete possession of a scene but remains a fitful, if widespread, emanation of character. Throughout his works Marlowe's favorite objects of ridicule continue to be, of course, Christian religion and gross excess of any sort. On the latter score, it is much to the credit of this subjective dramatist and poet of the bolder passions that he has objectivity and sense of balance enough to laugh at the exaggerations in his own writing. Sometimes, as in *Hero and Leander*, he even amuses himself by manufacturing them whimsically.

Thus except for those relatively infrequent cases in which a pure spirit of play is uppermost, Marlowe's humor

is predominantly critical, a weapon of attack against men
and ideas. Nevertheless its intellectuality is not of the broad
philosophic sort which dissects a whole civilization or regards human frailties under the aspect of eternity. Aimed
at specific, limited objectives, it directs our eyes to certain
immediate abuses in the life Marlowe knew. We do not
glimpse prospect beyond prospect of comic meaning
opened to us by a pregnant phrase or ridiculous attitude, as
we often do in Shakespeare. Nor, one must add, do we feel
in Marlowe the almost divine mildness which tempers
Shakespearean comedy with the realization of human fellowship and a common human destiny.

On the contrary, we are obliged to raise the question
whether Marlowe's humor is not ultimately vindictive.
Obviously this is a problem of the gravest difficulty. When
a writer satirizes an idea, a custom, an institution, he may
do so because on purely rational grounds he rejects it as
unsound or because he hates it emotionally for its effect
on himself or on others. Often all these motives, and others
with them, are present in subtle combinations. One can
appreciate how obscurely the intellectual may shade into
the emotional, the selfish into the altruistic, among the
causes of critical laughter. Nevertheless, I cannot avoid the
impression that in Marlowe's case malice is the first and
ruling factor. Within limitations which I have discussed
elsewhere, the emotional in Marlowe seems to me stronger
than the rational, the subjective than the objective, the
egoistic than the altruistic. It must be significant that his
humor is everywhere so hard in tone and so notably lacking in kindliness. What single character in all of the dramas
is capable of really good-hearted laughter? Those who
laugh do so in a baleful strain, instinct with pride of power,
moral indifference, or a savage gladiatorial joy. A humor
that intended well to humanity could not always have reveled

in destruction, without ever showing the positive aspect of its sympathy. I believe, therefore, that as a general thing Marlowe's laughter was malicious in the worst sense and came from the worst side of his nature. He laughed where he hated; he lacked the high faculty of laughing also where he loved. His more humane sentiments and deeper vision belong to what is serious in him, and are essential to his tragic genius. But it is not well to set up too sharp a dichotomy between his tragic and his comic gifts with respect to their morality, since even the former never completely escaped the circumscription of egoism.

Had Marlowe been interested enough in satire to treat it as a separate form and to discipline himself in its construction, his genius might have shone as brilliantly in this field as in tragedy. He had many of the qualities of a great satirist—the brains, the sense of humor, the anger, and the power of devastating expression. These were attaining a growing realization in his work up to the time of his death, and there is no reason to doubt that the process would have continued. The prophecy may be ventured that at his full stature Marlowe would have equalled or exceeded any other satirist of his age in the deftness of his multilateral scorn, seasoned with flights of whimsy and, above all, a saving power of self-ridicule.

12. THE EVOLUTION OF MARLOWE'S CHARACTER

FROM TIME TO TIME IN THE FOREGOING CHAPTERS Marlowe's ideas and emotions have been traced back to ultimate origins in the particular constitution of his psychology. His views on ethics and politics, for example, were explained by a theory of his basic aloofness to human affairs. Occasion is now ripe for a more ample statement of this theory, comprehensive in scope and supported, as well as may be, by a detailed interpretation of the changing qualities of his work. To stop short of some such theory is, I think, to be left with a mere miscellany of fragments. We must seek a final principle.

Briefly, the sequence of Marlowe's dramas is, in its most fundamental terms, a record of the discovery and expanding perception of the world outside the self, accompanied by an increasing identification of the self with that world. The Marlowe of *Tamburlaine* is a man who lives, psychologically if not literally, exiled from humanity, alone with the transcendent forms of his imagination and the hopes of his passionate ambition; the Marlowe of *Edward II* and *Hero and Leander* has moved a long way towards the world of human affairs and sympathies.

What we miss especially in *Dido*, the earliest of the plays, is the immense and pervading consciousness of the self

300

which the other dramas teach us to expect of Marlowe. This fact suggests that the drama is a very early one, written a number of years before *Tamburlaine*. The inference is that Marlowe was then in that period of youth, common to many sensitive spirits, when the personality is not yet fully aware of its own identity as against the world which surrounds it. At this period passions and disappointments are of course felt, but there is still not the keen sense of the individuality from which they emanate. Thus Marlowe to a certain extent throws himself into the frenzy of his Dido— and this was undoubtedly what attracted him in the theme— but he does not turn the situation into one in which the single ego opposes the world, as he was later to do in his four great plays. He does not, for instance, bring out nearly the full possibilities for Dido's struggle against the destiny which snatches Aeneas away from her. He might have made of this another such despairing conflict of the individual with a hostile universe as he painted in *Faustus*. Instead, he hardly makes Dido aware that it is the gods who are the ultimate cause of her suffering. The issue is not yet clearly seen because the idea of the self has not definitely emerged into consciousness.

Of the manner of this emergence we have no record.[1] Between *Dido* and *Tamburlaine* there is a silence, and when it is broken we hear the declamations of Tamburlaine's colossal ego, already at full growth.

In *Tamburlaine* the self is to a great extent alone in the universe, blinded in mists and separated both from God and man. The dominant note of the drama as far as religion

1. Tucker Brooke's suggestion (*Life*, p. 41) that it was Marlowe's moving from Cambridge to the more turbulent life of London which developed his qualities of wilfulness and iconoclasm is tempting. But since 1 *Tamburlaine* seems to have been conceived, and possibly written, at Cambridge, the awakening must have occurred while Marlowe was still a student.

is concerned is Tamburlaine's strength and self-dependence. He uses the idea of a Divine Power to enhance himself, since he alternately considers himself a scourge divinely appointed to devastate the earth and utters threats against the Deity. In neither case does he show the humility before God which is at the root of all genuine religion. Tamburlaine, like Faustus, conceives of God as a compelling force, a potential or actual enemy, not as a source and object of love. We must notice, however, that through the dominant tone of defiance in the play sometimes sounds, as if at a distance, a softer note of submission. The depth of poetry with which Marlowe writes Bajazeth's tragedy, the great laments of Zenocrate for the fall of earthly potentates, and Tamburlaine's final recognition of the necessity of death show that behind the veil of splendor and achievement the dramatist sees the face of universal human destiny and is filled with a sense of his own impotence. So the sense of weakness is already competing in his nature with the sense of strength proper to youth, each succeeding the other according to the mood. But the sense of strength is at this time prevalent.

Tamburlaine is aloof from man as well as from God. His quest of terrestrial power is only incidentally an entry into the affairs of the world; in its essence it is a lofty and remote aspiration, pitched in ideal regions. He does not consider himself a member of human society but stands far withdrawn as the sole and unique being of the world, regarding mankind much as a child regards the supply of colored blocks with which he builds beautiful houses. The most obvious instance is his ruthlessness to all who oppose his march towards world dominion. But it will be found that he also essentially lacks sympathy for the being he loves best—Zenocrate. When he sees her sorrowing for the danger of her father and her country, what touches him most is not the knowledge that she is suffering but the sight of her loveliness in tears. He is wanting in the power of suffering with others, or, indeed, of feeling with them in any real degree. They must come to him; he cannot go to them. And so when Zenocrate dies, his clamors are mere exercises in passion and have not the simplicity of a true grief. Similarly, when Theridamas mourns the death of Olympia he thinks of her loss in terms of vanished beauty, not of her pain or of his own loneliness and heartbreak. For Tamburlaine and Theridamas (and, later, for Faustus) the women they love are not so much human beings as symbols of or pathways to eternal Beauty, and love is less a matter of human tenderness than a reaching upwards to the inexpressible, a form of worship. Psychologically, such men are perfect egoists; they are immersed in the experience of their own passion; their emotions are highly abstracted, almost impersonal.

We must modify these observations by remarking that Tamburlaine is capable of warm friendship for a few, but we are also entitled to notice that this friendship is based upon a complete subservience of their personalities to his own. Tamburlaine is never called upon to show that real understanding which becomes necessary when there are differences of opinion and interest between friends. In short, such a friendship is not inconsistent with a very considerable degree of blindness and self-centeredness in the protagonist.

Beyond this narrow circle of friends lies for Tamburlaine a hostile world where ceaseless struggle for mastery is ordained by Nature. We find in all four of Marlowe's chief dramas this opposition between a central figure, with or without a few supporters, and the system which hems him in. With Tamburlaine, Barabas, and Gaveston, moreover, the social iconoclasm is intensified by the fact that they, like Marlowe, are of base or detested lineage. It is difficult not to conclude that this was the attitude of Marlowe himself and that he felt in varying degree not merely an aloofness but a positive enmity to the generality of mankind. I shall try to show that this feeling was mollified as he grew older.

Thus far the discussion has centered upon Tamburlaine as representative of Marlowe's personal qualities. But also from an examination of the minor characters and of the structure of the play we can learn something of the extent to which the dramatist faces away from mankind. These characters are on the whole so flat, so two-dimensional, so unparticularized as to indicate that Marlowe at this period knew little about human beings other than himself. There is in effect only one character in the drama, and that is Tamburlaine, who is fundamentally Marlowe. The other characters awake to temporary life only when they become like Tamburlaine—that is, when they have occasion to express either the defiant aspiration or passionate surrender which conflict in the temperament of the dramatist, and hence of Tamburlaine. Bajazeth, Zabina, Zenocrate, Theridamas and the rest are mere platitudes except when they are illumined by these emotions; even their utterances are not differentiated, and what one says might well have been said by another. In brief, Marlowe is here not a creator of character but a recorder of his own inner experience, which he distributes among his dramatis personae without transmuting and individualizing it as a dramatist should.

There are a few hopeful exceptions to these generalizations, however. The cowardice of Mycetes and Calyphas, particularly the latter, the madness of Zabina, the devotion of Zenocrate and Olympia are described with a certain power of insight—a power which already promises the far more skillful characterizations of *Edward II*. But the traits mentioned are still close to the periphery of Marlowe's nature.

Again, whatever his sympathy with Tamburlaine, Marlowe is objective enough to set forth clearly the hostile judgments which the normal social being would pass upon his pride and ambition. So he gives to the lesser and antagonistic characters a morality quite opposite to that of the central figure. They subscribe to a code of ethics which is that of order, duty, law, and social rights, and which condemns the depredations of Tamburlaine. It is they, and not he, who voice doctrines which we recognize as those of accepted Elizabethan ethics. In subsequent dramas we shall watch this social morality acquiring a more prominent function, but the present play is so constructed as to give it only a very subordinate place. For by virtue of the brilliant and commanding light in which Tamburlaine strides gigantic, flinging his shadow over the world of the drama, this condemnation of his opponents serves only to heighten his stature and carries no conviction in its own right.

In summary, then, *Tamburlaine* reveals Marlowe as primarily self-sufficient, remote from both God and man. He stands upon the mountain peaks questioning the stars and thinks himself either the darling of the gods or their equal. Human beings are shapes of which he is dimly aware as floating in the shadows on the boundaries of the clear daylight of his own consciousness. Nevertheless, there is in the drama a muted strain of recognition that human power is ephemeral and of nascent understanding of other men. In this strain lie the seeds of future development.

Faustus repeats many of the elements already noticed in *Tamburlaine*. Here again a single giant figure, consumed with the hunger for empire, is at war with an inimical world order; again the theme is laid high in the empyrean, far from the ordinary pursuits of men; again the men themselves, other than Faustus who is essentially Marlowe, are but vaguely realized; again the power of sympathy for anyone save the protagonist is at a minimum.

But in spite of all these similarities, *Faustus* is different from *Tamburlaine* in one significant respect: it shifts the emphasis from the strength of the self to its weakness, from victory to defeat. *Tamburlaine* may be called a drama of exultation which happens to end in death, whereas *Faustus* is a drama of spiritual death which happens to begin with exultation. The latter drama is, among other things, an utterance of Marlowe's fears for his own destiny as a free-thinking rebel from the laws of a Christian cosmos. But the important fact is that an unfolding in Marlowe's nature now leads him to choose the theme of the helplessness of even the most titanic human ego before God. He could not have written *Faustus* without feeling this impotence far more keenly than he did in the earlier play. Tamburlaine's arrogance is indeed overthrown—if death in the midst of victory be an overthrow—but Marlowe depicts his fall with none of the agonizing truth, the intensity of personal realization, which characterizes that of Faustus. As has been said, *Tamburlaine* stresses the success of ambition, *Faustus* its failure.

We must observe, however, that though Faustus confesses his weakness in the hands of the Deity, he remains unreconciled. He is led shrieking off, shattered by superior power but without love in his heart. Tamburlaine has the same disposition to look upon God as a repressing force, potentially an enemy. *Hero and Leander* speaks of Fate rather than God.[2] In fact, nowhere in Marlowe is God considered a dispenser of love and mercy; at most, he is legislator and judge who effects justice upon earth. For Marlowe, as for many another man, the way to see God as

2. First Sestiad, lines 167ff.

love might have been through the worship of beauty. He was intensely spiritual, as most poets are spiritual, in that the outward and visible impressions of beauty in women and in nature created in him states of exaltation which rose far above the physical world which gave them birth. They differed from the religious ecstasy only in not being directed towards a Supreme Being. Had Marlowe considered beautiful forms as the immediate products of the Creator's hand and looked consistently beyond them to that Creator, he would have been the most religious of men. That he failed to do so is a tragic circumstance for which the Elizabethan view of Christianity was probably responsible. Religion in that era still taught men that the world of the senses, whereby beauty must enter in, belonged to the Devil; so that in order to love God it was necessary to scorn the world. This dichotomy appears significantly in *Faustus* when Helen, the incarnation of earthly beauty, is summoned up to seduce Faustus from his desire for God.

The recognition of the powerlessness of the self before God has important, if indirect, consequences for Marlowe's relations with men. It constitutes an advance towards greater fellow-feeling for mankind, for the sense of one's own weakness is the strongest incentive for associating oneself in act, sympathy, and thought with others of the race, while the sense of strength has the contrary effect.

In the main, however, *Faustus* is still basically unsocial as being a colloquy solely between Faustus and the ruling powers of the universe, in which other human beings drop away and are forgotten. It is left for the later dramas to give to the idea of human society its proper emphasis.

The Jew of Malta begins this process and embodies some remarkable changes. For one thing, although the Barabas of the first two acts is touched with the grandiose dreams of Tamburlaine and Faustus, the atmosphere of the drama on the whole is that of the world of men, not of some luminous world of the imagination. We have to do here with daily intercourse, with trade, religious intolerance, revenge, petty greed, politics, and the like.

On the psychological side, there is a growing realism in the depicting of the environment and the people, including a reduction of the disproportion in size which existed between Tamburlaine and the personages among whom he moved. Barabas takes account of the psychology of the people with whom he deals and meets them on a footing of equality in a way never condescended to by Tamburlaine, or by Faustus, for that matter. Moreover, these minor characters are drawn with far greater discernment. We no longer feel in them the strain, the wild rhetorical striving, the woodenness of the lesser people of the earlier dramas; they have steadiness and normality. The portraits of Ithamore, the courtesan, Abigail, the friars, Lodowick, Mathias, and the rest exhibit some excellent strokes. These signs indicate a growth of objective insight into human nature.

On the ethical side we can list several new elements. Barabas is Marlowe's first "Machiavellian" villain. In drawing his character Marlowe associates for the first time the egoistic aspiration of his former great personages with contrivances of malignity and treachery which the drama authentically designates as villainy. The novelty here consists both in this new association and in the acceptance of the moral standards of society in calling it evil. *Tamburlaine*, the drama, had not held Tamburlaine up for condemnation; and *Faustus*, while officially regarding Faustus as the worst of all possible sinners in his offense against God, had required for him pity, not hatred. Barabas, on the other hand, is an object of abhorrence by the drama not merely as a Jew but as a scoundrel.

Again, the play depicts Barabas' ruin at the hands of the

society whose laws he has broken. Marlowe is here for the first time introducing human society as a factor which enforces its moral laws successfully against the unrestrained egoism of the protagonist. Tamburlaine had defied them without retribution, and Faustus, if he had violated them at all, did so in a far different sense. This recognition of the power of the moral sanctions of the community is a tremendous gain in realism.

It will not do, however, to overstress the advance made by this drama towards objectivity. Subjective elements remain in plenty. Thus Barabas, especially he of the first acts, has much of Marlowe's sympathy. With him, as with Tamburlaine and Faustus, it is still a case of one against the world. He retains something of the appetite and the vision which distinguish his mighty predecessors. Furthermore, Marlowe uses him as a mouthpiece for criticism of Christian intolerance, greed, and hypocrisy. In other words, Barabas still stands for one side of Marlowe's nature: a dark intransigeance. The importance of the play from our point of view is, first, that this intransigeance now operates more strictly within the everyday sphere, and, second, that it is assigned to a lower position both psychologically and ethically, while around it grows up a host of observations and sympathies contrary to it.

If we now look backwards for a moment we see that *Tamburlaine*—with the reservations noted—shows egoistic ambition as subject neither to God nor man; *Faustus* shows it as subject to God but not to man; and now *The Jew* shows it as subject both to man and to God acting through man. *The Jew of Malta* is thus a symptom of the rise, both psychologically and ethically, of the idea of human society in Marlowe's perception.

In *Edward II* Marlowe comes still more to dwell among mankind. Edward's ruling passion is for another human being rather than for some impersonal and remote ideal as was true of Marlowe's earlier heroes. The emotions treated by the drama—friendship, love, hate, pity—are those which men have for one another. Furthermore, Marlowe brings back his scene from distant countries to his native England and deals with political issues still significant for his own age. Curbing his love for wonderful events set in misty regions, he now traces with increased fidelity a series of historical happenings. Imagination is directed now to the interpretation of character and the skillful linking of cause and effect, less to bodying forth the forms of things unknown. This alteration brings losses as well as gains. Marlowe cannot be all things at the same time. As he travels towards the objective world he necessarily travels away from that other world where no man came but him. If he grows in the poetry of humanity he dwindles in the poetry of ultimate aspiration.

We can measure the extent of the evolution by considering the characters of the play, the proportions between them, and the way in which the dramatist allots sympathy among them at different times.

Edward, Gaveston, and Mortimer are in effect segments of a split-up Tamburlaine. The ambitious element of his nature is given to the latter two, the amorous to Edward and transformed into an intense friendship. There is thus no longer the one great protagonist as in all the previous dramas but a number of striking personalities. The qualities bestowed upon them, however, are not much changed.

Edward, for instance, is not an entirely new kind of Marlowe hero. His ardor for friendship is the same as that of Tamburlaine for power, and in his weakness he resembles Faustus. As I have said, the fact that his ardor is directed towards another man is a sign of humanization; but on the other hand it must also be recognized that this friendship is still of a very translunary nature. Edward neglects the duties of his office, scorns the world, and sacrifices his crown for Gaveston. His devotion lacks balance, the easy give-and-take existing between men to whom friendship is but one of the loyalties of a normal life. He has a singleness of soul, a fervor, and a possessiveness which are admirable or blameworthy according to the point of view but which at all events betoken a man not well reconciled to the world of men.

Edward shows this psychology in his relations with others, for he loves only his successive friends and is shut away from sympathy with or understanding of the remainder of the characters. He lives in a solitude of friendship. There is still between the central figure and the organized world the old conflict which is traceable through *Tamburlaine*, *Faustus*, and *The Jew*.

But here, even more than in *The Jew*, society's side of the struggle, as represented by the barons' condemnation of Edward's unkingliness and Gaveston's base birth, is set forth with a truth and fairness approaching impartiality. The figures of the nobles and the deserted Isabella are not mere dim adjuncts of the passion of Edward for Gaveston, as they would have been had this play been written at the time of *Tamburlaine*, but complete persons who have strong arguments for their wish to break the friendship. The barons are to be likened to the champions of the social order opposing Tamburlaine. The salient distinction, however, and one which is of the greatest import in the tracing of Marlowe's development, is that in *Tamburlaine* the ethics of ambition is so favored by the playwright as to far overshadow the ethics of society, whereas in *Edward II* the two antagonists are well balanced and the conflict of sympathy as well as of power is severe. The equities weigh so evenly on both parts that it is impossible to say that the drama, at least in the first acts, takes sides either way. Marlowe is here seeing egoistic passion in its true relation to the consequences it has for actual life, and not solely as a divine exaltation vibrating *in vacuo*.

The later acts of *Edward II* are, like *Faustus*, a drama of defeat in which the sense of weakness is emphasized and the dominant appeal is again to pity—pity which is a social force drawing men together. We see how far Marlowe has come since *Tamburlaine* by noticing that the captivity of Edward under ambitious Mortimer is like that of Bajazeth under Tamburlaine, but with an exact reversal of attention and sympathy. We pity Bajazeth and feel that Marlowe did also, but this pity is, as it were, only smuggled in and seems almost illicit; what is legal and demanded is our admiration for Tamburlaine's magnificent obduracy. Now in *Edward II* young Mortimer takes the place of Tamburlaine and adopts a philosophy of strength which, admitting some distinctions, is nevertheless substantially that of Tamburlaine. Here we yield him still a certain homage, but the emphasis is now entirely the other way, and it is to the sufferings of his captive, Edward, that Marlowe now directs our sympathetic attention. Before the play ends, however, Mortimer once more takes the center of the stage with the grandeur of his passing. Thus the old worship of selfish power remains in Marlowe's nature side by side with the new realization of the evil it entails.[3]

The Massacre at Paris is so perfunctory a drama as to add little to our knowledge of Marlowe. We can but remark that the exponent of egoistic ambition, in this case Guise,

3. Miss Bradbrook (*Themes and Conventions of Elizabethan Tragedy*, Cambridge, 1935, pp. 163-64) has well said: "That Marlowe, who reduced the human feelings to a minimum in *Tamburlaine*, should have come to rely on them so much has caused little comment; yet it seems remarkable enough, particularly when at the same time he maintained the completely unfeeling 'Machiavellian' attitude also, in the character of Mortimer."

is clearly branded as a villain and is vanquished by the forces of moral good. The most arresting observation to be made is that he is not the protagonist of his play as was Barabas of his; that honor must go to Navarre if to anyone. So for the first time the character driven by a ruling passion is not the central figure of the plot. Marlowe's one-man formula, which began to crumble in the more evenly balanced personalities of *Edward II*, here further disintegrates. But Guise is still given the most radiant poetry of the play.

Hero and Leander has the air of being an interlude, a pause between battles. In it Marlowe puts aside for the moment the great issues of life and chooses an idyllic theme which he treats with frequent playfulness. Since there is no occasion for intruding his personal passions as in the dramas, he deals for the most part objectively and with calm restraint. The beauty here expressed is the nearer beauty of terrestrial things as contrasted with the sublimity of the *Tamburlaine* period. It is significant that Marlowe is now objective enough to indulge in an interlude of this kind, but the very fact that it is only an interlude should prevent us from construing the piece as an entire change of heart on Marlowe's part.[4]

Some of the individual passages in the poem are of extreme interest as expressions of Marlowe's own opinions. There is that notable comment by the poet which runs:

> It lies not in our power to love or hate,
> For will in us is overruled by fate.
> When two are stripped long ere the course begin,
> We wish that one would lose, the other win.

4. Tucker Brooke also interprets the poem biographically: "*Hero and Leander* in particular has biographical significance. It forbids us to believe that Marlowe was fundamentally or finally intemperate, as Kyd called him, or of a cruel heart. Nor can we easily suppose that its placid beauty was achieved while the author was employing his less poetical hours as a libertine, a secret agent, or a revolutionist."—*Life*, p. 51.

And one especially do we affect
Of two gold ingots, like in each respect;
The reason no man knows; let it suffice
What we behold is censured by our eyes.

(I, 167-74)

Marlowe is saying that we lack the power to decide what emotions we shall feel, but he is not saying that these emotions need necessarily control our actions after we feel them. In other words, he is saying that Hero and Leander could not choose but love each other, but he is not saying that they were bound to yield to that love after it had arisen. The latter would be a complete determinism, whereas the former leaves room for a partially free will. The evolution of Marlowe's thought up to this point has been an increasing recognition of the control exerted upon the self by forces *external* to it, and now here we have an acceptance of control taking effect *within* the self by a determinism of the feelings, though not of the use to which the individual can put those feelings. The area of absolutely free action has indeed shrunk since the days of *Tamburlaine*.

A second important passage from *Hero and Leander* must be quoted:

When this fresh-bleeding wound Leander viewed
His color went and came, as if he rued
The grief which Neptune felt. In gentle breasts
Relenting thoughts, remorse, and pity rests;
And who have hard hearts and obdurate minds
But vicious, harebrained, and illiterate hinds?

(II, 213-18)

We hardly recognize the poet of *Tamburlaine*. Pity, which was once despised as a hindrance to the attainment of empire, is now extolled, while the cruelty which was strength becomes a sign of erratic mentality and lack of proper training. The words might have been spoken by a modern criminologist; the point of view is that of the good citizen who sees in the absence of pity a menace to the civilized community.

We should go utterly astray, however, if we considered this the whole Marlowe. It is, on the contrary, only the momentary resurgence of that comprehension of and sympathy with the behavior standards of mankind which we have seen coming to maturity in the poet's nature. That other fundamental strain of solitary and ruthless aspiration is still alive and will return to its own in those moods of bitterness when circumstances may cause Marlowe again to defy the world. The issue for him is whether in his future life he will merely oscillate between these two antagonistic attitudes, or one will displace the other, or there will be some kind of interpenetration between them. We have good evidence that the latter process has not yet taken place, for Marlowe has never created an important character who is both strong and kindly. His gentle, generous characters, notably his women, are weak; his strong characters, wrapped in the passions and meditations of the self, are at war with the world. Unless sweetness and strength become fused, Marlowe's nature will remain divided against itself, and the long process of advance towards the outer world which we have been tracing will be incomplete.

These passages we have just been considering are among the last Marlowe ever penned. He departs from us on that fatal day at Deptford with his problem still unsolved and thenceforth insoluble.

A brief review of what we have been saying may now be appropriate. *Dido* was written at a time before the idea of self had ripened into consciousness. Thereafter the sequence of Marlowe's dramas represents a gradual birth into the world of objectivity. This growth proceeds in two main directions: (1) realization of the actual limitations upon the powers of the ego; (2) the discovery of mankind.

The first of these recognizes first the powerlessness of the individual against the forces of the universe (*Faustus*); then the extent to which he is subject to check by others of his kind (*The Jew* and *Edward II*); and, finally, his inability to determine even what his own emotions shall be (*Hero and Leander*).

The second accompanies the first. Living beings, hitherto accepted without understanding, take on the aspect of humanity. Marlowe is able to see farther and farther into the characters of men and the conditions of their lives, and to depict both with increasing verisimilitude. At the same time, the growing sense of his own frailty throws him into greater sympathy with them and he begins to feel himself more one of the race and less a unique creation of Nature. He becomes more conscious of their system of values and to a larger extent adopts them as his own. His characters dwindle to the size of human beings and are seen more truthfully in relation to the community. But even to the end he does not lose all of his psychological aloofness or his disposition to outbursts of egoistic aspiration hostile to the civil order.

Up to this point we have been considering only the internal evidence afforded by the plays and poems. Now what of the biographical evidence?

It appears at once that the scanty external evidence we have in our possession is not of the kind which would either support or destroy a theory of the playwright's development. It falls into three classes: (1) information about specific events in his life; (2) the opinions of his contemporaries who knew him; (3) the documentary evidence of his anti-Christian beliefs. The first dates for us a few definite happenings like his appearance at the Newgate session in 1589 in connection with the killing of William Bradley,[5] but reveals so little about his inner nature that it is impossible to say whether any changes were going on in it. The second gives us judgments most of which are mere summaries of personal impression gathered from contacts with the poet for which we cannot set any exact date. They consequently tell us nothing about the successive stages of his mind. Many of them, moreover, like the elegies of Nashe, Thorpe, Peele, Petowe, and Drayton,[6] upon Marlowe's death are simply tributes to Marlowe as a poet, not as a man.

The third is concentrated largely within the last two years of his life, and is applicable, moreover, to but a single specific topic of his thought and emotion. We know that in his last years Marlowe was a crusader against Christianity, and we may infer with considerable certainty that his attitude was already well formed when he graduated from Cambridge without ordination, but of the manner of its formation and subsequent evolution no external proof is forthcoming.

The result of all this is that we may form a general estimate of Marlowe's character and thought based on external evidence, but we cannot say from it whether or not any evolution is taking place. Sufficient significant details continuous in time simply do not exist.

It may be asked whether the external evidence is not at least enough to prove that Marlowe never was the solitary and otherworldly individual I have here supposed him to be, since he is known to have had acquaintance with many

5. Mark Eccles, *Christopher Marlowe in London*, pp. 41ff.
6. Quoted in Tucker Brooke's "The Reputation of Christopher Marlowe," *Trans. Connecticut Acad. of Arts & Sciences*, XXV (1921-22), 350-408.

prominent men in London, including Raleigh, Thomas Walsingham, Chapman, Nashe, Royden, Harriot, Warner, and Blount. Several answers may be made. In the first place, he may have come to know many of them only as he himself grew fonder of company and more in harmony with his surroundings in his later period. In the second place, and more fundamentally, everything depends upon the nature of his relations with these men. We have nothing to show that he was really intimate with all or many of them. For Walsingham, to be sure, he probably had a genuine friendship, since he visited him at Scadbury in 1593; and the dedication of the *Hero and Leander* undoubtedly shows that Blount was very much attached to him. But we have no such proofs for the other men. This has already been shown in the discussion of Marlowe's relations with members of the hypothetical School of Night.

The laments of the other poets for the dead Marlowe are, as I have remarked, really votive offerings to his poetic genius and do not necessarily imply friendship. Again, surely Marlowe's mission for the Privy Council in 1587, problematically continued as spy work in later years, does not show him moving with normal fitness in Elizabethan society. Resort to the underworld has never been considered the mark of a man's harmony with life.

The point I wish to make, accordingly, is that all these latter relationships are quite compatible with aloofness in Marlowe. The aloofness to which I have referred throughout is a psychological one which persists even during ordinary social intercourse; I have never intended to say that Marlowe lived the life of an anchorite. It is of course true that such a man does not seek or enjoy company as much as do most other men; he finds only a few friends to whom he devotes himself with correspondingly greater vehemence. But when he has imagination, passion, and intellect, as

Marlowe had, he never lacks society. To him are always attracted men who are strong enough or curious enough not to be driven away by the alien temper of his soul.

Changes in character are such mysterious and incalculable things that speculations as to their causes are likely to be rash. I should like, however, to hazard a few ideas on this subject before concluding this chapter.

The growth of personality in Marlowe, as in all men, is the result of the interaction of external circumstances with those innate tendencies which make up the spirit's internal destiny. As regards the external circumstances which may have influenced him we are pretty well ignorant: we do not know what sorrows, what disappointments, what unexpected acts of kindness, what absorbing friendships may have helped him in his drift towards humanity, or what betrayals, what contempt for human pettiness and hypocrisy, and the like may have retarded it.

But there are two internal qualities which may have assisted the process: Marlowe's sensuousness and his reason, both evident in his works from the earliest period. The former impresses him with an invincible sense of the reality of the physical world and thus prepares him to understand the reality of the existence of other men who inhabit it.

The latter is extremely important. The progress which Marlowe makes towards the outer world has an intellectual as well as an emotional side. We have hitherto given most of our attention to this emotional aspect by which Marlowe gains in community of feeling through the deepening recognition of his own weakness. But we must also notice that his strength of reason compares, analyzes, and synthesizes his observations of men and institutions and leads him to make others. Knowledge of a thing is per se an approach to it and, moreover, breeds further curiosity. In addition, knowledge sometimes arouses sympathy for the thing

known, just as sympathy is likely to create a desire to know
the thing sympathized with; so that the two elements of
consciousness stimulate each other. On the other hand,
knowledge may produce disgust instead of sympathy. To
move closer to the world of men is inevitably to see more
and more things worthy of dislike, contempt, or hatred.
Hence the growth of Marlowe's satirical humor. Hence its
increasing range and malice. From its greater frequency
in the later plays, especially in *The Jew of Malta*, we can
gauge the rise of Marlowe's critical faculty sitting in judgment upon the deeds of other men. In so far as it shows
that the playwright's interests are becoming more mundane,
it is a step towards society; but in so far as it is lacking in
sympathy, it is a maintenance of the original aloofness. At
this, moreover, we need not be surprised. Only a complete
humanitarianism would accept everything without criticism,
and Marlowe, even more than most men, will never reach
that extreme. We here face the question, which it is not
necessary for me to debate, whether a certain amount of
this critical aloofness, operating rather according to abstract principles than to immediate human sympathies, is
not essential to the progress of the race.

Again, reason has a profound ethical function in making
the self aware of duties to other men. It detects the similarities between the self and others, and by a necessary logic
argues that under like conditions like principles should
apply to all.

Most men become stronger in reason as they grow older.
At the same time, emotion becomes less volatile and more
settled. The physiological and psychological changes which
go with advancing manhood will help to account for Marlowe's history. In some degree most sensitive men have the
same experience. Their youth is a time of storm and stress
when they see nothing clearly, being rapt away in dreams